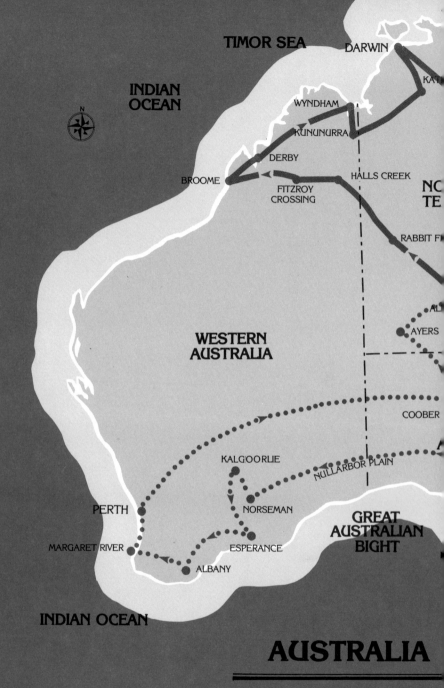

TIMOR SEA

INDIAN
OCEAN

N

DARWIN

KAT

WYNDHAM

KUNUNURRA

DERBY

BROOME

FITZROY
CROSSING

HALLS CREEK

NO
TE

RABBIT F

WESTERN
AUSTRALIA

AL

AYERS

COOBER

KALGOORLIE

NULLARBOR PLAIN

PERTH

NORSEMAN

MARGARET RIVER

ESPERANCE

GREAT
AUSTRALIAN
BIGHT

ALBANY

INDIAN OCEAN

AUSTRALIA

WINTER TOUR
SPRING SUMMER TOUR

0   Scale   500
kilometres

How To Get Lost And Found In Australia

by John W. McDermott

ORAFA Publishing Co., Inc.
Honolulu, Hawaii

First Published 1980
Second Edition, July, 1984

Orafa Publishing Company, Inc.
1314 So. King Street, Suite 1064
Honolulu, Hawaii 96814
U.S.A.
©1980 John W. McDermott

ISBN: 0-912273-07-0

Typeset by Studio Graphics, Inc. Honolulu
Reprinted by Fairfield Graphics, Pennsylvania

John W. McDermott's other books in this series
How to Get Lost and Found in California and Other Lovely Places
How to Get Lost and Found in The Cook Islands
How to Get Lost and Found in Fiji
How to Get Lost and Found in New Japan
How to Get Lost and Found in New Zealand
How to Get Lost and Found in Tahiti

Distributed in the U.S.A. by
Hippocrene Books, Inc. 171 Madison Ave., New York City 10016
Distributed in Australia by
Kingfisher Books, Pty, Ltd. Brixton at Wangara Rds., Cheltenham 3192, Melbourne
Tower Books, 505 Pittwater Rd., Brookvale NSW 2100 Sydney
Distributed in Continental Europe by
Roger Lascelles, 3 Holland Park Mansions, 16 Holland Park Gardens, London W148DY
Distributed in Hawaii by
Pacific Trade Group, P.O. Box 1227, Kailua, Hawaii 96734
Distributed in New Zealand by
David Bateman Ltd, P.O. Box 65062, Mairangi Bay Auckland 10

To Shirley
who waited on the dock when the ship
sailed away to Australia many years ago

Contents

List of Maps

Map Designer: Roger Suga

Australia — You Won't Believe It

All of Australia is divided into three parts. Sydney. The Other Cities. The Country.

This book is about The Country.

Sydney looks down on the rest of the nation as a place where the farmers play funny football, abuse the Aboriginals and don't take proper care of the kangaroos.

The superiority attitudes of Sydney put everyone's teeth outside the city Right-On-Edge. It leads to tummy pains usually caused only by English cricket writers.

If Sydney were cut off from the continent and allowed to drift into the Pacific Ocean, it would not be a bad thing, they say.

To Sydney with its three million people out of the country's fourteen million population, with headquarters for finance and communications within city boundaries, it really doesn't matter. The power is there.

The Other Cities — Melbourne, Adelaide, Brisbane, Hobart, Perth, Canberra and Darwin — have a separate sense of pride, nurtured by early days of city-state isolation.

All the cities are worthy of books, many of which have already been written.

Our mission was to explore, with several exceptions, places outside of the urban areas. The Country.

What a huge treasure we found!

Our travels covered two separate periods of time totalling about eight months.

The original concept was to go to Australia during the June or July winter for a bit of skiing. That was all. "Oh, no," we were told. "That is the time to do everything north of the 22nd parallel, the Tropic of Capricorn, before the summer when it is 'The Wet' — too rainy in many parts and certainly too hot in others."

So in June and July we toured the Great Barrier Reef. Flew a Bush Pilots Tour in a DC-3 up Cape York to Thursday Island. Did a sixteen-day safari from Alice Springs through the Tanami Desert in the Centre to the pearl centre of Broome in Western Australia, back through the incredible Kimberley District to Katherine Gorge and up to Darwin.

We drove from Sydney to Canberra, skied at Thredbo in the Snowy Mountains and went to one of those "funny football" matches in Melbourne. And went home.

In November we returned for a six-month tour starting with the famous Melbourne Cup, bought a car, the "Green Pony" a Ford Falcon Station Wagon, in Sydney and drove up the coast and down the coast, inside and out, from one side of the country to the other. In addition to driving, we planed, bused and boated, went by foot, horse and camel on separate side trips.

A cross-section of activities:

1. Went gold-panning, sapphire-hunting, opal "noodling" and thunder-egg digging.
2. Visited over fifty wineries.
3. Played six "Royal" golf courses, among many others.
4. Attended glamorous horse races, funny horse races.
5. Stayed on four different farms as part of farm holidaying.
6. Landed a twelve-pound trout at Lake Pedder in Tasmania.
7. Took a two-day horseback safari into the Bogong High Plains of Victoria.
8. Did a five-day, whitewater river raft trip.
9. Rode half-a-dozen antique steam railroads.
10. Drank, ate and slept in countless country inns and country pubs.
11. Houseboated on three rivers and one lake, including a paddle-wheel houseboat.
12. Took a three-day gypsy-caravan-and-Clydesdale-horse safari.
13. Hiked up (part way) Ayers Rock.
14. Completed a two-day kayak safari down the South Esk River.
15. Roamed over mountain tops.
16. Attended folk festivals and beach carnivals.
17. Drove across the Nullarbor Plain.
18. Drank fifty cases of beer . . . at least.

Oh, yes, we had sneaky visits to cities.

19. Attended a ballet and an opera in the Sydney Opera House.
20. Visited the War Museum in Canberra.
21. Enjoyed the Festival Centre in Adelaide.
22. Admired the pretty girls in Perth.

The list goes on and on.

The biggest discovery we made, after being in and out of Australia for more than thirty years — mostly in cities — was that there is an entirely new Australia to be found out in The Country.

The Country is beautiful. We fell in love with pretty birds, then the trees and then the clouds. Why hasn't anybody written a book about the spectacular clouds of Australia? Add the thousands of miles of magnificent beaches. Thousands of miles of rivers and mammoth man-made lakes. Dense rain forests, misty highlands, and green, green valleys to counterbalance the arid, flat plains.

That was a new Australia to us.

Make no mistake. This is not a gentle land. The Country is tough. Millions and millions of acres are desert dry, parched, twisted, hardened and flattened with age. On the surface, worthless dirt. Underneath: gold, copper, uranium, coal, nickel, precious stones, oil.

To make a living out of this land you have to be as tough as the land. The root characteristic of the people in The Country is still a basic, rock-hard durability.

If you go to war, go with an Australian from The Country.

Mostly our adventures were of the participating type, not spectating — the difference between skin diving on a reef and going to an aquarium. More and more we are finding that people are looking for family holidays which put them into action.

Australia is an unbelievable land, made for action, made for sportsmen.

Our experiences are but a sample of things to do . . . particularly in The Country where a different, exciting Australia will be found.

Note: prices in the book are in Australian dollars and reflect the general costs in 1984.

Distances and weights are a problem. The metric system, relatively unused in the United States, is used in the book to denote modern distances. Miles are used in historical cases.

Sometimes, particularly in heights, the English measure is used. A 1,500-foot cliff at Mt. Buffalo sounds better in feet, doesn't it? A five-foot ten-inch beauty queen shouldn't be described in metres.

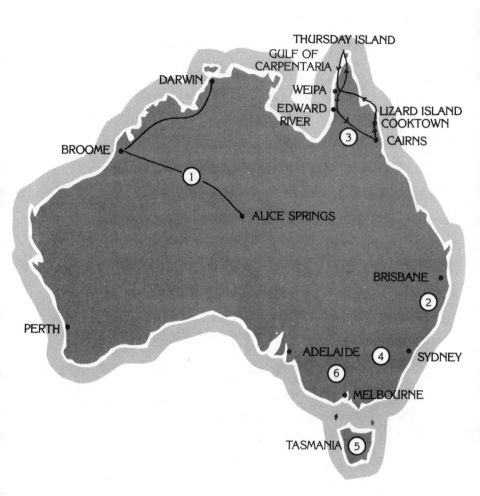

THURSDAY ISLAND
GULF OF
CARPENTARIA
DARWIN
WEIPA
EDWARD
RIVER
LIZARD ISLAND
COOKTOWN
BROOME
CAIRNS
1
ALICE SPRINGS
3
BRISBANE
2
PERTH
ADELAIDE
SYDNEY
4
6
MELBOURNE
TASMANIA
5

SAFARIS

1. DESERT SAFARI
2. WHITE WATER SAFARI
3. BUSH PILOTS' CAPE YORK SAFARI
4. BOGONG HIGH PLAINS HORSE SAFARI
5. SOUTH ESK RIVER KAYAK SAFARI
6. HORSE & WAGON SAFARI

1. Take a Safari

If you are sitting in New York or Auckland or London and planning Australian safari adventures, you are brought face to face with the reality of the size of the country.

For example, when we finished the Bush Pilots' Safari in Cairns, Queensland, we then had a 1500-kilometre flight to reach Alice Springs, the starting point of our Desert Safari through the Northern Territory and Western Australia.

When we finished the Desert Safari 3200 kilometres later in Darwin we flew from the capital of the Northern Territory to Sydney, capital of New South Wales via Adelaide, capital of South Australia, a journey of over 3,700 kilometres to start our ski exercise.

A little hop south of Melbourne, capital of Victoria, to Hobart, the capital of the island state of Tasmania, for our Kayak Safari, was an almost-nothing 1000-kilometre round trip.

Fortunately TAA and Ansett, the principal domestic air carriers, offer overseas visitors substantial, pre-paid discounts.

If the dimensions of the country are immense, so are the choices of action.

You'll find organised safaris of every description waiting to take you everywhere on the continent, offering every sort of experience.

(The Lady Navigator turned down a chance to go sky-diving. Instructions on Saturday. Jump on Sunday. Cost $80.)

These safaris, or tours, are proven and popularised by years of know-how. The guides are experts in their particular crafts.

You can be out in the open having an unforgettable adventure, often at a price less than that of a ho-hum tourist day in a city.

Six such safaris brought us into intimate touch with Australia.

(I promised to take her picture on the way down, too.)

2. Desert Safari by Bus

The Australian Tourist Commission publishes an excellent booklet entitled *Your Travel Planner...AUSTRALIA.*

Included in the eighty pages are two sections on Coach Touring and Adventure Tours. Listed are thirty-seven Coach Operators and thirty-five Adventure Tour Operators.

Coach Operators in the majority of cases run air-conditioned buses with built-in toilet facilities, hot and cold refreshments, lay-back seats. The buses reach selected hotels or motels by nightfall providing rooms with private facilities and restaurants.

On the other hand, the Adventure Tours go in a type of vehicle that is toughly sprung to handle rutted tracks. The toilet facilities are behind bushes and the sleeping accommodation are two-person tents. The travelling cook gets together the grub and you are expected to help with the camp details.

I remember at Victoria River Crossing, a restaurant-pub out in the middle of lonesome country, where our adventure vehicle, a converted Bedford truck, stopped at the same time as a beautiful, immaculate Mercedes bus.

We were in the second week on the road and we were dusty, wrinkled, ragged. We had accepted our scruffy condition as a way of life. We were broken-in.

The Mercedes passengers were starched. Clean. They wore little bus tags on which their names were printed.

The two groups looked at each other like two stray dogs. Each group sniffed and turned away, each feeling terribly superior.

"Did you see how they were travelling?" we said to each other. "Sixty miles an hour down the highway. Sleeping in hotels. They don't see *anything*." (Our truck's top speed was thirty miles an hour.)

Undoubtedly the other tour was saying, "Did you see those poor creatures? Have you ever seen anything so scrungy? What makes people descend to such levels? They don't see *anything*."

Frankly the Lady Navigator and I are strong on creature comforts and the idea of doing a sixteen-day camping tour through the Tamani Desert and The Kimberley would have been very low on our list.

However, well-meaning friends in Sydney signed us up for the tour and we couldn't turn our back on it. Fortunately.

So there we were in Alice Springs waiting for Bill King's Northern Safari bus to pick us up at the Ansett office. Nervous.

We knew only that the first night would be spent in a caravan park. We had arrived early in Alice Springs and drove out to look at Greenleaves Tourist Camp. Goodness.

We had never stayed in a caravan park. Common toilet and shower facilities. Goodness. Not since the military years and years ago.

Later we were to look back at Greenleaves as a symbol of luxury. But then after sixteen days we were experienced safari veterans. Yes, broken-in, indeed.

Arriving early in Alice Springs turned out to be a pleasant experience.

I expected Alice Springs to be a dry, dusty, shanty town with three wooden stores leaning against each other for support, and one pub. Maybe two pubs.

Not at all. Alice Springs is a modern, going-strong town with an eye-catching mall, many new government buildings, a major hospital. And lots of pubs.

Fortunately among the new additions are new accommodations because Alice Springs is the jumping off place for Ayers Rock and tends to get very crowded. Reservations are strongly recommended.

Among the new places to stay we found the Outback Motor Lodge, Alice Springs Gap Hotel and the White Gum Holiday Inn.

The swankiest place to stay is the new 75-room Federal Pacific Hotel-Casino Resort outside of town. Gambling. Golf. Tennis. Swimming. Sheraton is building another hotel next door.

Our first pleasant experience was to find the Centre for Aboriginal Artists and Craftsmen on Todd Street, the main thoroughfare in town. We had glimpsed pieces of Aboriginal art before and were not overly enthusiastic. But this!

We were wide-eyed. "Sand-paintings" in earth-tone geometric designs. Excellent carvings. Graphics of animals painted on bark. We bought piles of stuff and were grateful that the shop took American Express cards . . . and shipped purchases.

In Alice Springs we found a most amiable source of information in Brian Price of the Northern Territory Tourist Board.

He pointed us in many good directions.

We rented a "mini-moke" consisting of four wheels, a petrol tank and a canvas top. The barest sort of transportation.

We dropped into the Panorama and Museum, a painted 360-

degree mural of the countryside around Alice Springs. Went to the Stuart Auto Collection. Inspected the operational district head-quarters for the famous Royal Flying Doctor Service. Took a picnic lunch out to the Old Telegraph Station, the original "Alice Springs."

We had another most pleasant lunch at Turner House, an establishment started by two young men to "please the local people of Alice Springs." Here we had our first bottle of Houghton's White Burgundy (pronounced Hortons), a soft chenin blanc wine with a touch of tokay.

We also paid a call on our first-ever camel farm.

Although the safari was to take us back to both the Old Telegraph Station and the Camel Farm we wanted to enjoy both attractions on our own. At that time before moving on to become a full-time camel safari guide, the Camel Farm was run by Noel Fullerton, a grey bearded man with black hat, plaid shirt and dirty jeans.

Noel Fullerton was a non-stop verbal encyclopaedia of camel information.

"In 1922 there were 20,000 camels in Australia. Camels used to be the automobiles and the railroads of the Outback. The bush is still full of wild camels. They are the healthiest camels in the world. We sell Australian camels to Arabia now.

"I sent my last lot to Japan. It costs $85 to $300 to catch them in the bush and haul them in. A broken-in camel is worth $1,000 ... $2,000 if it is broken for over two years. I sent two by air to a Masonic Lodge in America for their camel corps.

"The camels are used in films and TV commercials and we do camel rides here on the farm.

"Ten years ago I bet another fellow with camels that my fastest camel could beat his fastest camel. He took the bet but never showed up. Anyway, that gave birth to camel racing and every year in Alice Springs our camel races bring the Lion's Club over $10,000.

"There are now four major camel races in Australia. The largest is in Perth with prize money of $20,000. I'm taking sixteen camels to Perth. Eight to win and eight to get in the way of the competition. There will be twenty camels in a race over a quarter-mile course with a flying start. It is something to see.

"Marindy Mick over there is the fastest camel in Australia in my opinion. How fast? That camel has been clocked at forty-two miles an hour when chased with a Land Rover."

(I later paid a dollar and rode Marindy Mick around the corral.

It was like riding a furry hiccup.)

"These animals are gentle. Tame. You have to be careful of the males in rutting season. They have been known to tear a man's arm off.

"The earliest camel was in North America, believe it or not. Fossils only eighteen inches high have been found dating back millions of years.

"The first camels were brought to Australia in 1840. Perfect animal for transportation in the desert country. The hump is not a water tank as most people believe but is for food storage. These animals weigh fifteen hundred to two thousand pounds and seventy of them made up a camel team.

Fullerton was an articulate authority on the Aborigines and recited stories at length of the white man's abuse of the natives. He told stories of many Aboriginal customs.

"In one tribe if a boy slept with a woman before he was officially declared a man by the heads of the tribe he was punished with mutilating cuts, a front tooth was knocked out and he was circumcised with a stone knife.

"I bring my girls' boy friends out here and relate the same story and tell them that I belong to the same tribe."

A rare guy.

Noel Fullerton now operates a camel safari company with seven-day and fourteen-day excursions on camel into remote parts of central Australia: Rainbow Valley, Finke River, MacDonnell Ranges. About $600 a week includes tent accommodations, all meals, bedrolls. A rare experience into places untouched by wheeled vehicles. The brochure says no camel experience is necessary. (You learn in a hurry.) Bookings are made through Adventure Travel Centre, First Floor, 28 Market Street, Sydney.

Saturday was the start of our bus safari.

We were waiting somewhat apprehensively early afternoon at the appointed place at the appointed time.

No one showed up at the appointed place at the appointed time.

Half an hour. An hour. An hour and a half.

We had checked out of our room and there wasn't another room to be had and we were thinking of an emergency plan when the safari bus showed up.

The driver with a shaggy mop of blond hair, a huge blond moustache and booming manner said a late plane had delayed our pickup as we claimed the last two empty seats.

Don Nayler was the name of the driver and Viv Leisk was the cook. There were eighteen passengers, generally of a retirement age and all from Australia with an exception of a media buyer from an international advertising agency in Melbourne, another young lady from New Zealand and a man from New York who was a central European immigrant and who really should have gone to Miami instead of Australia.

We had a good group. Acquaintances started slowly but in a sixteen-day safari there was time for friendship to mature. Having an older group of Australians was particularly rewarding. They were on the trip because of their love for the country. Knowledgeable people.

One couple specialised in bird watching. He had recorded seeing over four hundred birds in Australia. (The Reader's Digest puts out an excellent book on Australian birds.)

A pair of elderly sisters were rock hounds and had a machine in their home to polish rocks.

Another couple knew the name of every bush and tree.

If you had a question, you could count on receiving an accurate answer.

Don Nayler was the perfect driver-guide. He had been a drover, a gem miner working his own claim. He recited facts and figures of the countryside we covered but never too much at a time. And he recited poetry. Shakespeare or Australian doggerel.

Later in the trip, sitting in the shade by a small lake with a waterfall in the background, sipping a "tinny" — a can of beer — I asked the reason for his penchant for poetry and he garrumphed, "Arr, John, it is a shortcut to a woman's heart." Pause. "And sometimes it works."

Splendid bastard. (In Australia all male persons are called bastards. What kind of bastard depends upon the intonation of the speaker.)

That first afternoon we returned to the restored buildings of the Old Telegraph Station, Fullerton's Camel Farm then on to Pitchi Ritchi, a strange collection of sculptures by artist Bill Rickett, remains of gold digging equipment from gold fields, water tanks carried by camels, etc.

At one spot was recreated "The Prospector's Dream," a mine glinting with precious metal. In October, 1872 at Hawkins Hill in New

South Wales, a gold mass, not a nugget, was found that was five feet high and two feet wide and weighed six hundred and thirty pounds! It took twenty men and a horse to bring it to the surface. The largest gold mass ever found in Australia.

Our tour took us to the Anzac Hill War Memorial and then to the caravan park. A back entrance led us into a spot reserved for the Bill King Safari trucks where tents were already erected.

The two-person tents had vinyl floors and were equipped with cots, sleeping bags and burlap sacks used to store wool but used, in camping, as extra insulation which we needed for the first half of the trip.

The brochure copy said that if passengers wanted to help with the camp it would be appreciated but wasn't required.

The truth of it was, without the passengers' help in preparing food, washing and drying dishes, packing and unpacking, the safari would never have been able to complete the schedule.

However, the Australians pitched in with a cooperative spirit by second nature. The women simply assumed chores around the camp kitchen. The men took over from Don after the first day, packing away the tents on top of the truck and loading and unloading the ton of bags in back.

Participation was part of the adventure.

That first night we had chicken and white wine (wine was served with every evening meal) and ice cream for the first and last time.

And we froze. Fortunately we also read in the brochure copy that desert nights could be freezing and to be prepared with warm night clothes. Like a track suit. In Alice Springs we bought track suits and slept in them for most of the trip.

Day Two, leaving Alice Springs a petrol station sign read "328 miles to BP service"... a hint to the vastness of the country.

The Northern Territory, five times the size of New Zealand, is a huge hunk of land which had only been granted "self determining" governmental status the year before. With 65,000 people in Darwin, the capital, and 21,000 in Alice Springs, it left a lot of land to be occupied by the remaining 38,000 people. Of the total 124,000, 25% are Aborigines.

One-third of the land is desert, that is, it receives less than fifteen inches of rain a year.

The Northern Territory is proud of having the highest beer consumption in the world. Alcoholics Anonymous was disbanded in 1969 for lack of support.

We were headed first across the Tanami Desert. It would take us three days.

Then we would work our way across the state of Western Australia to the pearl farming town of Broome on the Indian Ocean, north to Derby and across the northwest part of Australia, called The Kimberley to Wyndham, facing the Timor Sea, back into the Territory to Lake Argyle, Katherine Gorge and to Darwin. The trip would cover over 3,200 kilometres (2,000 miles).

The second day on the tour and the first day out of Alice Springs we drove on a straight-as-string, red dirt road that stretched endlessly into the desert. You could see to the horizon in all directions.

The Tanami Desert is not the Sahara of white sand. It is filled with bush, gum trees, tough shrubs, wattle (acacia trees). An occasional windmill marked a government-drilled bore to bring water to the cattle.

In three days we saw no more than twenty vehicles, one store, one ranch house. In three days we never saw or heard an airplane.

You have to give the desert enough time to come to you. It then takes on a rugged serenity of its own and a beauty and colour you cannot duplicate. You begin to enjoy the desert for its silence and its remoteness.

The first two nights we made bush camps.

Tents erected on the flat land next to the road, a campfire built, the kitchen work and serving tables spread out, the butane stoves connected.

The sunsets were beautifully clear followed by a full moon. The Southern Cross constantly visible.

The first night in the desert Don made "damper" after dinner. He rolled and punched the dough, placed it in a covered iron skillet, set it in a hole in the ground surrounded by coals and then covered it with dirt.

An hour later the damper was ready and we had it for dessert covered with jam. All the fun of Boy Scout camps rushed back again.

The best part of bush camping is the dawn. To get up while it is still dark, put a couple of pieces of wood on the remaining coals of last night's campfire and then watch the first touch of pink touch the eastern horizon and spread gradually from orange to gold and then to the yellow of a full sun slanting across the tents ... lovely, untradeable moments.

Day Three we stopped at The Granites, a former gold field where water was more precious than wine. Remains of old buildings and an old crusher are all that is left.

We saw flying turkeys and pink cockatoos worth a fortune in the United States and termite hills over six feet high.

We stopped for a cold beer at Rabbit Flat, the most remote store in Australia. Its nearest competitor is 464 km down the road.

Bruce, the proprietor, came to this location ten years ago when there was nothing. Open, vacant land. He built a petrol station, a store, bar and restaurant and camping facilities with running water . . . and toilets.

The Aborigines drive from a hundred kilometres away to get petrol and to get drunk.

"The rule is they pay for their tucker and petrol first. Then they can get on the grog."

It gets pretty rough. The store is a small fortress which can be closed off with only a pass-through for money in exchange for grog.

A stranger finds out in a hurry that the question of Aborigines in the Outback is a delicate one. "The reporters won't write about it and, if they do, the editors won't print it," host Bruce said.

The front of the corrugated building was a mess of empty beer cans.

"There was a party yesterday," the pub-keeper explained. "It only lasted six hours. Sometimes parties last days and nights. Once a mob of fifty Abo's drank up $2,500 worth of grog. The politicians down south don't know what goes on."

Bruce who was born and raised in country where tall trees grow and where creeks run year around with clear water said he could no longer live any place but at Rabbit Flat.

That afternoon we visited a canyon with Aboriginal paintings including one used in Eric Von Daniken's *Chariot of the Gods*. The author maintained the drawing represented a visiting spaceman. Shielded in the cliff of the canyon walls the protected painting in red, dark browns and cream whites indeed looked like a childish drawing of a helmeted spaceman two feet tall.

We took pictures of the sign saying that we were entering Western Australia and we drove past a huge brush fire only minutes from blocking the road . . . a roaring, leaping yellow-tongued fire puffing huge black clouds into the sky.

Anna, our bus, developed trouble. The fan began to tick against the front radiator. It got louder and louder. We inched along hoping to make the homestead where we were to spend the night.

It was getting too bad. Don stopped the vehicle, went underneath, and came out from under with grim news. The engine mounting was cracked. The engine was slipping down and the radiator fan was coming in contact with the radiator. If the mounting broke, we would face a stay of unknown duration.

We drove on ever so slowly in an attempt to reach our homestead destination and, hopefully, welding equipment.

Finally at eleven p.m. the safari stopped. We would try to solve the problem in the morning. Everything, said Don, looks better in the morning. We had been on the road fifteen hours.

We had rice and creamed tuna standing around the campfire and turned in. It was one a.m.

The next morning Don huddled with the other Australian males — I hum a lot during these crisis situations — and they came up with an ingenious solution.

First, the engine was jacked up into its original position. (The tyre jack was too short but they made a successful platform out of the steel rim of the spare tyre.)

The steel cable from the front end winch on *Anna* was then passed around a bolt inserted on one side of the engine mounting, passed under the engine and fastened to a bolt on the other side of the engine mounting. The winch was then tightened, trussing the engine into its original position.

This make-do device lasted until the bus returned to its home base in Alice Springs, 6400 kilometres later!

Anna's patching took up most of the morning and it was almost noon by the time the safari reached the cattle station of "Carranya," a property comprising one million acres.

The attraction of the station after two nights in the middle of the arid desert was hot water.

At the homestead we paid $1 each for using the single shower, everybody lining up, taking turns, whooping with pleasure. We also had tea for 60¢ and scones at 40¢ and biscuits for 20¢ each. The toilet was free.

I told the good-humoured, pretty-eyed station wife that the Lady Navigator and I had showered together and we should only be charged $1.50. She said that having someone scrub your back made it more pleasurable and we should be charged $3 instead of $2. You never win with women.

Nearby was Wolf Creek Meteor Crater, a crater exceeded in size only by Canyon Diablo in Arizona which I had seen as a child. Remarkably similar. The only difference in the Arizona crater was the obvious slanting angle at which the meteor had entered the earth which you could tell from the canyon walls. The Wolf Creek Crater looked like the meteor had entered the earth straight down making a perfect circle almost a kilometre across and fifty metres deep.

We are toilet trained in the twentieth century tradition. Running water. Tiles and mirrors. Comfort combined with delicacy.

In the bush you go to the toilet with a shovel and a roll of toilet paper. Women to the left of the road. Men to the right.

It is enough to tie up your plumbing for weeks.

The first time the Lady Navigator set off resolutely into the scrub Don called after her: "Be careful of the snakes and mine shafts!"

She stopped as if she'd hit a stone wall. Shuddered. Then STOMP, STOMP, STOMP into the bush, eyes glued to the ground.

We never walked louder and looked at the terrain more carefully than we did on the desert safari.

At the end of the fourth day we rolled into Halls Creek, population about one hundred. A pub. Several stores. A modern municipal building. Ice cream cones for half of the safari passengers. Iced beer for the other half.

Anna carried an Esky and we learned when we touched civilisation to buy fruit juices and beer and soft drinks to store in the Esky, Australia's favourite ice-chest.

We camped at Caroline Pool outside of Halls Creek and the next morning visited Old Halls Creek, the original gold mining community of Western Australia, where abandoned buildings made of tree branches and mud (wattle and daub) are crumbling in the sun.

Halls Creek is interesting historically because here was found the first gold in payable quantities in 1886 in the Far West. It was the beginning of a continuing discovery of vast quantities of the precious metal from the Kimberley 3,200 km south through Leonora, Kalgoorlie to Norseman.

In the Halls Creek area is the "China Wall," a ridge of nearly pure quartz looking like a jagged wall of white glass, said to be three hundred million years old.

At Halls Creek we headed west on Highway 1, still a dirt road and by now we were seeing the red rock formations of the south Kimberley. (The Kimberley area is nearly twice the size of Great Britain.)

Fitzroy Crossing was our turn-off to Geike Gorge National Park on the wide-flowing Fitzroy River, a pleasant relief from the long desert experience. We arrived in mid-afternoon, pitched our tents, had a cold water shower and chatted with John Savory, the park ranger, in front of his riverside tent.

"This whole campsite," he said, "will be twenty feet under water during the summer when the Fitzroy is in flood.

"You see, the catchment area of the Fitzroy is four hundred kilometres to the east and two hundred and forty to the west. When there is a two-inch rainfall, the total volume of water is awesome and the river is running strong enough to fill Sydney Harbour in four hours.

"Where the river enters the ocean a few 'k' below Derby, the fresh water extends over one hundred kilometres out to sea.

"Even now there are spots in the river seventy feet deep. Good swimming."

Any . . . snappies?

"Crocodiles? Sure, they are all along the river banks but these are fresh water Johnson crocodiles. Not dangerous. But when you go on the boat trip tomorrow upstream, just don't dangle your fingers or your feet in the water."

We didn't go swimming either.

During the time of our desert safari, "Skylab," the empty American spaceship, was on its way back to disintegrate on earth but no one knew precisely when or where.

That night about eight o'clock in our camp a safari mate pointed up and said, "Look!"

There across the southern sky we could see what looked like a fast moving star, bright and close. It was "Skylab" on what — we didn't know at the time — was its next to last orbit around earth.

At one a.m. the pieces of the space vehicle, shattered by re-entering the earth's atmosphere, scattered themselves across a swatch of Western Australia's southern desert from Albany through Esperance to Rawlinna.

The ranger's wife with a radio gave us the news the next morning.

The response of Prime Minister Malcolm Fraser to the United States president's message of concern is worth repeating:

"Dear Jimmy. Thank you very much for your message. It appears we can all breathe a sigh of relief. While receiving Skylab is an honour we would have happily forgone, it is the end of a magnificent technological achievement by the United States, and the events of the past few days should not obscure this.

"If we find the pieces, I shall happily trade them for additions to the beef quota."

The temper and independence of safari cooks is inherited from the tough-as-leather reputation of drover cooks.

Passenger: "What time do we get up tomorrow morning?"

Viv, the cook: "When I call you."

No more questions.

During the night I heard a loud roar outside our tent and I pointed a trembling torch through the flap opening into the round eyes of a mooing cow who was wondering what this silly contraption was doing in her traditional path to the waterhole.

The major attraction of the park is the ranger-conducted boat trip into the rocky Geike Gorge.

We had a soft, sunny morning. Perfect sight-seeing from the flat-bottomed scow which was pushed by the ranger's boat.

We saw black swans and fantastically feathered egrets and Willy Wagtails, little birds with big fantails, and tiny crocodiles sleeping on old tree branches just above the water line. Crocodiles which can lengthen to six feet and live two hundred years.

Fairey martin birds were busily building nests under the overhang of 100-foot high cliffs.

The ranger pointed out figures in the river-carved rock. A white elephant. An indian chief's head. A profile of a sharp-nosed, pugnacious-jowled Richard Nixon.

Fossil shells studded the cliff walls. How old? Millions of years.

The two-hour tour costs $5. Great bargain. Over two thousand fortunate campers take it every year.

As we were leaving Geike Gorge for Broome we passed an ancient Holden parked high in the branches of a tree. Its door was splashed in white paint: "The '68 flood."

Gag? True? Who knows. In Australia you are never sure.

After dark we entered the Broome Caravan Park, council-owned and operated.

Our park site was on grass! A proper concrete cooking complex for Viv and hot water showers, even washing machines. Luxury.

It was not until the morning light lit the park that we realised we were camped on the edge of the Indian Ocean. We had crossed half of Australia through the desert, and had reached the sea. After the desert, the amount of water in front of us was almost incomprehensible.

Like great explorers we had made it!

Broome, on Roebuck Bay, is one of the many colourful small towns of Australia. Its primary industry is pearl farming. Luggers come into the tiny wharf on thirty-foot high tides to be left on the muddy bottom when the tides retreat.

On the beach were two refugee boats from Vietnam and the remains of Dorniers destroyed in one of the three strafing raids made by the Japanese during World War II.

We visited a pearl shell factory where shells are stacked in steel drums and local artisans turn shells and pearls into better-than-average pieces of jewellery.

Broome's "Chinatown" consists of a few stores and restaurants, a hang-over from the early pearling days when two thousand Chinese divers were imported to exploit the rich beds of pearl shells at the bottom of Roebuck Bay.

Pearl shells were used for making pearl buttons until the use of plastics eliminated the pearl button industry. Oysters are now used for cultivating cultured pearls and the shells go into costume jewellery.

Divers in the early days also were brought in from the Torres Strait.

The population of Broome today is wonderfully diverse. Chinese, Torres Strait islanders, Aborigines, white stockmen and many Japanese.

The Japanese who strafed Broome during World War II returned to initiate and control the cultured pearl industry.

In Broome the Shinju Matsuri Pearl Festival takes place in August starting with a float parade and ending a week later with an all-day beach carnival and barbecue.

I had a long talk with shopkeeper Yuen Yee, son of Y. Wing, the founder of Y. Wing's store whose sign reads: "Delicatessen. Confectionery. Chinese Food. Ice Cream. General Chemist Lines."

Mr. Yee was born in China and when he arrived in Broome he couldn't speak English. He still doesn't read or write English but he has two children in school in Perth and another one in school in Sydney. The educational bill is $10,000 a year.

"Hard," said Mr. Yee, "but worth it."

Our morning tour of Broome included an hour at Cable Beach, an immense, dazzling stretch of white sand facing the Indian Ocean where we relaxed with a refreshing swim in the waves.

(Nude swimming and sun bathing is around the corner of the northern rocks I discovered during a beach walk.)

At Lighthouse Point, a place of stratified coloured rocks, we saw reproductions of dinosaur tracks. The original tracks can be seen at low tide thirty feet off shore. It is estimated that these ten-feet tall, carnivorous animals existed one hundred thirty million years ago.

An abandoned DC-3 used to serve as the Broome Tourist Bureau headquarters, perfect for this odd-is-normal community, but they had to move because of booming business. I asked if they moved into a "747" but the answer was negative. Too bad.

Broome has character.

Oh yes, there is a snack shop called the Chip Monk where you can get an Hawaiian Burger for $1.90 which consists of meat, onion, egg, cheese, ham, pineapple with a salad on the side.

Also pearl shell meat, deep fried in beer batter, for 40¢.

On our last night we visited The Cave, a bar in The Tropicana Hotel where men played pool and drank together.

This "mateyness" of the Australian men was described in detail to us by our young media buyer from Melbourne who obviously didn't approve of it at all.

Those who stayed in camp and avoided the dens of iniquity said they were rewarded by the moon coming up over the low tide mudflats of Roebuck Bay in a single shaft of red light quite unlike anything seen before.

The next day marked our second week on the road, and we left for Derby, a town of 2,500, flat, dusty, dry and a centre for cattle with an airport and a seaport.

Outside of town is the Boab Tree Prison.

The boab tree looks like a giant bottle with small branches that go squiggling off in all directions. It is a comic opera tree.

This boab tree was so large that they used it at the turn of the century to imprison lawbreakers before taking them into Derby for trial.

(Derby is pronounced *der-bee* and not like the British *dar-bee*.)

The Spinifex Hotel in Derby has the Spinifex Bar (air conditioned with television), the Public Bar, the Saloon Bar and the Garden Bar plus the usual Bottle Store.

We had a cold beer in the Garden Bar.

The Gibb River Beef Road links Derby to Wyndham.

Once the only way to get cattle to market was in huge cattle drives over the ranges. It was slow, expensive. The cattle lost much of their condition.

The situation gave birth to a unique enterprise, "Air Beef." The cattle were slaughtered and dressed in the field and the beef was air freighted to market. The effort was marginal, however, and when the Gibb River Beef Road was completed it meant that motorised road-trains could more swiftly move cattle to Derby on one side and to Wyndham on the other side of the King Leopold Range.

The Kimberley is rugged country. We thought the mountain ranges on the map signified forests and greenery but, instead, it was more gum trees and wattle. Also, we learned that the desert we had gone through had had an unusual amount of rain and appeared greener than normal but The Kimberley country had had a drought and was dryer than usual. Sort of evened out the greenery.

The name "Kimberley" immediately suggested the famous diamond mines of South Africa and by coincidence in August, 1978 there was a major find of diamond "pipes" in the Australian Kimberley, a discovery which led to the establishment of a mining operation now producing over two million carats of diamonds annually.

Our destination for Night 8 was Windjana Gorge National Park, an outcropping of limestone cliffs on the Lennard River. In the same area is Tunnel Creek National Park named after a 750-metre tunnel dug through the limestone of the Oscar Range which you can walk through. A strong flashlight is recommended.

This area served as a base for "Pigeon," an Aboriginal outlaw who was talked into taking arms against the white man by a renegade that Pigeon and a white constable had captured. The caves around the gorges made perfect hideouts. Finally in the Tunnel Creek area Pigeon was cornered and lost his life . . . a story which is recounted in a book, *The Outlaw of the Leopolds.*

We arrived in the Windjana Park in time to investigate the Aboriginal paintings on the cliff walls and to take a swim in the Lennard River.

It was a peaceful spot. Green, shady trees overhanging a deep, calm pool. A sandy river bank to enter the water.

The picture was somewhat marred by the still, brown logs with eyes a bit farther down river. Crocodiles.

Mind you, these were Johnson fresh water crocodiles, a descendant, it is said, of the dinosaur. It is a protected reptile. It is shy, you are told, and you want to believe it.

When you are going swimming in the same pool, the fact that a Johnson fresh water crocodile has never been known to attack a man . . . doesn't make any difference at all.

You take the fastest swim of your life.

You hardly need a towel when you get out.

Walking back to the campsite, swimmers pass you on the way to the pool.

"How was it?"

"Great!" you answer heartily. "Fantastic! We could have stayed in forever."

The dawn departure was delayed six hours.

Leaving the pasture *Anna* hit a concealed rock in the tall spinifex grass, breaking a spring bolt and pushing the front wheel back into the fender guard.

Disaster. It was unfixable.

But thanks to that same incredible Don Nayler-ingenuity, aided by his Australian passengers and with outstanding help from Michael Kosarotov, the local ranger, *Anna* rolled out of the park.

It was another superb repair performance.

Don in his gruff manner said later that the only breakdown that is major is the one where they have to come and get you!

The day was gone when we finally pulled into Manning Gorge. But some more "firsts" had been recorded. A huge wedge-tailed eagle with a seven-foot wing span took off from his perch on a tree like a lumbering airplane to fly alongside the bus, landed on another tree and kept repeating landings and take-offs to everyone's delight.

We saw our first emu, the ostrich-like bird and wallaby, the small kangaroo.

Manning Gorge in the morning light was gorgeous. The river water clear and inviting.

Don, when asked if he had been swimming said, "Did I ever. Skinny dipping at pickaninny dawn. My, yes!"

The Manning River was a most photogenic visual. The varied coloured sandstones in the pools made it look like a Japanese garden. The evergreen trees in front of the limestone rocks reflected in the river waters in that soft morning light were bits of artistry begging to be painted, to be put on film.

Everybody was enthralled.

Even this scenic masterpiece was to be topped.

After leaving camp we backtracked a few miles down the road to Gavan Falls which we should have visited on the way to Manning Gorge but couldn't because it was too late.

I have three pictorial books on Australia and I can't find Gavan Falls in any of them.

I promise you that it is the most perfect waterfall you have ever seen. Not tall, it is probably thirty feet high and glides down terraces in two falls into a perfect circular pool one hundred feet around. Pandanus trees and green ferns look twice as thick because they see themselves in the mirror-clear waters.

It is a jewel . . . a four-star, breath-gasping jewel.

Camp 10 was at Joe's Waterhole on the Campbell River. We sat around a huge bonfire and ate a curry dinner.

The pink dawn over the river in this most remote area was so peaceful. Probably less than a thousand people see Joe's Waterhole during the year. It would be our last day on the Gibb River Beef Road and the last hard day of dusty driving.

Before noon we had dropped out of the Barnett Range and could see the Timor Sea in the distance and before noon we had reached paved road and were on our way into Wyndham, a port city for shipping beef. A guide book lists as one of the special places of interest the meat works during killing season. That's it.

We were grateful that our stopping schedule had eliminated Wyndham and moved up our stay at Lake Argyle.

Outside of Wyndham we drove into Marlgu Billabong, a bird sanctuary, which was birdless due to the drought, and then went to the Grotto, a gorge which was almost waterless.

By contrast, the little modern city of Kununurra with green grass and water sprinklers thanks to the waters of Lake Argyle looked like a piece of green heaven. Modern municipal buildings, souvenir shops, motels . . . and water sprinklers.

Outside the Kununurra is Hidden Valley, a cul-de-sac of tall sandstone formations layered with colours.

The dirt road leads through a Disneyland of fantasy shapes: a chapel, a giant monster. It was late afternoon and the sun was just topping the tallest of the formations.

The valley is estimated to be three hundred million years old and was a favourite site for Aboriginal ritual meetings.

Lake Argyle Tourist Camp, thick with tents, was dark by the time we reached it.

No matter, we were a gang of professional campers by now.

A washing machine! We had dirty clothes in hot water before *Anna* had stopped.

Formerly all thumbs and stumbling and stopping, our tent now went up in zip-zip time. Cots rigged. Sleeping bags out. Into the hot shower.

We all had our routines.

Ed, the retired executive, shaved on the left front fender of *Anna* with a hot mug of water and a straight razor. The red-headed newspaper man was as meticulous as a cat and carefully scrubbed behind his shining ears with a washcloth.

I laugh now looking at my notes.

By this time the safari had seen emus and eagles and kangaroos and so many gorgeous big and small wild birds that it is difficult to count the number.

What produced the most chatter among the Australian passengers? Seeing a wild donkey.

Lake Argyle and the multi-million dollar Ord Dam which made the immense water scheme possible was completed in 1972.

What was once only country for grazing now has the potential of becoming farms for rice, safflower and cotton although an ambitious American cotton plantation failed due to the devastation caused by boll weevils.

The waters of The Kimberley rivers had drawn the attention of eastern cattlemen in the nineteenth century.

The original explorations, the staking out of vast tracks of virgin territories on maps, the duration of incredible overland cattle drives to bring livestock into the country, all are captured in an excellent book, *Kings in Grass Castles* by Mary Durack, granddaughter of "Paddy" Durack, the pioneer founder of an empire . . . a king in a grass castle.

We later met and fell in love with the authoress, now Dame Mary Durack Miller, in Perth where she is working on a sequel of the Durack legend which will centre around her father, Michael Patrick Durack, Paddy's eldest son.

Argyle Station, the family homestead, is at the bottom of Lake Argyle. Also at the bottom of Lake Argyle is, potentially, part of the diamond deposits found in The Kimberleys.

In a paddock above the lake the original Durack homestead has been reconstructed and is a pioneer museum. A plaque nearby was erected by Mary's father who camped first on this site on May 8, 1886 when he was twenty-one.

Lake Argyle is already a popular vacation area as proved by the tent population at the camping ground. The huge expanse of water — eight times the size of Sydney Harbour — houses sailing boats and fishing boats, water skiing boats. The lake is stocked with catfish.

We left Western Australia and re-entered the Northern Territory travelling beside the Victoria River.

In 1883 the Victoria River Downs Station was the largest cattle ranch in Australia covering thirty-five thousand square miles. It has since been reduced considerably in size.

In relating statistics, Don-the-guide and former drover, harrumphed about absentee ownership. The straggly little brown cattle showed lack of reinvestment by the owners, he said.

We camped by the river that night. Across the bridge from a small pub and a caravan park.

After dinner we walked to the pub and I took a towel. After a couple of beers I asked the bartender how much he charged for use of the caravan park's shower.

"Six bob if I see you. But I probably won't see you."

I did. He didn't.

At the prosperous little cattle town of Katherine (population 2,500) it was Show Time. Exhibits, carnival rides, horse races. The town was bustling the day before the Show. The day of the Show the town shops were closed. Everybody goes to the Show.

We drove the few miles out of town to Katherine Gorge National Park and camped in a neat section reserved for touring buses such as ours with a fenced off grassy area complete with picnic tables and concrete barbecue pits.

Among the attractions were tame kangaroos and a pair of emus to eat out of your hand and to pose for pictures.

Next to *Anna* another Bill King tour bus pulled in.

Our earlier experience with the Mercedes air-conditioned bus was repeated.

We eyed their equipment, their driver, their cook and in the subsequent huddle quickly agreed that we had the better bus, the superior driver and the more competent cook. (You think we asked them what they were going to have for dinner? You bet we did!) It was no contest. Marvellous.

Katherine Gorge as a national park is properly developed.

There are information kiosks to tell you about the birds and the plants; the many recommended, developed hiking paths are mapped out and the walking time is detailed.

One walk suggested returning down the Katherine River on an air mattress which sounded like fun.

The principal attraction is exploring Katherine Gorge on a ranger-conducted boat trip which takes two hours and costs $7.50. Another boat trip takes all day and costs $32.

The fifty-six kilometre-long gorge is considered one of the scenic highlights of Australia's Top End.

Over a period of twenty-five million years the river has sculptured its channel through rocks leaving high cliffs on each side.

We took the two-hour scenic ride up the gorge on a cloudless morning. We passed through Butterfly Gorge, by Jedda Rock.

We saw more Aboriginal paintings on the cliff walls.

"These red and yellow colours were derived by the Aborigines from ochre, dried iron ore powder. Brown and white came from the trees and limestones. The powders were mixed with lizard oil and applied with fingers or the tips of feathers," the ranger-guide said.

It was a peaceful way to spend the morning.

Our Last Camp. Number fourteen.

We couldn't have found a more idyllic spot.

Edith Falls is part of the same area as the Katherine Gorge but is was reached after two hours of driving, skirting the park and then cutting into the bush on a dirt road. It was worth the effort.

A tranquil pool under the shadow of a cliff, a tumbling waterfall, a fringe of shade trees around the edge of the water — everybody in for a swim!

We climbed to falls higher up the river and they were even prettier. Scenic pond with marble stones. Rock slabs that slide into the clear water. Surrounding ferns. Most satisfying.

We met a Czechoslovakian in the pool. He had escaped his country in 1968. Over an electrified fence. Two bullet wounds. He left behind a wife and child he'll never see again.

He was part of a surveying team for a new sealed road into Edith Falls. It will cut seven kilometres off the present track. Good and bad.

Sitting in the shade of a eucalyptus tree with the tinkle of waterfalls in the background, Don, the poet-driver, told about his childhood, his schooling, his drover days.

We were mesmerised by his monologues. Gruff. Honest. Droll. Self-effacing. Lyrical.

It was our best camp.

At dawn we rolled toward Darwin. The Top End it is called.

The countryside was dotted with former World War II airfields.

Before noon we were at a caravan park outside of Darwin with hot and cold running water and everyone did a quick laundry.

Over lunch the Lady Navigator took a quick "most satisfactory" survey among our companions.

The men voted Gavan Falls, the Tanami Desert and Geike Gorge as the highlights of the trip.

Strangely, no one picked Katherine Gorge and we surmised that it was probably a let-down after seeing Geike Gorge first.

The safari exceeded the expectations of the women in every way. Among their highlights were: the bus breakdown in the desert (!), seeing country they wouldn't drive through themselves, Gavan Falls, Broome and Cable Beach.

The girl from New Zealand said that the country was drier than she expected which contrasted with Viv, the cook, who was enthralled with everything in the desert.

"I visited New Zealand once," Viv said. "It was nothing but mountains and rivers and lakes. Boring!"

We left our last can of macadamia nuts for Mr. McDonnell who recovered our lost wallet in the Ansett airline offices and gave Don-the-singer-driver a tape of Hawaiian music to play on *Anna's* tape machine.

At the airport Don said, "I have to leave now. I'm getting misty."

A Japanese national took the sixteen-day Kimberley Safari. He didn't speak or write any English but somehow communicated with sign languages and gestures and nods of the head.

He was given a "Your Comments Please" form at the end of the trip and he wrote in English: "Bloody good, mate." We'd second that.

The 1984-85 brochure of the Bill King's Australia Outback Hotel and Motel Tours did not include the tour we took through the Tanami to Broome and through the Kimberley to Darwin. The new tours are mostly the swept up kind on air-conditioned buses with hotel-motel accommodations.

I would have hated to have missed the little-boy thrill of sleeping under the desert stars, the campfire, the cooked-in-the-open grub.

Fortunately there are many tours of all kinds available, on camel, on horse, in canoes, on rafts, as well as four-wheel vehicle where tents and sleeping bags are still the accommodation.

We were to sample all of them and we vote for adventure travel as the way for opening the doors to the best part of Australia.

Darwin

However, we moved from the caravan park to the Travelodge Hotel and abandoned ourselves to the luxury of room service: roast chicken, white wine, vodka tonics. A tub bath followed by a shower shampoo.

We watched the satellite TV broadcast of the final round of the British Open until two-thirty in the morning.

Swam in the hotel pool. Steak lunch. We loved it.

Although our stay was limited — and self-indulgent — it doesn't take too many sensitive antennae to know that Darwin has to be ranked as one of the more gutsy little cities of the world.

As the capital of the Northern Territory with 65,000 people, it has its own pride in being the biggest frog in its own small pond.

World War II was a mixed blessing. Nearly half of Darwin was destroyed. Bad. Nearly 10,000 servicemen crammed the area. Good and bad. A sealed road was opened to Alice Springs. Good.

The postwar period was a boom time.

Then on Christmas Eve in 1974 a cyclone called "Tracy" which was forecast to veer off harmlessly to sea, bore straight down on Darwin, destroying five thousand of the city's ten thousand homes. A night of horror.

Today Darwin is new and fresh and bustling.

The brightest edition on the scene has been the Mindil Beach Hotel-Casino Resort.

With something over one hundred rooms, the hotel is connected by air-conditioned walkways to the casino.

Blackjack, roulette, dice, baccarat, slot machines and bingo games are part of the action. We heard, but couldn't confirm, that in action-starved Darwin the casino reached the dollar volume in one month that had been forecast for the entire year.

Oh, yes, and there is a Las Vegas type girly show. In Darwin.

When we were in Darwin a tragedy occurred.

"Sweetheart" died.

Sweetheart was a twenty-foot, one-ton crocodile whose fetish was chewing off propellers from outboard motors of fishing boats.

In one attack he took on the Northern Territory's leading crocodile expert who had gone out to check on the Sweetheart attacks.

The authority was about to abandon a boat search in Sweetheart's favourite lagoon when suddenly the monster appeared out of the murky waters, grabbed the stern in his awesome jaws and started to shake the boat from side to side.

Just as suddenly he broke off the attack and disappeared.

That did it. Sweetheart had to be moved.

A special net trapped the crocodile who was tranquillised for the move to a remote lagoon. A floating log forced him underwater. Sweetheart drowned.

It was suggested editorially that Sweetheart's giant body would be preserved and displayed at the city's proposed $6-million museum. We hope with an outboard motor dangling from his chops.

3. Whitewater Safari in a Rubber Ducky

Driving north from Sydney along the coast, the newcomer with a mental picture of Australia as a land of wide deserts and lonely animal life, kangaroos and spear-carrying Aborigines is stunned by the beauty of bountiful rivers bordered by lush forests.

The rivers are created by waters running off the cliff-face of the New England Plateau, part of the Great Dividing Range which extends from Victoria through New South Wales to Queensland.

On one of these rivers, the Nymbodia in northern New South Wales, Nymbodia Whitewater Expeditions has set up rafting safaris on what they claim is the finest whitewater river on the continent and through some of the most breath-taking, natural, unspoiled landscape of Australia.

That's what we were committed to on a Sunday in late November.

We had practically memorised every word in the *River Rats Handbook* distributed to us in Sydney at the time of signing... "everything you need to know to have an exciting *rapid* love affair."

All went according to the book.

We were met at a highway rendezvous point two miles south of Coffs Harbour and directed to a warehouse where a swarm of people were busily unpacking, repacking, loading a Land Rover and a small bus.

Two sixty-litre plastic drums, usually used for home brewing, were given to us for our rental sleeping bags and the standard gear provided: an air mattress called a "lilo," plastic plate, cup, knife, fork, spoon and a roll of toilet paper.

Into the drums went the recommended pack items: plastic ponchos — we would be travelling during the "wet" — a sweater or jumper as the Australians say, an extra pair of tennis shoes, our oldest T-shirts, two quick drying bathing suits, a pair of jeans for the evening around the campfire, a hat with strings over which a plastic helmet could fit, two pairs of socks — one to wear at night, one to wear in the daytime to protect the ankles — necessary underclothes and personal articles. Camera and film.

Camera and film! Would you believe on such a trip that I would

25

leave the camera and film in the car? The lovely Lady Navigator never mentions it.

You are forbidden the bringing of alcoholic beverages, firearms and portable radios. They don't mind a *small* medicinal flask for use of an evening. I forgot that too.

Our party totalled nineteen including four professional guides.

We piled into the two vehicles and took off for a three-hour ride up to the Dorrigo Plateau to the headwaters of the Nymbodia River.

In the bus there was an immediate breaking out of beer by some of the Australian males who would be going through that particular Australian purgatory, beerless days.

Two hours out of Coffs Harbour we stopped at Ulong, a tiny mountain village and went into the Ulong Ex-Servicemen's Club. Dutifully signed the registry, bought beer at the bar and dutifully put the change into surrounding poker machines which carried a sign: "Poker machines may only be reserved while (a) obtaining change (b) using the toilet facilities."

At the bar expedition members, passengers and crew, began trading names and home towns. We were the only non-Australians.

The passengers included a band leader, a financial editor, two airline stewardesses, one just-finished university graduate, an engineer and his wife, a truck operator and his girl friend, an accountant, a maitre d' and a young barrister.

Arthur was the expedition captain, a smallish, extremely muscular, moustached character, constantly smoking. He was strong enough to carry the world on his shoulders if it were required. He would command the largest of the three rafts assisted by John, a tall, lithe young man who, in the summer, led the company's bush treks in New Guinea.

Peter Kelly, our raft commander, was as Irish as his name suggests, curly of hair, mercurial of temper, an extremely competent boatman.

Ross, another handsome youngster, had the third raft.

With every one knowing each other and warmed by the refreshments, we set off in comradeship instead of being a pack of strangers. Our road led to the top of the mountain and through forest trails and stopped.

Descending to the river could only be done in the four-wheel-drive Land Rover which would mean shuttle trips.

We were in the first group to bounce down the steep slope to the river camp. A lovely spot. The Cod Hole. A large sand beach faced a calm, two-acre river lake with scenic cliffs and a forest on the far side.

A small, cascading waterfall fed fresh water into the pool.

"It's great swimming," said Arthur, a remark which produced an immediate scramble for the individually numbered plastic drums and swimming suits.

On the beach were three deflated Avon rubber rafts, one fifteen-feet and two thirteen-feet. One of the small rafts was inflated and floated into the pool.

Peter paddled the raft to the falls, dragged it over the rocks and then, with four passengers inside, he ran the raft through the falls. It slithered through, bending over and around the rocks.

"How much air do you put in the rafts?" we asked Peter later.

"The proper pressure is two and a half pounds per square inch which makes the raft resilient enough to give when it hits a rock and not so hard as to produce a puncture."

He wasn't using an air gauge. "How do you know when you reach two and a half pounds of pressure?"

He thumped the side of the raft. "It *sounds* like two and a half pounds."

For an hour, joined by the other expedition members, it was swim time and then everybody settled into the first camp.

A large, blue nylon cover was stretched across a nylon line to create a simple A-frame tent. The advance material said you could ask for an individual tent which we should have done but didn't.

We picked a spot on the beach to ourselves — too near the fire we found out later — pumped up our air mattresses and made ready for the next day.

The management provided six flagons of wine for the trip with the warning that sometimes the wine only lasted the first night. In our expedition it only lasted one night.

After a good dinner of grilled lamb chops, potatoes and green salad — nothing tastes better in the open than grilled lamb chops — a couple of hardier members got stuck into the wine. They finally finished it in the early hours of the morning after much singing and joke telling and raucous laughter. Near the fire, of course.

(I had revenge the next evening. Because of the threat of rain, I moved into the blue nylon "hotel" right next to one of the revellers of the night before and I snored loudly in his ear.

"I didn't sleep a wink all night," he snivelled.)

When the drinkers finally did cover the fire and go to their sleeping bags, the fading quarter of a moon also disappeared leaving a canopy of touch-me stars.

At dawn the sleeping bags were wet with dew.

The camp slowly came to life. Bedraggled sleepers emerged to scratch, stretch, yawn. A few shaved. Several took a morning swim.

Breakfast came in stages. An orange. A cup of tea or coffee. A bowl of hot porridge or cold cereal. Sausage and eggs and toast. Solid breakfast.

Breaking camp and the organisation of the rafts proceeded at a leisurely pace. Never any sense of pushing for time or frantic efforts to meet a deadline. I had taken off my watch on arrival and put it into the bottom of my plastic container and it didn't come out again until Thursday night. Measured time was of no consequence.

What counted was a chance to be out in the wilderness, on a river which was never seen except by people who came by river, in air scented only with the smell of gum trees.

"Stop the bus" said the band leader from Sydney on the drive to camp. "I won't go any farther until I see the air I'm breathing."

Across the middle of each of the two smaller rafts was placed an iron frame floored with wire mesh. On these the food containers, an "Esky" with fresh meat, the nylon tent and individual drums were stacked and roped down securely. One container was designated as "the camera drum."

Each member donned a red life jacket and a yellow plastic, made-in-Japan hockey helmet. Everybody was given a paddle.

"All we ask," Arthur said, "is that you follow instructions. The dangers are small but obey the rules. In fifty river trips we haven't lost anyone yet and we don't want to start with you."

We listened very carefully.

"You've all promised that you can swim. That might be necessary.

"First don't use your life jacket as a cushion. If you cut it on the raft or pierce it with a rock on shore, it will become saturated with water in the river *AND ACT LIKE A CEMENT JACKET*."

Not a noise.

"If you are thrown out of the raft — and it happens — don't panic. Be prepared to spend five to ten seconds under water. Don't hold on to the raft. Point your feet downstream, straighten you knees, tighten your buttocks. Float to the bank and get out of the water.

You never know what is around the next bend. Don't try to swim against the current."

No one moved.

Arthur continued: "The biggest danger is being sucked under the raft. If the raft is stuck against an obstacle, don't push it from behind or pull it from in front. In shallow water if the raft goes over you the weight of the raft will hold you under. We have thirty seconds to get you out.

"Our accident count to date is one dislocated shoulder, one sprained ankle and two bloody noses. We don't count cuts and bruises.

"Everybody ready? Let's go."

The rafts were pushed out into the stream led by Arthur in the big raft and started the drift down river with slightly apprehensive passengers on board.

From Cod Hole, where we spent the first night, to the first rapid was less than an hour. All hearts were pitter-pattering but once through the swift whitewater ride it became routine. No, not routine. The water in the river was very low and we spent hours out of the raft pulling it through the shallows. A rapid meant a fast passage down river.

The company never cancels a trip. They did cancel twice their first year and both times the rains came and a potentially fine trip was lost. Also trips that have started out on a low river on Monday have finished in flood runs on Thursday.

The biggest thrill the first day was The Waterfall, a straight, four-foot drop.

The drill of a major drop called for an initial riverbank reconnaissance by Arthur. The camera drum was opened and cameras were passed back and forth for the people on shore to film the first boat as it was slowly pulled by the current into the narrowing rocky wall and then faster and faster and then . . . *whoosh* . . . over the edge to shrieks, laughs, finally loud hand-clapping.

Then the passengers of the first boat took over the cameras to film the next raft.

At midday a previously patched seam on our raft parted on contact with an underwater rock. All three boats beached while our raft was repaired. It became lunch break. Sandwiches. Peanut butter. Sliced tomato and cheese.

The weather was perfect. Warm sun and inviting water made swimming a natural part of every break. People were constantly in the water throughout the expedition.

In the first afternoon we were also out of the rafts more than in them, putting the crafts over the slippery rocks, banging ankles, sliding, trying to keep from falling down.

We were relieved to pull into that night's camping beach.

"How far have we gone, Arthur?"

"We've only covered six and a half miles. If the river had been up another six inches, we would have done nine miles."

The steak and mashed potato dinner with salad was wolfed down by the starving passengers.

What you do after dinner is skip rocks across the river.

A wedge-tailed eagle wheeled slowly high in the sky and, when night came, fireflies appeared in the dark forest.

Despite a few drops of rain that night, the river fell another two inches and after a breakfast of scrambled eggs and sausages the organisation of the camp and the rafts moved a bit more quickly to make up for the time lost the day before and we soon were paddling downstream.

"The Gully," a major drop just around the corner provided the initial excitement. A roller coaster ride which bent to the right, down a chute, and then sharply turned left.

You go at a drop paddling to keep the raft in the proper heading. At the edge of the drop, you ship your paddle, grab the straps of the raft and lift your feet to the raft sides to keep the rocks from bruising a foot. The action produces a mess of bodies in weird positions.

Day Three was spent in great part in making portages not only around but up and over giant rocks. Shoving and heaving. "One-two-three — pullll!" echoed from the three rafts.

It is the kind of tough work at which Australian men excel . . . the tougher it is the more they come together and get it done. The more grinding, the more demanding, the dirtier, the more impossible, the more the genuine "mateyness" pays off.

Mid-morning of Day Three we brushed a tragedy.

Our raft was stuck in a narrow wedge of high rocks, the water rushing from behind pinching her bow tight in the wedge.

Peter ordered everybody off the raft to the rocks on the side. In stepping off the slippery rubber pontoon, the Lady Navigator's feet went out from underneath her and she disappeared under the raft! There was a split second of instant, paralyzing panic.

Then Peter let out a yell. I jumped out of the raft to do what I don't recall. All I could think of was "thirty seconds."

Just then in the pond below the stuck raft the bottom of a red bathing suit bobbled on the surface and slowly righted itself and there was the Lady Navigator, wide-eyed, scared, stunned, with a "who-pushed-me" expression on her face.

There had been enough space in the wedge below the raft and enough water pressure to blow her clear.

What a frightening moment.

The next excitement came at "The Pinnacle."

The Pinnacle called for quick manoeuvring. A severe right turn into the rapids, a sharp left turn into a five foot drop between two solid walls of granite, followed by an immediate right turn.

We negotiated the right turn ... good ... then the left turn ... good ... over the falls! And there the raft, made too flexible by its leakage, stuck firmly between the granite walls where the waterfall cascaded down on us and wouldn't let us go.

We were solidly stuck and pounded by the water. The occupants of the first raft, though, were hanging over the rocks yelling and laughing. By this time a fine bit of rivalry had developed.

"Rock the boat," yelled Peter.

We rocked and rocked and he jumped up and down furiously. Gradually the raft began to turn and with a final, giant jump, *Peter went straight through the raft.* The whole front bottom gave way ... but we were free.

For the second consecutive day lunch time was spent repairing our good ship "Lolly Pop."

After repast and repairs all rafts were portaged a few hundred yards over high rocks and the drums were floated through the unnegotiable rapids and collected in the clear water pond below.

High on the cliff-face were remnants of a kayak attesting to the fury of the Nymbodia in a flood. The canoeist was saved by being helicoptered to a hospital.

"During the flood there are only three places on the river where you can beach," said Arthur. "What took us two days to cover is run in an hour and a half during a flood.

"Oh, yes, it is a thrill," he went on. "You never know what will be around the next bend. What you really fear is a log across your run. A raft can't go over a log. It goes under it. . . taking off everything on top, including you."

Our raft continued to leak as we limped into camp at "High Beach." To everyone's relief we found a sandy niche above the "hotel" and after a beef stew dinner, we slept the sleep of the exhausted.

Day Four.

The highlight was paddling through the Nymbodia Gorge — towering cliffs looking over an expanse of placid, deep water.

After the gorge it was a long day of fierce portaging taking much time and effort, pulling, hauling, shoving: "one, two, three."

But the compensation was having the time to taste the beauty of the pristine wilderness, to savour the silence between bird calls. Virgin country. Scenic. Unspoiled.

That night it was Peter's turn to cook and we had Kelly's Stew.

Unique.

The meat had gone off and Peter compensated by using almost everything that was left over. Potatoes, carrots, cabbage, canned beans, packaged dry vegetables, tomatoes . . . and chilli powder. The diners, especially the crew, hooted and made pointed comments about the concoction . . . and ate it all.

Day Five, the last on the river. Everyone now a pro, knowing when to paddle, when to get out, when to pray for open water.

We had several good runs before cliffs slowly started to spread out . . . a couple of patches of long, quiet water . . . the third raft made a sail out of the blue nylon tent . . . and there were frequent water fights between rafts with buckets, paddles.

About mid-afternoon we turned the last bend and nosed into a grassy bank. It was our pick-up landing spot. It was all over.

Arthur's raft had already banked and its occupants had been picked up.

We waited leisurely for almost two hours in the warm sun. Pleasant. Made sandwiches out of what didn't go into Kelly's chilli. Have you ever had a pickled onion-peanut butter sandwich?

Finally the Land Rover returned. Yes, with a case of cold beer, of course. On the vehicle we loaded twelve drums, two iron frames, two Eskies and twelve expedition members plus the driver. Bodies inside, outside, topside, riding on fenders.

The solid vehicle inched up the narrow, twisting road — how it made it when it rained we don't know — slowly reaching wider and wider roads until we were on a paved highway. At the Coutts Crossing pub we joined the others for more beer, peanuts and "jaffles" — toasted sandwiches.

It was almost dark by the time our small bus picked us up for the long ride back to Emerald Beach, a caravan park, where we showered and then reboarded the bus for the "Captain's Dinner" at the pub in Woolgoolga.

We arrived at ten. The pub had been waiting for us since six. But that is the way of the river.

The pub closed by law at eleven and the evening was too short. But we shared a couple of drinks and last laughs. We had become a river rat family. That, too, is the way of the river.

Certificates attesting to our successful passage on the river were handed out and each certificate bore a special "degree" awarded by the raft commander.

On the Lady Navigator's certificate Peter wrote: "Hull Inspection."

We opted out that night for a motel instead of a caravan park and again, gratefully, accepted all the discomforts of hot water and a double bed.

You can make reservations on the Nymbodia through the Adventure Travel Centre in Sydney. The Adventure Travel Centre also offers several rafting and canoeing experiences. It is best to write for a free brochure. The address again: First Floor, 28 Market Street, Sydney.

4. Bogong High Plains Horse Safari

In the heart of the Victorian Alps 400 km northeast of Melbourne is the little cowtown of Omeo — pronounced as in Romeo — population 400.

In summer Omeo hosts a number of trout anglers. Winter skiers driving from Melbourne to Mt. Hotham pass through and sometimes party at the two-storey Golden Age Hotel. During annual stock sales the hotel is wall-to-wall with cattle buyers and sellers.

We were in Omeo overnight prior to a two-day trail ride into the Bogong High Plains. Actually the ride was a four-day outing but our schedule permitted us only half the trip.

The Golden Age was our first country hotel experience. Overhead light in the room with a pull chain. Bathroom down the hall.

Because there were obviously few guests in the hotel, we went down to dinner expecting the bar lounge to be empty but instead the room was packed with local people having a night out. Porterhouse steak $3.20. Strawberrry Moose (sic) 60c.

Before dinner Lorna Peterson came across the street from the chemist shop were she worked and introduced herself as the wife of Frank Peterson who heads the trail rides.

The safaris, available from November to June, she explained, are really tailored to fit the request and the experience of the riders who frequently put together their own groups. Some riders even bring their own horses.

Everything is provided for on the ride except sleeping bags which can be rented. The total cost for the safari is only about $45 a day per person. A great bargain.

After dinner Frank Peterson came in and introduced a Melbourne couple who was going on the ride. They had brought their own horses.

Frank had a beaten-up cowboy hat on, which he never removed, a rather beaten-up face with a nose that was undecided whether to go east or west, broad-shoulders, firmly set. You wouldn't want to argue in a bar with Frank Peterson. Lorna, his wife, was a good looking angel.

The next morning we gathered about nine at the hotel . . . eventually moved to the Peterson house outside of Omeo where we were joined by a young man and two young ladies from Melbourne who had been rained out of a camping trip and decided to ride instead. There would be eight of us on the trail. Lorna would drive the jeep with trailer carrying all the bedding and grub and meet us along the way, first for lunch, and then later for dinner.

Saddles, bridles, food boxes, grain bags, a case of beer and sleeping bags were loaded into the jeep and trailer and we took off for the paddocks outside of town where the horses were herded together and saddled.

I drew a pinto named Tonka and the Lady Navigator was given Hardy, a bay.

Starting a two-day trail ride when you are hazy in memory about which part of the horse goes first is a bit jittery but by eleven-thirty we were clip-clopping peacefully down the macadam road and then up a dirt road into the bush, through groves of towering eucalyptus trees . . . all alone except for the sound of horses and birds singing . . . trailed by two of Frank's happy, panting dogs.

We rode along faint trails and roads, across pastureland, almost always ascending. It was a warm morning and in less than two hours we came to a woolshed where the jeep was parked in the shade. Cold beer and a pile of excellent cold chicken, salad, tomatoes, buttered bread and cheese were served.

After lunch the horses were eager to get on the trail again. Tonka pulled constantly at the reins trying to get in front of the other horses. A goer.

Frank's horses were accustomed to the mountains, surprisingly strong. The couple who brought their own mounts kept behind, not pushing them because the horses had been trained on flat land.

The woolshed dropped below us rapidly. In the timber country the dogs cornered a porcupine-looking creature called an echidna. Frank dismounted and picked up the spine-covered creature to show us its long, sharp claws. A startled tiny face peered out from its furry center.

We sloshed through the Cobungra River where a couple of men we had met the night before in the bar were fishing and picnicking with their children.

Through more forests and across more plains and there under the shade of the tree again was Lorna. Afternoon tea.

For the best part of an hour the horses had a chance to rest and cool off and then we started on the last leg of the day up the golden hills and eventually to the Bundara River where we met a couple of stockmen. They had been catching frogs because that night they were competing in a "frog walloping" contest.

Frog walloping is trout fishing with tiny live frogs tied to the end of the line. The pole is anchored into the bank and then the fishermen lean back and get stuck into the grog. The record fish is not recorded but we were told the unofficial record for grog was three cases of beer and one bottle of Baileys Irish Cream.

Along the last mile of road by riverside — most picturesque — we saw wedge-tailed eagles wheeling in the sky. Average wingspan: seven feet, six inches.

We came to an ancient wooden woolshed, grey with age, where we again found Lorna and the jeep. The horses were unsaddled, their backs washed down from the grime of the saddle sweat and dirt and turned out to a paddock where they rolled in the dirt and grass with great ecstasy.

The young trio went swimming and I went fishing downstream. A picture-book river. Quietly flowing, twenty feet wide, with deep pools alternating with shallow ripples, tree shaded. Little fish jumped near my feet but never touched my prize Christmas-present brass spinner or red fly which I eventually lost by snaring in an unreachable bush. A peaceful end to a twenty-four kilometre ride in the saddle.

Evening "tea" was the best T-bone steak we tasted in Australia served with peas, onions, potato and cold beer. Not bad for "roughing it" in the bush.

Half a dozen country neighbours dropped by to share the beer and to gossip with the visitors and it was well after dark when we finally worked out territorial rights in the woolshed and found places for our sponge mattresses and sleeping bags.

Sleeping in a thirty-year-old woolshed is like sleeping in the armpit of an old ram — unforgettable. The wind blew through the tarpaulin. The old walls creaked. Holes in the walls were so big we could see the stars.

McCoy, the farmer whose woolshed had provided our cover, had lost $2,000 the year before in lost wool and replacement costs for sheep killed by dingos, the native wild dogs.

The dingos mate for life and hunt as a family. Sharpened by a kill-or-be-killed existence, the creatures are incredibly cunning, killing first in one part of the country and then quickly moving to operate in another part of the country, always moving.

Killing for the joy of it, the dingo savages sheep in bunches leaving them mutilated and dying. The farmers hate them as much for their unbridled slaughter as they do for the economic loss.

In the Omeo Hotel bar a state-appointed dingo hunter was pointed out to us. A bushman with a hat worse than Frank's and a weather cragged face out of which poked the butt of a handrolled cigarette. He would kill probably fifty dogs a year, we were told, mostly with steel traps, seldom if ever with a gun because a dingo is an almost invisible animal. Steel traps may be cluck-clucked at by humane societies but don't voice any objection to an Australian farmer.

At dawn I was first up and back on my pretty river to watch the world come alive. The tripping water over the round river rocks. The chirping of birds. The wind dancing with the trees. I took my fishing rod but never put a line in the water. Just sat silently on the bank in the stillness. A small body moved out into the stream. In size and shape it resembled a mongoose but it had a flat bill . . . a duck-billed platypus.

The camp came awake slowly. A few of the riders had gone over to the McCoy homestead and played cards until early in the morning.

Ham and eggs and potatoes for breakfast prepared us for the longest ride of the four days. Preparations were casual and it was not until eleven o'clock that we finally were packed and saddled and out the gate on the road into the hills.

Frank told us we would be riding a fairly steep grade for the first three miles.

We climbed higher and higher and the horses breathed harder and harder. The woolshed diminished to a speck in the valley below us.

We flushed a fox and gave it a short chase. Then we flushed two kangaroos. The dogs went yelping uselessly after them.

Higher and higher. Through forests of tall gum trees which gave way to snow gums, evidence that we had reached the high country, the Bogong High Plains.

We were starting to get hungry again and thinking of food when there was a loud shout from up in front of the line of riders and the heavy, hurried thumping of horse hoofs.

The Lady Navigator had been riding at the front of the line with Frank and I thought, "Migawd, she has fallen under the raft again."

The first thing we saw coming into a clearing was a mountain corral. Frank was on his feet running to one side of the enclosure. Beyond was the Lady Navigator still on her horse and not underneath it nor bucked into a tree top.

"Brumby!" Frank yelled. "Bar the front gate!"

He had reached the back gate and was standing in the middle of the opening, arms spread, hat in hand as a waving flag and inside the wooden, rough-tree-fenced corral was a wild horse. We formed a line at the front gate and then swung it closed.

I had always thought that a brumby was a knock-kneed, skinny, blotched-coated, starving orphan of the high country.

Not a bit of it. Inside the corral was this magnificent bay, shining black mane, wide, wild flashing eyes, flaring nostrils, stampeding from one side of the corral to another, pulling up short and crashing to the other side.

It was thrilling just to watch him.

He had come inside the corral for the salt lick, the bait used by brumby hunters in the mountains.

Eventually the front gate was pulled back and away he thundered, the earth shaking under his hooves. Gad.

We munched sandwiches in the corral and talked of nothing but brumbies.

Our next rest stop was at a log cabin ready for any occupant. Sugar and flour stowed away. Ashes in the fireplace. Frank had used the hut with others many times when they had hunted brumbies which was done more for sport than money. The cabin inside and out looked like a set for a motion picture.

During the rest of the afternoon ride across the green pastures of Dinner Plain, Round Plain and Mt. Niggerhead, we saw over twenty wild brumbies, their coats sleek by the green feed of the plains.

As daylight faded across the mountain tops, fog began to roll in. Temporarily we were lost.

Finally dropping down the other side of the mountain we came to a road which led us to Towanga Hut, an idyllic corner of a valley called Pretty Valley with a small stream running through it, sheds for shelter and a corral for the horses.

We had ridden some twenty-four kilometres the first day and over forty km the second.

They *peeled* us off the horses.

Every bone ached. The hair had been rubbed off the inside of my calves.

Fog now enveloped the camp. The chill of the mountain was warded off by billy tea and a small fire. We were due to meet a pick-up car at the dam causeway at six-thirty.

We said good-bye to riding pals with regret but, deep down, the idea of riding two more days at thirty kilometres each day didn't make us too envious.

(A month later we learned that the fog had stayed in the mountains and the ride without visibility was shortened.)

When the car picked us up at the dam, we thought it would be a short ride back to Omeo. It took us two and a half hours of steady driving! We had come that far. What made the biggest impression was that we drove *down* past the ski complex of Falls Creek at 6,000 feet. We had been that high.

It was nine o'clock when we reached our home at the Golden Age Hotel and Alan Faithfull, the hotel manager, came up with a bottle of sherry, waited until we had had deep soaking baths before personally cooking steak and vegetables. He opened a bottle of good red wine and gave us Camembert and port and, yes, we slept very soundly.

Riding alongside Frank on the second day I finally asked him what had happened to his nose.

"Oh," he shrugged. "Bar fights. Broken three times. Used to be a heller. Come home with shirt torn. All bloodied up. Getting calmer as I get older."

Alan, a native of the area, said that the graziers put their cattle into the high country for summer feeding and when autumn came they mustered the cattle down to Pretty Valley, where we had met our pick-up car. There would be four to five thousand head of cattle.

"To see the riders cut out their own cattle from that giant herd and muster them away is one of the great sights of the high country," he said.

Across the street from the Golden Age is a picture of the original hotel, an ornate, three-storey wooden structure which was destroyed by fire. The new hotel had been built in the early fifties.

Alan Faithfull leased the hotel. Obviously the bar trade sustained the operation. "Last week we did have a holiday but my payroll came to $1,500."

The post office in Omeo is a classic building. And the city gaol is a log cabin that has been in use since 1863. A sign at the entrance to the police compound reads sternly:

STRICTLY POLICE BUSINESS ONLY
OFFICE AND LOG GAOL STILL IN USE
AND NOT OPEN FOR PUBLIC INSPECTION
SO PLEASE DON'T ASK. VIEW FROM ROADWAY

Adventure Travel Centre also offers high country horse trekking in the high country of New South Wales. Duration is from three days to six days. Current costs are from $240 to $495. Previous riding experience is advised. Frank Peterson's address: Omeo, Victoria.

5. Bush Pilots' Safari

The first whiff of the Bush Pilots' Airways Tour to Cape York, The Top of Australia ... to Cooktown ... to Lizard Island ... to "Old T.I." (Thursday Island) had such a ring of romantic adventure to it that the Bush Pilots' Tour immediately went to the head of our list of things to do.

We must, however, confess to a hobby interest.

We belong to a growing crowd of people known as "Cookie Groupies." We worship at the cabin door of Captain James Cook, the supreme navigator. If our desire to share the scenery and experience of one of Cook's most dramatic moments is too enthusiastic, skip lightly through the next few pages.

I remember my initial kindle of interest in Cook was at the museum in Christchurch where there was a huge wall map detailing the three voyages of Cook. I was stopped by the vastness of his expeditions.

On returning home I called a historian who referred me to my first book on Cook. That led to J. C. Beaglehole's *The Life of Captain Cook* which in turn led to the Hakluyt Society's four volumes of *The Journals of Captain James Cook* (3,370 pages!).

I then spent two London weeks in the Public Records Office in Kew Gardens reading original Cook journals — a tingly experience — and travelled to Marton-in-Cleveland to visit Cook's birthplace.

On a pre-dawn Valentine's Day we pilgrimaged down a lava road to Kealakekua Bay in Hawaii to the site of Cook's death and watched the sun come up on the last scene of his life. He had been struck down at that very spot in the same morning light one hundred and ninety-nine years before to the day.

We stood on the ground at Point Venus on Tahiti where he built his celestial observation post and fort and we visited Gisborne where Cook made his first landing in New Zealand.

Captain James Cook is a major hobby interest.

On Cook's first voyage after accomplishing his mission in Tahiti and rediscovering and mapping New Zealand, he came within a thread of losing his ship in Australian waters. It was to be his closest call in three voyages.

North of Cairns while threading its way through the uncharted

Great Barrier Reef under full sail and a full moon, the *Endeavour* ran onto a coral shoal at high tide.

We would fly over the exact spot on the first leg of our tour.

Our BPA Tour to Cape York assembled at dawn at the Cairns Airport.

Our equipment was a venerable DC-3. Twenty passengers, all Australians, shared with us the common problem of trying to recall the last time we flew in a DC-3.

(I originally thought that the BPA Tour would consist of a pilot in a Piper Cub, sleeping bags and canvas water bags.)

Our craft was made in 1942 in Tulsa, Oklahoma and was originally operated by the U.S. Air Corps, then it was bought by Philippine Airlines, followed by New Guinea's Papua Airlines and finally was acquired by Bush Pilots' Airways.

Members of BPA, incidentally, call themselves "Bushies." Their infectious family spirit adds a big degree of satisfaction to the tour.

The single pilot turned out to be a crew of four: a captain fittingly named Cooke; Hayward, the first officer; Jan Lassen, the hostess and our tour leader, Wendy Walsh, a delightful, knowledgeable lady in love with all aspects of the Cape.

She apologised for her tin whistle which would be blown once for assembling passengers and twice "as a suggestion that it was a good time to go to the lavatory because I know the best loo's on the peninsula."

It was a perfect day for aerial sightseeing.

Immediately after take-off we could clearly see Green Island in the distance.

We flew up the coast looking down on Port Douglas and Daintree River and Cape Tribulation named by Cook "because here began all our troubles."

The DC-3 then turned toward the open sea and after a few minutes the captain directed attention to the port side to see Endeavour Reef, the spot where Cook nearly lost his ship.

The coral shoal, a patchwork of greens, was more than an acre in size and completely underwater. Of the thousands of acres of coral in the Barrier Reef, this coral head is probably the most famous.

After the *Endeavour* hit the reef, fifty tons of ballast, casks and stores including six cannons and carriages were heaved overboard. Twenty-three hours later the ship finally floated free.

If the coral had truly ripped the hull open, the ship would have gone down in minutes. It was a chance that Cook knew he had to take. Later, when the ship was beached, a broken-off coral head was found plugging the major hole.

Fortunately, three pumps were able to keep up with the leakage until the ship was fothered, a technique of using a sail, bolstered with wool and oakum and sheep's dung, like a huge bandage, pulled over the hull plugging the holes.

The *Endeavour* limped into a river harbour where the ship's company spent seven weeks repairing the damage.

The site is now occupied by the village of Cooktown.

The plane turned back to the mainland and landed at the Cooktown Airport, a dozen miles out of town.

We boarded two light airplanes – triple-engined Trislanders – and again flew out to sea passing over the vast spans of white silica sand of Cape Flattery and landed on the sand airstrip at Lizard Island. As if to dramatise the island's name a metre-long lizard slid off the airstrip's apron into the brush fringe. At the parking area an outhouse-sized wooden shack with a busted toilet in view bore the sign: "Lizard Island International Airport."

In a tractor-drawn wagon with a red and white striped canopy we toured the brown-coloured, treeless island which supplied another exciting page in Cook history.

After completing his repairs in the river, Captain Cook anchored at Lizard Island and, accompanied by Sir Joseph Banks the botanist, climbed the 1200-foot hill on the island to try and spot a passage through the reef.

Through the haze after a second climb he could see a gap in the wall of coral and determined to take the *Endeavour* through.

As he approached the reef the wind failed and the current took the vessel within a wave's length of the coral, a wave's length from being pounded to pieces by the thundering seas.

A slight wind saved the ship which went through a second opening "like a mill race on an outgoing tide."

After the frightening coral reef, the journals reported that the officers welcomed the dangers of the open sea with relief in what Banks called "this crazy ship."

Lizard Island is home for only two enterprises: a marine research station and an exclusive lodge with twelve guest rooms, lounge, bar, kitchen and dining pavilion.

The green, perfectly clear waters and the white beach at the lodge are beautiful. The island is a "mother ship" location for deep-sea fishermen because the marlin grounds are but minutes away from the harbour. Jack Nicklaus and Lee Marvin have both landed huge marlin while staying at the resort.

In the roofed and screened recreational-barbecue pavilion we had "elevenses" of fresh fruit and champagne. Delicious.

A signboard listed the record fish caught at the resort, the largest marlin, a 1,323-pound black marlin; the largest tuna, 147 pounds.

Lizard Island is a special place we would recommend to friends. Small. Nice ambience. A beautiful, get-away-from-it-all honeymoon resort.

In high season the American plan rate runs about $280 per day per couple. Not bad at all.

On the return to the mainland the two Trislanders did slow pass-bys so each load of passengers could take front-of-the-album pictures of each other. Typical of the thoughtful planning by BPA.

At Cooktown Airport we boarded buses for lunch and a town tour. Our driver-guide was a marvellous character called Hans Looser. "I am a born Looser," he would say.

He came out from Germany after World War II at the invitation of his cousin.

Hans' only geographic reference was an old gold-rush map of Australia on which the only cities were Sydney, Melbourne . . . and Cooktown. At the time of the 1890 gold-rush Cooktown had about 40,000 people, sixty-five pubs with licences pending for thirty more. Palmer Kate's and French Charlie's were renowned places of fun, sin and wild living. Half of the population was Chinese.

When the gold ran out, so did the people and by the time Hans arrived it was a ghost town with but a few hundred people remaining. He was stunned.

"I don't blame my cousin. How could you describe this land."

His first attempt at farming failed and he moved into Cooktown to do everything and anything. He mowed the grass at the cemetery. Played in a band. Gave music lessons. Ran a theatre.

The ex-German corporal, for years, led the annual Anzac Parade and when a righteous group protested at this anomaly, they were told, "No Hans. No parade." He was the only one in town who could play the bugle.

When he returned to Germany on a holiday, parade officials pre-taped his music.

He is a jolly man, always cheerful and an excellent guide. He apologises for his English saying that it is not the fault of his German accent but the fault of the Japanese-made loudspeaker.

We had a pleasant lunch with wine at the Endeavour Inn and then went to the river-front where Cook beached his wounded craft on the 18th of June. He actually entered the harbour on June 16 but was unable to reach shore because of gale winds.

The forced stay at Cooktown had its reward.

No previous explorers had the enquiring minds or the abilities of Cook and Banks and they spent the seven weeks in profitable research.

Their journals contained the first full description of this new continent, the details of the land and the bush, the Aborigines, the fish and the animals.

The scientists were intrigued by the strange animal with the short front paws and long tail which didn't run but hopped. The kangaroo. They tried to capture one to take home but even Banks' greyhounds couldn't catch one of the bounding animals.

The ship's company feasted on duck and clams and ate turtle — "feasted" Cook reported. All food was divided evenly. "The meanest person in the ship had an equal share with myself or any one on board, and this method every commander of a ship on such a Voyage as this ought ever to observe," he wrote in his journal.

Cook found the native tongue "soft and tunable." He described in his journals the use of body paint and was plainly shocked by the nudity: "On the other side of the River about 200 Yards from us, we could very clearly see with our glasses that the woman was as naked as ever she was born, even those parts which I always before now thought nature would have taught a woman to conceal were uncover'd."

The historic cannon at the waterfront is unrelated to Cook. During a time of Russian expansion near the turn of the century, the people of Cooktown thought they, as the largest, nearest population centre in the northern part of the continent, were threatened by a Russian invasion.

The city council pleaded with Brisbane for help.

Brisbane was sympathetic and sent one cannon, one officer, and two rifles!

Happily, there was no invasion.

We visited a local craft factory and ended the tour at the James Cook Historical Museum and the Joseph Banks Garden. For Cookie Groupies, that is where the tour should begin.

An excellent display details the history of Captain Cook's three voyages and his life story from birth at Marton-in-Cleveland to Kealakekua Bay. There is a model of the *Endeavour*, a model scene of the *Endeavour* on the shore and, most important, one of the six cannons Cook jettisoned to lift the *Endeavour* off the reef.

Cook had marked the spot with buoys hoping to return and recover the valuable arms but later was concerned only with saving his ship from the menacing reef.

Efforts by historians to reclaim the cannons were unsuccessful until 1969 as the two-hundredth anniversary of Captain Cook's arrival on the east coast of Australia approached, an American team from the Philadelphia Academy of Natural Sciences equipped with the electronic technical gear capable of searching out hidden metal found the cannons buried under three feet of coral.

Distribution of the restored cannons was decided by the Commonwealth Government. The one allotted to Queensland was turned over to Cooktown in time for the official opening of the James Cook Historical Museum by Queen Elizabeth on 22 April, 1970.

The six-foot, ten-inch cannon has an embossed "G.R.2" on the top of the barrel indicating it was manufactured during the reign of King George II. The number "2" on one side is the manufacturer's serial number. On its breach are the numbers "11-2-15" signifying hundred weights, quarters and pounds — or a weight of 1,303 pounds.

Chiselled on the trunnion end are the initials "J.C." thought to stand for Joseph Christopher, the gunfounder, and the embossed letter "D" for the town where he worked.

The wooden carriage, of course, had disintegrated in the ocean but a faithful reproduction was made, including the use of red paint, a colour commonly used to camouflage spilt blood.

In 1971 Norman Innes-Will, the museum's curator, inspecting the storage site where Cook off-loaded the *Endeavour* found a cast-iron cannon ball lodged in the bank. It fits the cannon in the museum.

We found Mr. Innes-Will at the desk when leaving and hearing our American accent he fervently asked, "You don't have a Kennedy dollar, do you?" He is an avid numismatist. Our negative reply brought a sigh. "Actually what I want most is a genuine piece of American Indian wampum." He sighed again. "I understand they are making instant wampum now in Maine."

The museum has other intriguing displays. A Chinese joss house. Communication equipment. Also memorabilia of the beloved "Streak O'Rust" the railroad that ran inland for sixty-seven miles to the goldfields.

The Queensland gold-rush was started with the discovery of "colour" on the Palmer River on the 29th of June, 1873. A party of prospectors produced a hundred and two ounces of gold in three weeks.

James Mulligan, a fearless prospector and the leader of the expedition, claimed a rich reward for the discovery of a major goldfield.

Before the alluvial gold ran out the prospectors recorded fifty tons of the precious metal although it is estimated that twice as much was not recorded, and not taxed, much of it returning to China in the bones of the honourable deceased.

Getting to the goldfields was a problem. Rugged mountain escarpments, bogs, jungle growth were only part of the challenge facing the prospectors. The fierce Merkin tribe, avid cannibals, fought in the "Black War" until their near extinction.

Getting stores to the goldfields by bullock or horse teams cost one hundred and twenty pounds sterling a ton. Eventually the cost came down to fifteen pounds sterling but it was still expensive.

A railroad would have been a god-send. In 1884 the mayor of Cooktown turned the first sod ceremonially to start construction. A torchlight parade followed.

In 1888 the third and last section was completed to Laura making a sixty-seven and a half mile track. It was a hellish railroad to keep running. One timber-bridge crossing over the Deighton River, a span four hundred and seventy feet long and forty feet high, would go fifteen feet underwater during a flood!

The line seldom showed a profit. As the gold disappeared passengers and cargo dwindled and gradually the tiny railroad fell into disuse. In 1961 the line was sold for salvage.

On our way back to the airport we stopped at the Cooktown cemetery. The early settlers died so young. One corner was reserved for the Chinese.

We left Hans Looser and Cooktown with regret. Nice guy. Engrossing historical town.

From Cooktown we flew over Black Mountain, a tumbling mass of black rocks ... a superstitious mountain to the Aborigines; over a fleet of shrimp boats and then across the Cape York peninsula; over the minute village of Coen once a scene of gold-rush activity and later a World War II airfield, one of many that dotted the northern country.

Wendy put together a "sweeps" on the landing time at Weipa, our destination, with the understanding that the winner had to shout for drinks at Thursday Island the next day.

We descended to the airport with the last rays of sun. Below us the open bauxite diggings provided a landscape of red dirt patches alternated with freshly planted trees. A matching red sunset was vivid and splashy.

The Albatross Hotel in Weipa is a modern, air-conditioned, two-storey, concrete block structure.

It was Saturday and Saturday night is dinner-dance night at the Albatross Hotel and it takes on the colour and enthusiasm of a mining town dance. Stand back!

The music was taped but the dancing was genuine and wild. I can still hear the stamping of feet to a tune called *Rah-Rah Rasputin*!

Sunday morning we flew up the coastline of the Gulf of Carpentaria, over a beautiful mosaic of beige sand-bars and blue and green tidal pools.

We flew so low we could spot turtles on the water and even turtle tracks on the smooth white sand beaches.

On a lonely beach we saw the burned out debris of two U.S. Thunderbolt fighters which had been forced to land during the war. A padre heard the engines and put out a search party for the flyers. He took them back to his mission but when they established contact with their units, the pilots were ordered to return and destroy their aircraft. At the airport in Weipa is the four-bladed propellor from one of the airplanes.

The Cape York peninsula is a solid mass of thick, green forest with occasional flashes of rivers and lakes. The hostess spotted a crocodile in a river below us.

"You don't go swimming in these waters. Sea snakes and sharks and crocodile and other wigglies and snappies discourage you," she said.

The crocodile is particularly dangerous because of his ability to memorise the habits of his potential prey. A Cooktown lady took her Great Dane and another canine pet for a daily swim at the same place and the same time. Crocodiles got them both.

The same fate awaited a Weipa worker who swam in the same place in the river for two weeks.

Not that the crococile is a huge eater; he takes his victim to an underwater home and nibbles at the carcass from time to time. Makes you shrivel up in your reading chair just thinking about it.

Wendy, our brave leader, said she planned to spend her vacation in the area camping out.

Wasn't she afraid?

"Oh, I plan to move my camp from time to time," she said.

I'd move my camp back to Sydney.

An hour's flight from Weipa carried us to the tip of Cape York. To the Australians on board the jutting piece of land below, previously seen only on maps and read about since childhood, was a highlight. Our bush pilots made several passes so everybody could get the souvenir photo.

The east tip of Cape York is interesting because of a curious thread of historical circumstances. The area was first visited by Captain Cook in 1770. William Bligh, a member of Cook's third and last voyage, made his first landfall in the same area on his famous voyage in the open boat — the one in which he was put adrift with nineteen men in 1791 off the islands of Tonga. Two years later the *Pandora* returning from Tahiti with mutineers from Bligh's *Bounty* struck the Barrier Reef and sank. Those who were saved landed in the same general locale.

Shortly after leaving Cape York we landed on Horn Island, boarded a bus and then a launch for a ten-minute ride to Thursday Island. (The origin of the name is obscure.)

"Old T.I." sounds like what it is . . . a romantic leftover from yesterday.

Situated in the middle of the notorious Torres Strait named after a Spanish navigator who passed through the reef-island-studded strait in 1606, it is still headquarters for the famous Torres Strait pilots.

Pearl luggers ride at anchor in its harbour. Once a flourishing industry, pearl diving like that of Broome is now for oysters, future homes for cultured pearls.

During its heyday Thursday Island's pearl industry attracted a wide cross-section of races: European, other Torres Strait islanders, Polynesians, Micronesians, Melanesians, Mainland Aborigines, Filipinos, Indians, Chinese, Japanese. They all came. Many left. A polyglot society remains.

Christianity came with members of the London Missionary Society in 1871. The event is celebrated with an annual festival called "The Coming of the Light" on the first of July.

Our visit was on Sunday . . . the first of July. We were in luck.

We first visited the Catholic church, one of the few buildings not harmed by the last cyclone. Its original walls were papered with copies of the Sydney Morning Herald. On the wall back of the altar is a partially finished painting by Father Sing, a well-known religious painter.

Next door is the Church of England's Cathedral which officially is called the Church of All Souls and St. Bartholomew. Unofficially it is more commonly known as the Quetta Memorial Cathedral.

In 1890 the *Quetta*, a British India steamship sailing in the Adolphus Channel off Cape York on a clear moonlit night hit an uncharted rock and sank within three minutes. Out of two hundred and ninety-three people on board, one hundred and thirty-three lost their lives. It was the greatest shipping tragedy in Australian history.

From the church came the sound of lyrical voices lifted in song. When asked when the pageant would take place, Wendy just shrugged. "On Old T.I. time."

Eventually the clergy in white robes and the Bishop in richly embroidered robes led a parade of parishioners through the streets of Thursday Island preceded by an altar boy swinging an incense burner and followed by the singing congregation.

Although it was an Anglican church celebration, the Catholic padre joined the parade and we joined too until the parade turned off the main thoroughfare. At that point we went back to a corner pub where the winner of the Weipa landing "sweeps" was buying cold beer.

The parade returned to the church grounds for the pageant.

From the church steps we watched the re-enactment of the landing of the three missionaries and their reception by the Torres Strait islanders.

As an elder of the church read a narrative of what was happening, the natives danced and sang.

When the pageant was over, baskets of food were made ready for lunch but we dined at the Grand Hotel, an ancient wooden structure. Huge buffet of prawns, baked chicken, curried chicken, grilled white fish, salads, two kinds of rice, a sparkling white wine and a still white wine.

A highlight of the Thursday Island visit was the State school's sub-teen dance team performance. The mini-ambassadors had danced on tours as far south as Sydney. What great stuff and what a great way to retain their cultural pride.

A quick tour on the back of an open truck around the island — eagles nest in the towers of the Overseas Telegraph Corporation — and it was then back in the launch, the bus, the airplane and back to Weipa.

On the way we flew over Possession Island where Captain Cook landed, planted the British flag and claimed the east coast of the continent in the name of King George III.

The next morning we were scheduled to take an industrial tour of Weipa.

Industrial touring I put on the same exciting level as watching coloured slides of someone else's vacation.

However, Weipa was a curiosity.

Bauxite, the basic ore for aluminium, was found in the area in 1955, a discovery which later proved to be the largest bauxite deposit in the world.

An international consortium of companies was formed called Comalco which obtained an eighty-five year lease on the Aboriginal land from the Queensland government, built the town of Weipa in 1965 and today supplies twenty percent of the world's bauxite requirements. It's huge.

To the Australians it was of intense interest because Weipa has been the focus of much controversial publicity. Charges of raping the land ... foreign investors using up the country's resources ... ignoring the rights of Aborigines ... environmentalists jumping up and down on hot skillets. A field day for headline hunting.

I had an illuminating, slightly disturbing experience at the beginning of the tour. When the public relations guide saw that I was taping his remarks, he wanted to know, not in a particularly friendly manner, if I were a writer. On hearing an affirmation the guide relayed to the group the bitter experiences he had had with the press of Australia. The group responded sympathetically and a couple of passengers gave personal examples of their own negative experiences with the press including one chap whose inference was that yellow journalism was communist inspired. I felt very lonely.

For two and a half hours we inspected the model mining town, the golf course, the supermarket, the theatre and the twenty-three hobby clubs that keep the isolated inhabitants occupied.

We saw how the ore is open mined to an average depth of ten feet and then is crushed, washed and graded in an automated plant and then loaded into ships in the deep-water Albatross Bay and shipped to Gladstone, to Europe, to Japan.

The most admirable part of the operation was to see how the top soil is removed, the ore taken out, the top soil replaced and potentially productive trees are planted.

Comalco had planted over 130,000 trees in its regeneration program. The truth appeared that the mining operation was leaving the land in better shape than they found it.

And paying $7 million in royalties annually to the Queensland government.

While we toured the mining operation, our bags went to the airplane for departure south, down the east coast of the Gulf of Carpentaria.

The west coast of Cape York is country touched by the early explorers. Carstenz named Pera Head in 1623. Cape Keer-Weer received its name from Jansz in 1606. Matthew Flinders reported on the red bauxite cliffs in 1802.

Most of the coastline is Aboriginal reserve land and we landed at Edward River to visit an Aboriginal settlement, have a barramundi barbecue and visit a crocodile farm.

We landed on a shell-grit runway parallel to the beach. The aluminium shed terminal sign said: "Edward River: res area 466198h, pop 331, rain 1780ml, temp 15° 37°C."

Another sign: "You are entering upon an area set aside as a reserve for the Aboriginal inhabitants of the state. Unauthorised entry on such reserve is illegal. Penalty $200."

We travelled by open truck to the village centre, past the pub which is open three days a week, past the Anglican church open all the time, past the butcher shop and stopped at a grassy area where there was a buffet table laid out.

Beyond was the government administration office, store and post office.

Presiding over a concrete barbecue stand was the village Anglican priest, a large man who confessed to the love of good food, grilling pieces of fish and beef.

At one time the community was run by the church.

"There was a dairy then and the village was almost self-sufficient. Now we have the government. A bar. They'll tear themselves up tonight and the sisters will be up till all hours piecing them back together. Bah! It is all corrupt. Last year we had a school teacher who bootlegged illegal spirits to the people. Made a fortune until he was caught. You know his attitude? 'It was there for the pickin's. Why shouldn't I?' Terrible. See that sweet old woman over there selling grass bags? She'll take that money and drink it. By midnight she'll be a thing demented."

After lunch we toured the Applied Ecology Edward River Crocodile Farm. First the concrete beds where the baby crocs live, then the breeding, high-fenced lagoon where one hundred female crocodiles lay their eggs in tall grass surrounding the lagoon waters. Lastly we saw the site of a future lagoon where crocodiles will reside until age four and then will be harvested for their skins.

The target is to harvest about four thousand crocodiles a year from several satellite farms run by the Aborigines.

(The Australian members of the tour expressed grave doubts of the Aborigines' ability to successfully run any complex operation without supervision.)

At the breeding lagoon there were giant lady crocodiles, ten, fifteen feet long. The skin of one of these monsters, valued by the girth of its stomach, was estimated to be worth $700.

Returning to the community green the village inhabitants staged a dance symbolising a kangaroo hunt. I think. A dozen Aborigines in various costumes and in various body paints clapped and sang while another Aborigine took the part of the kangaroo. Chased by a dog. I think.

Afterwards we were told that such dances sometimes come off and sometimes they don't. What the dances mean are never too clear either. And the Aborigines don't tell.

It was late afternoon when we returned to the airport and almost time for the canteen to open. The inhabitants were beginning to gather.

A bushman subsequently told me, "They drink like there is no tomorrow. It is like a death wish."

Government run. What price equality.

The padre said over the barbecue. "A team of physicians said the inhabitants have deteriorated so fast in the last ten years that in another generation they will have disappeared."

The last leg of the BPA Tour consisted of exchanging addresses, drinking beer from the airplane's bar and examining certificates attesting to the experience. The certificate said that we were members of a highly selective and adventurous group that had flown 1,838 kilometres (1,149 miles) on the BPA Top of Australia Tour, and, as such, had viewed magnificent, rugged scenery, and witnessed many fascinating aspects of northern Australia, both past and present.

Below us the lights of Cairns appeared. In the distance a bushfire lit a mountain top.

The Bush Pilots' "Top of Australia" Air Tour operates every week from the end of May through September — only eighteen tours annually.

The tour price is about $599 each and includes everything but personal gifts and drinks.

It is an absorbing trip conducted by a pack of fine "bushies." Get an early reservation.

6. Kayak Safari Down the South Esk River

"You tip over your kayak. When you are upside down in the water, slap the bottom of the kayak three times with the flat of your hands to show you are in control, then place your hands behind the cowling and push yourself out. It's simple."

Although the preliminary idea sounds a bit spooky, it is simple. The water of the South Esk River is only slightly cool, very green and slapping the bottom of the kayak seems to take an inordinate length of time, but it is simple.

The "capsize drill" of our scheduled two-day kayak trip down the Tasmanian river was the first lesson in the expedition.

The recommended dress was a pair of long, light trousers over a bathing suit, an old sweater of quick-drying wool and tennis shoes. You are told at the very beginning that you might be wet all day.

The expedition organiser provided a red crash helmet, a red and yellow buoyancy vest, a yellow nylon windbreaker and a huge red diaper-like thing which slips over the cowling edges to make the canoe water-tight.

In the complete uniform we looked like something that was going to be shot out of a circus cannon.

Actually the first lesson was how to shoe-horn yourself into the canoe.

For more than an hour after that drill Paul, our guide, gave us instructions on how to sweep, how to fairy glide, how to back paddle, how to stop quickly.

The technique of efficiently pushing a kayak through the water, feathering its blades smoothly, demands more skill and practice than one thinks.

We had started from "Pleasant Banks," our farmhouse stay in Tasmania at nine in the morning, had gone to Paul's farmhome in the hills overlooking the Launceston Airport. Into tight water-proofed bags we crammed our change of clothing, sleeping bag and pad, tent, eating utensils and toilet necessities.

Everything but our personal items was supplied and the only extra cost was for the sleeping bag at $3 each.

With the canoes on a trailer behind a Land Rover we headed for the little village of Avoca where there is a small landing on the South Esk.

After our initiation, we packed the canoes. The small, compact rolls of gear fitted into each cranny front and back. We lunched on sandwiches and hot tea provided by Paul's wife, who drove the Land Rover and trailer back to base camp.

It was one o'clock by the time we pushed off and pointed down the South Esk River, a portion of which has Grade One rapids.

Rapids are graded from zero to six according to their difficulty. Grade Six is tantamount to a rocky waterfall.

At the first good Grade One rapid, the water funnelled through a small chute near the right bank under a large tree limb. When we reached the bottom of the chute, it was imperative to make a strong sweep with the right blade to keep from bashing into the tree limb. Easy.

Paul went first, down the chute, swept strongly with his right paddle and the kayak swung smoothly to the left and into the quiet pool of water beyond.

I followed with confidence. Down the chute. Swept right blade. The kayak didn't turn! Frantically swept again. Here came the tree branch. Crash. Splash.

I was in the river. Paddle floating. One shoe floating. Kayak filling. Damn.

Always catch your kayak first. Capture paddle. Capture shoe. Splash through the waist-deep water. Empty kayak. Put on shoe. Breath deeply. Slip into kayak and set off again.

It was the only capsize of the trip.

The problem we found at the end of the first hour was not the capsizing or the paddling or the sun or the water. The problem was in the unfamiliar sitting position with legs stretched straight out front from the hips and little room to bend the knees. The ham muscles start to cramp and the legs want to know what is going on outside.

Our next trip will be preceded by (1) losing every ounce of extra weight, (2) leg exercises to extend and relax the leg muscles and (3) sitting, Buddha-fashion, in the lotus position for hours on end.

The river, which was not more than twenty feet wide, was serene, tree-lined, uninhabited. Just what we had hoped for.

Until it was almost dusk we paddled peacefully down the river crossing an occasional series of small rapids where the river bottom was only inches away from the canoe bottom.

We made camp in a clearing on a bank about ten feet above the river. Just beyond, the river curved beneath shaded trees and rippled over rocks providing a picture postcard visual with stereophonic sound.

Our nylon tent for two consisted of an outer tent, an inner tent, a nylon floor, mosquito net, zippered flaps. With sponge rubber mattresses underneath the nylon sleeping bags it made a cosy home.

Dinner was a surprise. The first course was a hearty soup. The second course was braised lamb with peas and gravy which tasted perfectly fresh. Very tasty. Alliance Freeze Dried from New Zealand. Excellent.

What was for dessert? Cheesecake, of course.

A strong wind blew up a chill but we were soon in our downy sleeping bags. With new-found muscles needing rest, deep sound sleep came easily.

Once during the night I was aware of snuffling noises near our tent but a shout from Paul's tent drove off what we learned later was a Tasmanian Devil, a terrible looking—but harmless they say—scavenger unique to Tasmania. Then silence.

The Tasmanian Devil is a nocturnal, carnivorous marsupial, the size of a badger, who hunts among sheep herds and poultry pens. We were told the chilling account of the animal's ability to eat a horse down to the hoofs.

Much later I heard the far-off sound of roosters crowing. At the first pink of day I was out of the tent to claim half-an-hour of dawn beauty for myself.

River fog hung low in the valley above us but not over our camp giving a surrealistic background to the landscape. Two wallabies, startled at my appearance, went pogo-sticking off into the bush. Thump, thump, thump.

Kookaburras gave their hyena laugh in the distance.

Overhead a V-formation of long-necked birds headed north, high, high in the sky.

Far off Mt. Nicholas was still shrouded in black, outlined against the morning pink sky and as the sun slowly moved up piercing the fog, the mountain came into view.

The soothing sound of the river ripple was the only noise.

The camp came alive. Rumpled but alive.

Breakfast was left-over cheesecake to clear the pan for frying bacon and eggs. The smell of bacon and eggs on a morning riverbank camp-fire has to be one of the most tantalising, pleasing smells in the world.

Cleaning, striking camp, repacking into plastic rolls and then into canvas bags, storing each bag precisely into each canoe took the best part of three hours.

It was ten o'clock before our kayaks were at the river's edge. Paul gave us a "seal launch." With the nose of the kayak pointing straight into the water, paddle ready, he gave each of us a shove over the grass and into the river. Painless way to start. Like a seal.

In the distance dogs barked. We heard the sound of a stockman calling the dogs. It was the only other human voice we heard on the river.

We saw the manor towers of Eastborough, an imposing homestead; mid-morning, at the edge of a cliff above the river we saw a white farmhouse profiled against the blue sky. A line of fresh laundry flapped in the breeze but no human appeared to wave at the intrepid travellers. It looked like a stage set.

Many delightful river scenes floated by slowly. Large gum trees cast shadows on the banks where an occasional mob of sheep would stare at us in disbelief.

Once a pair of wallabies bounded up the hills and a herd of black angus came to their feet from a noon nap, watched us apprehensively as the three red and yellow floating bugs came closer and then they scampered into the bush, black tails swishing indignantly.

Paul had put plastic skegs on the stern of our kayaks to help keep us moving in a straight line. Sweeping the paddle evenly to keep going straight ahead is not all that easy.

We paused twice for a "brew up" — and a much needed leg stretch. Paul would build a small fire of twigs, arrange a wooden arm over the fire to hold the billy can for boiling the water and we soon had a cup of hot tea. Nothing finer.

Cheese, crackers, salami and fruit made lunch.

We headed down the river for the last time.

After three o'clock we pulled out.

To reach the scheduled pull-out was going to take too much time for the threesome so Paul sped off alone to rendezvous with the Land Rover. We had a leisurely hour to unbend, uncramp, swim, push and pull the empty kayaks up a thirty-foot bank to the road, tote ten sacks of clothing, food and equipment up, take another swim and a small siesta.

That night we camped in a large hotel-motel unit in Launceston. Carpeted floor. Coloured television. The luxury of hot showers and shampoos and room service bringing steak and wine.

Life was more enjoyable on the river.

Since our kayak expedition the touring company ceased operations. Too bad. Good concept.

It does underline a fact that adventure tour companies are often founded by inspired, competent young people who are strong in purpose but weak in finances. The return simply doesn't justify the investment in time, energy and expensive equipment.

However, like dandelions, when one expires another seems to take its place.

Check the state tourist office for the latest information on going-strong adventure tours that interest you.

Adventure Travel Centre, besides the Nymbodia River operation, also runs whitewater expeditions in other parts of Australia. In Tasmania the hairiest, wildest experience is the Franklin River World Heritage trip which takes ten days through one of the most spectacularly scenic areas of Tasmania. But it is a tough, unpredictable trip and applicants must submit proof of previous whitewater experience. Cost about $685, from December to March.

One of the most appealing adventures the company offers in Tasmania is the "Tassie Bicycle Tour." A ten-day tour of the North and East Coast with easy gradients, great scenery, and "little coastal villages with their excellent seafood cuisine." December through February. About $250 including everything but bike rental ($60) and food kitty ($90). Support vehicle, cook, guide, mechanic. What fun.

7. Clydesdale and Gypsy Wagon Safari

To take a covered wagon hitched up to a mammoth Clydesdale horse and go clippity-clopping through the unused roads of former gold mines in Central Victoria, a half day's drive from Melbourne, is a hearts-and-flowers adventure.

First of all you fall in love with the horse.

Ours was "Goblin," the star of the corral who was over twenty years of age but with the body, heart and lungs of a four-year old who pricked up his ears and stood tall at the sign of a camera. An animal who bluffed when tired, who made executive decisions at the first sign of a faltering rein, who inhaled a full sack of oats every day.

Brown and white with plate-sized feathery feet, and a greying mane, Goblin weighed in slightly less than one ton and stood seventeen hands tall. Much horse.

We were intrigued by the idea of a horse caravan, especially in the historic gold country and especially when the horses were Clydesdales. Once, spending a summer in Ireland we had been tempted by the gypsy caravans but a series of reported accidents caused by hills and high-spirited horses sapped our initiative.

We reported in to The Colonial Way, an operation run by Rod Dovey, a former chemical engineer who sold his own business and retired to the country to enjoy life. Starting in 1978 with one wagon and one horse he had expanded to three wagons and five rotating Clydesdales and contemplated a total of six wagons which was as far as he planned to grow in one location.

The location was at Bridgewater bordering the Loddon River.

Our temporary home was a covered wooden wagon which Rod had designed and had built with gas-fuelled refrigerator and stove, a settee arrangement which converted into a most comfortable double bed. There were various bunk arrangements to accommodate a family with small children.

It was ideal for a couple.

A shovel on the back of the wagon and a portable seat was the toilet equipment.

Then we met Goblin. Your first consideration in the caravan safari is the care of the horse. He is the first to water. The first to feed. He is curried clean of sweat in the evening and curried completely clean of dust in the morning and it becomes a routine of love to take care of your huge, oat-munching machine, constantly talking to him or keeping a hand on him so he knows where you are.

You quickly develop an affinity with the animal.

Once Rod had as clients a young couple who obviously were intent on a romantic interlude.

Rod's routine is to check regularly on his clients. See that they have no problems with harnessing. Brings out fresh supplies. Mother-hens his clients.

When he visited the young couple the first morning to see that everything was all right, he found in the doorway of the caravan an indignant young lady drumming her fingers impatiently.

"Where is your friend?" asked Rod.

Over in a grove of trees was the young man crooning over his Clydesdale whose coat was as shiny as a newly polished penny with immaculately feathered feet and brushed-to-the-last-hair mane and tail.

"He — is — still — cleaning — the — damn — horse!" was the terse reply.

Rod feels the success of the safaris is because they provide an entirely different, absorbing vacation. To learn how to harness and hitch up a Clydesdale might make grandfathers slap their sides with laughter but it becomes an art form.

In addition, routes are tailored to specific interests: wild life or bird watching, fishing, history, fossicking — who knows what roadside nuggets might have been unearthed by last night's rain?

The horse and cart safaris appeal to people who like involvement. It is a participatory vacation that has been enjoyed by older couples, honeymooners, families and affinity groups. Mostly, Rod finds repeaters in the professional and quasi-professional ranks who need a break from city pressures. They report that a week, the average length, is not enough.

Rod will "charter" a horse and wagon for four days but he knows from clients that they need a couple of days to wind down. Planning satisfying routes is easier with seven days' duration.

Note: During the Australian school holidays the caravans are booked out a year in advance.

At nine o'clock the next morning, after our car was stored under cover on the property, we were introduced to the mysteries of harnessing and hitching. So many straps. So many loops. So many odd pieces of leather.

When Goblin was finally and properly set to go, Rod took a plastic-coated map and crayoned over it a suggested route ending at Iron Bark Dam. (A "dam" is a muddy water hole.)

Close to eleven o'clock we left headquarters under a blessing of yapping dogs. Rod rode with us across the highway to head us down the first leg of the journey and then hopped out, saluted a "good luck" and returned home on foot.

We soon learned that Goblin with a speed rating of four kilometres an hour preferred two kilometres an hour unless one person was out in front, lightening the load and setting the horse an inspirational pace. So one of us walked while the other rode, theoretically to rein. Goblin didn't need any reining. He knew it all by heart.

The drill was to stop every hour to rest and feed the horse. A twenty-minute break after the first hour. An hour's break for lunch. Goblin had water and oats at every stop. It was a leisurely trip.

At our very first break Goblin, unchecked, jammed the wagon firmly against a stout post. He knows the way but he forgets about the wagon. Much trouble getting free of the obstacle. Then the Lady Navigator did the tea dishes and neglected the crayoned chart and I continued on the main road making a left hand turn. Should have gone straight ahead.

It was a two-hour mistake.

While we should have hit camp before 5:30, it was 7:30 before we finally unhitched Goblin.

Rod was there to show us the setting-up-camp routine.

The strain of the day melted in that final hour of the setting sun. The camp site was a pleasure. A nearby pond . . . surrounded by red iron bark trees . . . a split log to use as a bench to sit and watch a big, brown wallaby come out of the bush and drink his evening fill. Birds of all kinds wheeled around us, swooping to the water for refreshment.

When dark came and Rod had gone, we took the table out of the caravan, placed it in front of the log bench, set the table with tea towels and glasses, lighted the candle and opened the wine. A splendid opera on the radio provided majestic music under the stars —

huge stars. A glass of riesling. A lamb stew dinner. Our first night in the bush. Peaceful.

Small wonder that Rod's clients do not think one week is enough.

Gold prospectors looked for iron bark trees which grew in porous rock which indicated quartz-laden gold.

The bush surrounding Iron Bark Dam was pot-marked with century-old diggings of miners who once blanketed the area.

At nine a.m. Rod returned to watch us try to harness and hitch Goblin to the caravan. We succeeded ... with just a little bit of help. Rod also brought fresh milk and more beer and other forgotten essentials, part of the service. He takes fatherly care of his clients and his horses.

He then mapped out another route which would take us to a vineyard in the almost deserted village of Kingower. Today's population: 30. The 1860 population: 70,000.

The reason, of course, for the major population figure was gold.

In a field near the town on the 27th of August, 1857, a nugget weighing over 1,743 ounces was found. Named the "Blanche Barkly" it was the third largest nugget ever found in Australia. The fourth largest nugget, "Precious" was found in the same area by Chinese miners in 1871.

In those days the suppliers often made more money than the goldminers. Winemakers with European heritages quickly nurtured their vines to give drink to the thirsty.

The goldminers and the vines disappeared but in the seventies the vines were reintroduced to the Bendigo region. With Goblin leading the way we plodded into the Blanche Barkly Winery at Kingower.

Two brothers, Alvin and David Reimers, started with only nine acres but expected to expand to twenty acres from which they hoped to produce quality wines. A wine writer reported that their first cabernet of 1977 had the "muscles of King Kong."

A lot of loving care had been put into the winery which was built by hand using a hundred and fifty tons of local stone, half a metre thick. The old-world leaded windows had been commissioned but the storeroom door was an antique. Originally it had been the Kingower gaol door.

We left the winery and headed Goblin back into the bush.

And got lost again.

This time we were lost in a gradually disappearing uphill track with a mountain staring at us and trees closing in on each side. Damn. How to get the wagon turned around?

The one thing we hadn't found yet on Goblin was a reverse gear.

The day before, stuck against the post, I had tried the command, "Way back! *W-a-a-a-y* back!" No back. No way.

Now in the present situation, there was a small clearing on the right. If we could move the wagon past the clearing and if Goblin cooperated, we might be able to back the wagon into the clearing, turn around and try another track.

We brought the wagon forward to the proper position, guided Goblin over to the side so the wheels turned back towards the space at the proper angle . . . now if Goblin would only give us a bit of help.

I coaxed. I nudged. I pleaded. I sweated. No reverse. The impossibility of the situation suddenly made me frantic with frustration and I seized the reins tightly under the mouth and forcibly pushed the straps back yelling. "For Pete's sake, Animal, put your gear into rear! **NOW! WAYBACK, DAMN IT, I SAID** *WAYBACK!*"

He backed up!

The wagon slipped into the clearing and I pulled Goblin around in the other direction and we headed back down the trail. I was weak with exhaustion and sat slumped in the seat like a shot buck.

We clip-clopped back to the crossroad where we had made the wrong turn and finally — two hours late again — we made camp at Orchid Dam.

But what was this? Another Colonial Wagon was at the camp.

We preferred to be by ourselves again but this initial reaction proved to be wrong because it gave us a chance to share a campfire, a bottle of port and horse experiences — hilarious laughter — with a charming couple from Canberra and their bright, articulate son. They were enjoying every minute of a two weeks horse and wagon vacation. He was, at least.

The lady had told Rod that she was very experienced around horses so he gave the family Jack, a Clydesdale with more spirit and ginger than our mature Goblin.

"When we leave camp," said the father, "it is like a scene out of Ben Hur. The animal flies. I love it."

"Mrs. Hur" on the other hand, was so terrified that she left camp on foot an hour before the scheduled departure and walked down the route until Jack was vetted of his early morning energy.

The next morning when Rod appeared he took Jack under rein

and ran him in circles for ten minutes. "He decided that this wasn't going to get him anywhere and he behaved. Just needs a strong hand," Rod told us later.

Our last day was uneventful. When Goblin is going home, even we couldn't get lost again.

At one point we were trying to make up our minds whether to take the suggested long way home or take the shortcut. No decision was necessary. Goblin took the shortcut.

The second time around we would take more time and wouldn't travel every day. Find a spot, stay there. One couple Rod told us about had the right idea. They came late and left base camp at Bridgewater with only enough daylight for an hour and a half journey.

They arrived for the night at an idyllic riverside location . . . and didn't leave for a week. Loved the horse. Loved the wagon. Loved the camp. Never left. Had a marvellous vacation.

A week's holiday, horse, wagon and oats cost from $300 in low season to $420 in high season. For current prices and reservations write The Colonial Way Pty, Ltd., Bridgewater-on-Loddon, Victoria.

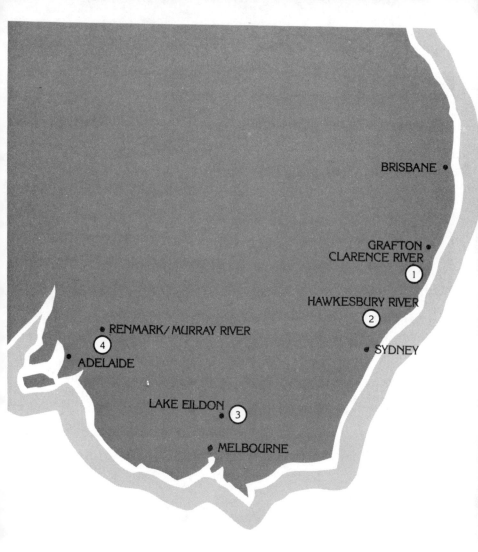

HOUSEBOATS

1. GRAFTON HOUSEBOATS
2. HAWKESBURY RIVER
3. LAKE EILDON
4. MURRAY RIVER/RENMARK

8. Houseboating on Rivers, Lakes and Harbours

The Lady Navigator was the deckhand and ready with a line for our first landing.

I gingerly nudged upwind toward the wharf. Slower. Slower.

"Go slower!" cautioned the deckhand.

I killed the forward power of the engine. The big houseboat moved inexorably toward the dock.

"Reverse power! *Reverse power!*" came from the deck.

Oh, *migawd*, reverse power. Where was the reverse power?

Ker—runch.

The forward rail touched the dock gently but firmly and slowly bent backwards, pretzel fashion.

Then the reverse power came on. Too strong! We lurched backwards toward the river bank.

Neutral gear. Forward again!

Panic . . . and finally, safe and clear in the river again, we looked at our poor front railing. A disaster.

It was not what you'd call a great beginning.

Note: you are told by all operators that driving a houseboat is like driving a car.

Wrong.

The blockhouse construction of a houseboat provides a sail against which the *lightest* wind creates a moving effect and a *strong* wind can put you at the corner of Third and Main Streets.

What we eventually learned is that you don't gentle a houseboat when the wind is blowing.

The master's touch is to know how to give the boat full throttle, forwards and backwards, how to whip the wheel around.

Still it is safe. Unlike a car you can't really get in serious trouble. You might bang into a shore or scratch another boat, you might even bend your railing but the only big hurt will be your pride.

"I told you to put it into reverse gear!" said the Lady Navigator.

Houseboats, like so many adventures, were not included in our thinking of Australian holidaying and when we read about houseboating on the Murray River we said, "Oh, yes, we must try that!"

What we thought was a unique opportunity on the Murray is fairly common. Floating holiday vacations are offered in many places in Australia.

We ended up trying four different houseboats . . . in a major river, in a harbour, on a lake and finally on the Murray.

All were great fun . . . and all were different.

For us, living out of a station wagon, living out of motel rooms and hotel rooms, a houseboat provided a wonderful feeling of floating freedom.

Every houseboat had a gas stove and a refrigerator — wow! we could do our own cooking! — toilet, shower, fresh water, fully equipped with cooking utensils and cutlery. We rented linen and blankets.

We had space and room to move around.

The sun would be out and we would cruise happily along without the strain of highway traffic, past houses, under bridges, anchoring and eating leisurely, drinking. Sometimes after dinner we'd take a mattress to the top deck and lie under the stars.

Marvellous stuff.

The Clarence River

Our first semi-hysterical experience happened on the Clarence River at Grafton near the northern coast of New South Wales.

We had gone to Grafton to see the last of the blooming jacaranda trees which transform the city into a stunning blue garden. There we stumbled across a small houseboat operation.

An inspection of the houseboat was impressive. Big enough to sleep eight, clean and neat.

In the thirty-five feet were three separate rooms, large and airy, completely equipped including linen.

"Why not take it out?" asked the proprietor. "She's full of petrol and ready to go."

"Let's go," said the Lady Navigator.

"We went grocery shopping, took baggage on board, stored our car and got instructions from the proprietor. "It couldn't be easier," he said. "It drives just like a car."

Initially we went downriver.

"We'll take our swim suits," said the Lady Navigator.

"Downriver," said the proprietor, "the mullet are running and the sharks come in after the mullet."

We saw lots of mullet jumping and we didn't go swimming.

After our beginning bent-railing disaster we docked successfully at Ulmarra and went to the Commercial Hotel and had a quieting beer.

Pub crawling in small river towns is another charm of houseboating we found.

That night, anchored in mid-river, with a dinner of lamb chops and braised carrots, potatoes and wine, we luxuriated in the off-by-ourselves feeling.

The next morning in the crisp sun we cruised upriver.

We were the only boat on the water.

We had driven along the Clarence River and found it to be one of the prettiest drives in New South Wales.

Pushing along leisurely in a houseboat was even better. Time was suspended. We waved at the cows. The cows mooed back. We waved at the passing cars. The cars honked back.

We moored here and there. Picnicked. Read. Watched the birds. Opened a cold beer now and then.

After twenty-four hours we tied up again at the bottom of the main street against the river bank . . . after two passes.

The proprietor came down to the houseboat in response to our telephone call, looked at the pretzeled railing and said, "Not to worry. That's why we are insured."

Our experience proved to us that a weekend or a week on a houseboat is a fine way to vacation in Australia.

The only such operation on the Clarence River today is the Grafton Leisure Hire Company. The telephone number is 066-426-284.

Call them for current information on prices and reservations.

Tell them the rail-benders sent you.

The Hawkesbury River

North of Sydney, less than a two hour drive, is the Hawkesbury River, the centre of a water playground second only to Sydney Harbour itself.

Hundreds of miles of navigable inlets, bays, coves, three national parks and several places to charter houseboats or cruisers.

We zeroed in on Holidays-A-Float at Brooklyn not too far off the Pacific Highway for our second houseboat experience.

We didn't receive the same tender loving care that we had received on the Clarence River.

The operator of the Holidays-A-Float, between talking on the telephone to his attorney and then his accountant, was able to squeeze out of drydock a river cruiser badly in need of maintenance.

The cost, payable in advance, was $155, another $5 for the linen, plus the cost of petrol, plus $100 on deposit to cover possible damages.

The boat promised at two o'clock was finally available at four-thirty. Advice on where to go, where to anchor, how to operate took about five minutes. Sloppy.

Nevertheless, being back on the water was exhilarating, and, once clear of Brooklyn, we headed into the broad Hawkesbury with wind-made whitecaps around us.

Our boat was twenty feet overall but had everything we needed on board. Gas stove. Sink. Fridge. Shower. Septic toilet. Dinghy.

Constant steering was needed because it tended to drift left or right and we made our way under the bridge of the Pacific Highway, past Milson Island, Prickly Point and into the calmer water of Berowra Creek weaving back and forth like a drunken driver.

As dusk descended we tried one anchorage . . . and the anchor dragged . . . tried another near an oyster farm . . . and it held. We settled in for the night.

I put a fish line over the side while the Lady Navigator put on dinner and one fish broke my line and another mullet was almost in the boat when it jumped out of the improvised bucket-net and escaped.

No one was around us. We couldn't see another boat nor could we see on-shore lights.

Even in the crowded waterways of the Hawkesbury that is the advantage of a houseboat. Not like a caravan or tourist park where your vehicle or tent is snore-by-snore next to the travellers near you. On the river you can be alone.

Listen.

By dark the wind died down. We put candles on upturned fire buckets, carried dinner to the outside deck, turned the radio to a symphony and with hunters' chicken and salad and Tulloch's white wine, lighted by candles and stars, we had one of our most memorable dinners.

Sometimes you are blessed by magic moments of genuine tranquillity.

That was one of those moments.

We heard the flop-on-water of a jumping, distant fish. We heard the last call of an evening bird. Gorgeous music swelled the night. The world can be so beautiful.

So can the dawn.

Calm waters touched with morning pink. Far off a boat at anchor with fishermen hunched motionless over their poles.

The first cruisers on the river appeared leaving white wakes and ripples.

Bacon sizzled filling the morning with nose-twitching aroma.

A good day on the river. We went upstream, past vacation houses, past water skiers.

At Berowra Waters we gently threaded our way through moored boats and made a successful docking — hey, hey, hey — and bought ice and cold drinks and shoved off again just like professional boatmen.

The weather report predicted thunderstorms and we returned to our original anchorage. By dark the winds began to build up. Lightning flashed across the sky followed by rumbling thunder and then pelting rain.

Our little bathtub boat rocked securely in the snug harbour and we settled down to a cozy dinner.

The next morning we chugged back to the starting point and turned the boat in, settled our petrol bill and set off for Sydney.

Next time we would be more thorough in checking the available houseboats on the Hawkesbury and we would take more time on the river. With so many places to explore, you should take a week.

Lake Eildon

Houseboat Number Three was a huge boat on a huge lake.

Lake Eildon is two hours north of Melbourne and is a man-made lake. How big? Three and a half times the size of Sydney Harbour.

The *Elfin Green* was a massive forty-five foot, eight-berth ship with a full-sized galley, stove, oven, big refrigerator, stainless steel sink, running hot and cold water. Two staterooms, large lounge, bar, settee which converted into a double bed. Tiled bath with shower and separate w.c.

The company, Lake Eildon Holiday Boats, located at Boat Harbour, runs a good operation.

Our vessel was clean, well-maintained. We received proper instructions on operating the boat and friendly advice on places to moor and the best places to fish.

We had one small problem which was easily corrected.

In writing ahead to have the boat provisioned — including a Christmas tree because it was Christmas Eve — there had been a misunderstanding. In the order form I turned in, I had requested a six-pack of beer. What we found on the boat were six *cases* of beer in *large-sized* cans.

The funny part of the story is that in Australia, home of the mighty beer drinker, the operators didn't think it at all unusual for a couple on an outing for three nights to order six cases of beer.

"You might have been expecting friends," said the young lady at the office taking five cases back.

Before we pushed off a young farming couple — friends of friends — came by and introduced themselves. Geoff and Bronwin Dobson. They brought three baskets of the reddest, plumpest strawberries ever grown, a carton of thick country cream and a bottle of white wine ... and an invitation to come out to the farm the next day for Christmas brunch.

He raised cattle and sheep and grew potatoes on a family farm in nearby Goulburn Valley.

We plied them with beer.

It was late afternoon by the time our new friends parted and we had just enough daylight to cross the lake and nose the *Elfin Green* into a gravel bank, snubbing it into shore with two aft lines tied at forty-five degree angles to lakeside trees.

We garlanded our Christmas tree with boat-made decoration. Strips of cellophane. Bits of aluminum. Foil-wrapped chocolates.

Christmas Eve dinner was brightened with a bottle of excellent cabernet sauvignon from Bob Roberts at Huntington Estate in Mudgee followed by a bit of blue cheese and a rich McWilliams port, a present from Glen McWilliams in Griffith.

Lovely. We also had for dessert a slice of new moon followed by the first evening star.

Christmas on the farm was just what it should have been.

Geoff picked us up about noon and apologised for being late.

"I would have been on time but she made me wash down the outside of the house," he grumbled. (Bron later admitted to the Lady Navigator that she had capitalised on "company-coming" to get a long-sought chore accomplished. Typical of feminine manipulation.)

On the way we stopped at a lookout to view Geoff's valley. A tree-lined river twisted gently through the property. Neat and green agricultural fields and grazing land. Picture-book stuff.

At the freshly washed, white farmhouse, we met Geoff's parents, his mother-in-law and sister Ann who helps run the farm.

A pre-luncheon beer was followed by family presents and even a thoughtful, desirable reference book for us: *Historic Places of Australia* which introduced us to a series of National Trust books.

The buffet luncheon table was set with handsome china and crystal glasses and platters and platters of food. Cold lobster. Prawns. Turkey and ham. A dozen salads. Paté. Cold vegetables.

Ann was responsible for a galaxy of desserts. Traditional plum pudding with hard sauce, heavy cream and brandy sauce. Two ice cream "puddings." One was made with orange juice and Grand Marnier and mixed with vanilla ice cream and refrozen. The other was like an Italian cassata, ice cream mixed with fruits and nuts. Also available were fresh strawberries marinated in marsala and port. A bowl of whipped cream to go over everything.

We tried every delicious dish.

After coffee and port, Geoff taking us back to the *Elfin Green* passed over the Goulburn River.

"When you come off the lake day after tomorrow, we can take you down the river in a canoe or take you water skiing on the lake."

In the *Elfin Green* again, we chugged east away from the sun looking for Big River Inlet. Past the dam. Past Jerusalem Inlet.

Finally, at dusk again, we admitted to ourselves that we were lost. We are always lost near the end of the day.

We pointed the vessel to the nearest bank, through a grove of dead trees coming out of the water, and tied up.

The next day we never moved.

The luxury of not doing anything. Read and wrote letters. Had a beer. Pored over maps. Had a beer. Hiked up a mountain. Played a little backgammon. Had a beer. Took a long siesta. Good day!

At dawn on the final day we were up and away for the three-hour run back to home port. Due in at ten o'clock in time to have the boat cleaned, fuelled, serviced and ready for the next party boarding at two o'clock that afternoon.

Running down Lake Eildon, we had a fat breakfast eating all the left-overs in the refrigerator. Packed, shaved, showered.

The big houseboat held a steady course by itself.

I made another terrible landing. The wind was blowing and I missed the dock and then came in sideways and then had to back up and came in half sideways. Finally a company man jumped aboard, zoomed the boat around to the other side of the pier and docked it as neatly and gently as putting down an egg. Maddening.

The Dobsons were waiting for us with water skis and a patched up canoe.

Our choice. Did we want to go canoeing or did we want to go motorboating back on the lake to a pub for a "counter lunch" and water ski going and coming. We voted for water skiing.

The Dobsons once operated a water skiing school and they were experts. He gave a demonstration with trick skis, spinning in complete circles, jumping waves, very professional.

The Lady Navigator after flunking the one-ski test showed the results of a misspent youth on two skis. After being splattered all over the lake, I finally was able to get up on skis and running — flying it felt like. Good fun with good people.

Lake Eildon is an excellent vacation area.

Being near Melbourne it is popular. Although there are six hundred houseboats on the lake, there is so much water to play in, so much shoreline (620 kilometres) that you aren't conscious of any crowd.

The Lake Eildon Holiday Boats, Boat Harbour, Eildon, 3713 Victoria has houseboats from twenty-eight feet to forty-eight feet renting from Friday-to-Monday weekend from $220 in low season for a smaller boat to $645 for the largest boat in the high season.

Murray River

Our last houseboat on the Murray River was quite properly the granddaddy of them all.

Liba-Liba Houseboat No. 19, docked at Renmark three hours northeast of Adelaide, was sixty-five feet overall with a twenty-four-foot beam. It had more floor space than most summer cabins. It was *roomy*.

With No. 19's size and weight I could have wiped out *miles* of docks on the Murray River, given enough time.

Fortunately an experienced skipper-boatyard-owner from Cape

Cod, an old friend, joined us in Adelaide for our cruise and we assigned him the job of captain. No bashed railings. No hard "hot" landings.

A unique feature of the Liba-Liba houseboats, and historically fitting, is that they are paddle-wheelers.

At one time, a hundred years ago, the mighty Murray River was a vital transportation means for people and freight in three states of Australia and fleets of paddle-steamers plied the river waters.

Indeed the owner of the Liba-Liba houseboats and their designer, Ian Showell, returned to Renmark on a paddle-steamer sixty-seven years ago as an infant with his mother and nurse.

Today the commercial paddle-steamers have all gone but Ian Showell, now a white-bearded, ex-military engineer often mistaken for either Burl Ives or Colonel Sanders, owns twenty-eight paddle-wheel diesel-driven houseboats, the biggest operation on the Murray.

His first boat, built at the time of his retirement from the military, cost $8,000. His newest boat is costing $60,000.

The original design used a Holden engine and an International Tractor transmission. Out of one hundred houseboats on the Murray only the Liba-Libas are paddle-wheelers.

"My first design objective was to create a boat with plenty of room. Cruising boats with family and friends and kids on board can get very small very fast," he told us.

He succeeded.

The awning-covered "front porch" of our houseboat measured twenty feet by twenty-four feet and was equipped with deck chairs, a gas-fired barbecue, an outdoor ice chest augmenting a ten-foot refrigerator in the full-sized kitchen.

We asked him where the tennis net was.

The lounge was equally vast and could be partitioned into two rooms sleeping four people comfortably. In addition, there were double-bed and twin-bed staterooms.

The bathroom and shower were tiled and spacious. The separate w.c. was located on the aft deck. Provided was a dinghy with oars, a cutting board for freshly caught fish, a bucket to catch river prawns.

Our boatyard captain shook his head in admiration. "He has thought of everything. Really well designed."

We had a relaxing time.

The recommendation was to go upriver, which we did, enjoying the native trees and the native birds with only distant homesteads in the first leg of the cruise as evidence of civilisation.

By evening we were at the edge of a bird sanctuary and we tied up early to a grass bank. The red-gold sunset through the trees looked like a forest fire.

In our willow-lined harbour we were comfortably out of the wind and enjoyed good wine with good food with an old friend . . . a perfect place for gossiping and catching up on what-happened-to-old-whatshisname.

The next day we followed the winding river which was now flanked by colourful cliffs.

Occasionally we would see another Liba-Liba houseboat with the paddle-wheel spray making a rooster tail of white water at the rear of the boat.

Once two houseboats passed us, filled with heartily drinking passengers. They belonged to the same club and were having a name-calling, whisky-swilling race, both boats making a froth out of the river.

Again we anchored against a tranquil bank. No one around us. Peaceful in the woods. The smell of lamb stew with fresh mushrooms wafted through the evening air.

At dusk we caught a river carp but threw it back.

On the last day we paddle-powered downriver, past Renmark, returning to the Jane Eliza Landing for the last night on board. We had a scheduled dawn departure to visit the local vineyards.

Superb.

If you want to charter a Liba-Liba Houseboat, ask now because they are 80% pre-booked. Three-fourths of the houseboats are repeat customers and they reserve their boats three years in advance!

Cost for the long weekend, Friday to Monday, starts at $220.

Liba-Liba Houseboats, Paddle-Cat Ltd., P.O. Box 1, Renmark, S.A. 5341.

Showell has started another houseboat operation at Wentworth in New South Wales which is farther up the Murray. Every year he holds "The Wentworth Safari" which sends a flotilla from Renmark to Wentworth two hundred kilometres through five locks and three states! Sounds like fun.

Renmark is also headquarters for the *Murray Explorer*, a new three-deck river boat, air-conditioned with bar and huge dining room and sixty-one cabins, all with private baths.

The *Murray Explorer* makes five-day tours up and down the Murray River which is another way of exploring the country while being waited on.

It also offers an overseas visitor a chance to make acquintances among many Australians.

We were impressed in a walk-through. Immaculate condition. Sauna and spa bath. Hair-dressing salon, gift shop.

Cabins on the top two decks are preferable, having windows on the river and doors fronting a deck.

The bottom deck (Lachlan) has portholes for windows and costs less.

About $450 is the full fare. Transport by bus is available from Adelaide.

The *Explorer* is not a paddle-wheeler but her older sister-ship, the *Murray Queen*, is. The *Queen* operates farther downriver between Goolwa and Swan Reach. Same price. Less luxurious.

A third motor vessel, the *Coonawarra,* based at Murray Bridge offers five-day cruise packages at about $398 for a cabin with private shower and toilet.

All tours can be booked through the South Australian Government Tourist Bureau.

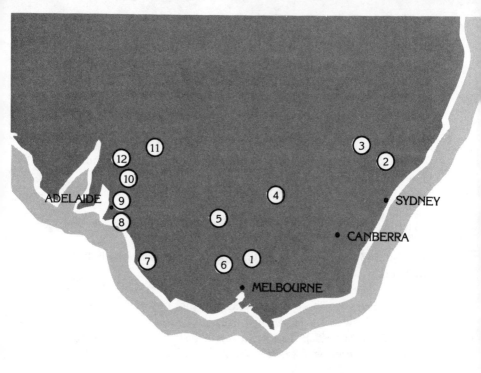

WINE DISTRICTS

1. RUTHERGLEN
2. HUNTER VALLEY
3. MUDGEE
4. GRIFFITH
5. SWAN HILL
6. GREAT WESTERN

7. COONAWARRA
8. SOUTHERN VALES
9. ADELAIDE
10. BAROSSA
11. RIVERLAND (Renmark)
12. CLARE

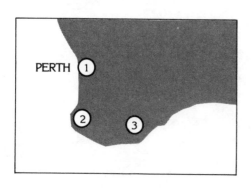

1. SWAN RIVER
2. MARGARET RIVER
3. MT. BARKER

9. Chasing the Grape

Granted, our research of Australian wines was an example of overkill.

"Many overseas visitors are not aware that there *is* an Australian wine industry," we said going to seventeen out of the twenty-one wine districts, blissful in the peaceful, God-ordered tranquillity of rolling rows of grape-laden, green-leafed vineyards.

"What a pleasant surprise the wine-loving tourist will have when he discovers the large number of different wineries: big wineries, small wineries, internationally-owned wineries, family-owned wineries," we said visiting over fifty of some three hundred wineries with their sweet-sour smell filling the musty air, surrounded by casks and vats and tubes and bottles. Church ground. A place for spiritual inspiration.

"What a delight the hard-core oenologist will have sipping and gargling and chewing and rinsing and appreciating the unappreciated high quality of Australian wines," we said as we sampled fortified wines, dry reds and dry whites, dessert wines, sparkling wines and ports and brandies.

Oh, how we worked!

We have had the good fortune to chase the grape in Burgundy from Lyon to Dijon. Followed the vines through the valley of the Loire. Stayed in St. Emilion and drove the country roads through the sandy countryside of Bordeaux viewing in the distance the mighty chateaux that invoke awe and reverence.

We have tramped and sipped our way through ancient vineyards of Sonoma and the shiny new wineries of Napa Valley in California and have done the wine crawl — all day — through the golden hills of New Zealand's Henderson Valley.

The temptation of adventuring too far, too deep, too long in Australia's excellent vineyards was too much.

Overkill, granted. But what a lovely chase!

Yesterday and Today in the Australian Vineyards

Wine has been part of Australia's heritage from the time of the first colonies.

So successful were the early wines, particularly the fortified wines

— the sherries, the ports — that the shipping of Australian wines to England was an important factor in Australia's early export trade.

Today the English market has been eliminated by the European Common Market. The local post-war popularity of dry table wines has created an entirely new industry in terms of volume and in the new technology of production.

We paid a visit to Dr. Bryce Rankine, head of Roseworthy Agricultural College's School of Oenology and Viticulture to get an authoritative background on Australian wine.

Dr. Rankine is tall, grey of sideburns, bright, animated. A charmer who graciously gave us much of his time.

"The per capita wine consumption in Australia has doubled in the last ten years to sixteen litres per head. In America I believe it is nine litres," he told us one morning in his office.

"In 1960 our national table wine production amounted to thirteen million litres. In 1979 the volume had increased to one hundred and seventy million litres. The dry white table wine volume alone is now over one hundred million litres.

"What you will find in your travels is that the swing to white wine has been so dramatic that there is now an over-production of red wine. I think this will balance out because the tendency is for new wine drinkers to try white wines first and as they learn more about wine and appreciate the nuances of wines they will turn to the more satisfying red wines.

"At the same time you'll find a dramatic drop in brandies largely due to the excise tax imposed on brandies which has been increased by more than five hundred percent in five years."

(Hard liquor is expensive in Australia. Nationally made vodka, for example, costs US$15 a bottle. It will make a sherry drinker out of you.)

"By world wine standards we are still comparatively small. Our total wine production is only two-fifths of California's production, for example. But we are continuing to grow.

"Today there are about three hundred registered wine growers who crush a minimum of ten tons each annually. The leaders, not in any particular order, include Lindemans, Orlando, McWilliams, Penfolds, Kaiser Stuhl, Berri, Tolley Scott Tolley, Seppelts, Yalumba, Wynns, Hardy.

"One of the unique features of Australian wine-making is that the average Australian winery produces the whole gamut of wines: sweet wines, dry wines, liqueurs, reds, whites, rosés while the average French vintner will produce only two or three.

"Significantly, the new popularity of wines has attracted the big companies. Australian breweries are buying into the industry. So have multi-national companies. Seagrams bought Saltram in the Barossa and Colgate-Palmolive has bought into Rothbury Estate in the Hunter.

"It has not been a bad thing because it has meant new and needed capital for more sophisticated equipment.

"Technologically, we have made giant advances in the last ten years in Australia. New techniques in refrigeration. New techniques in oxidation control.

"One future trend in Australian grape production will be the site selection in new areas, more to the south, in the cooler climates."

As he walked us back to our car he added a word of advice: "Overseas writers often get caught up in the romance of the boutique wineries and that is all they write about. The true story of Australian wines today is in the big wineries and the consistent quality of their production."

At the end of our tour of fifty wineries we remembered the good doctor's last words.

What we found and what an overseas visitor will find is that the larger the winery, the farther the visitor is removed from the winemaker.

You never get closer than sipping samples in a room with a salesman. That removes you from the heart and the heat and the fun of chasing the grape.

Winemakers are artists deeply and emotionally involved in their craft. Each is a poet without artifice. An alchemist. A priest.

Each believes absolutely that his wine is unique in its qualities, and, while colleagues are to be congratulated for their efforts, in his Temple exists The True Wine.

He preaches his dogma with feverish intensity and, if you show the proper respect and interest, the revelation can take many hours . . . and many bottles.

Winemakers are simply great people.

I remember Robert "Rob" Bowen, the winemaker at Plantagenet Winery at Mt. Barker, serious blue eyes, a full, slightly red beard.

A woman entered the winery smoking a cigarette.

"Hey, Lady, put out that cigarette," said the young winemaker-priest. "We are making wine in here."

(Don't sully my Temple.)

That's what you find in a small winery.

The Rutherglen Red

We timed our return to Australia and to Melbourne in time to take in the Saturday running of the Derby. Many of the favourite horses would take their last warm-up in the Derby before the famous Melbourne Cup race the following Tuesday.

On Derby Saturday a more tempting offer was put on our plate.

"The Rutherglen Red is going next Saturday. We can get you on board."

What is the Rutherglen Red?

"It is a two-day tour of the vineyards of the Rutherglen area which is famous for its fortified wines. You leave by train Saturday morning, travel to Chiltern, bus through the vineyards, dine that night at a club, tour the next morning, barbecue in the country at a vineyard and come home Sunday afternoon."

Rutherglen Red or the Derby?

We'll try a bit of the red, please.

The Rutherglen Red is a smashing two-day boozer.

Our introduction to the vineyards was a bath in champagne, a startling introduction to the Australians' ability to drink, a chance to meet gracious, honest vignerons, and a look at what must be one of Australia's prettiest countrysides.

The Rutherglen Red is a chartered train made up of ancient first-class coaches, a baggage car with food and wine, a forward disco-dance car for fun and games, and a diesel locomotive.

At the inception of the Rutherglen Red tour the locomotive was steam-powered in keeping with the spirit of the week-end but it took so long to get the passengers to their destination that it was too late to tour the vineyards and by then the passengers were too zonked to see the vines much less sample a bottle.

The train left Spencer Street station at 9:25 a.m. with the cheerful sound of popping champagne corks and passed-around pitchers of orange juice. Half-and-half is the suggested drink but one can only drink so much orange juice and gradually, as the scenery slipped by, the orange juice diminished, the noise level in compartments reached increasingly high decibel ratings, the laughter was loud and the goings and comings in the corridor was a continual parade.

Plates of fresh chicken sandwiches were passed around as blotters and the champagne continued its never-ending, never-ending flow.

It was a fully raucous party by the time the train stopped at Seymour Station for meat pies and railroad tea.

The men went straight to the bar and ordered beer!

As you know a meat pie is a round pastry filled with brown gravy and only brown gravy.

Once in 1939 an Englishman from Esher, Surrey found a piece of meat in his Australian meat pie and they awarded him a three-acre plot in the Simpson Desert to grow rabbits. They hung the baker. A piece of meat has not been found since that time in a railroad station meat pie.

My memory of Seymour Station is a bench filled with wide-eyed Boy Scouts watching the train depart.

The countryside north of Melbourne leading to Rutherglen is pastoral . . . cultivated fields, horses, sheep. It sped by the open window interrupted only by a passing congo-line of chanting passengers.

Champagne was now interlaced with jugs of iced riesling and box lunches with fresh roasted chicken. The tour operators were wisely keeping food as well as wine in constant reach of the passengers.

By the time we reached Chiltern it was almost one o'clock and we emptied out of the train into air-conditioned buses for separate rotating tours of three vineyards. The train would be washed out and shaken upside down for the return trip the next day.

One passenger had lost the use of his knees.

His colleagues, a group of football referees, dragged him to his bus like a knocked-out player. Which he was.

Greg Driscoll, the tour operator, shook his head. "That's the first one we've lost in eight trips."

The discovery of gold in Victoria in 1851 touched off a fever of exploration which included the finding of rich alluvial gold streaks between Chiltern and Rutherglen in 1858.

The gold was dug out by hand often to depths of three hundred feet and piles of dirt can still be seen flanked by pools of water which filled in the diggings when they ceased to be worked.

Vineyards were started in the same period and when gold-mining declined twenty years later the vines and wineries were flourishing.

At one time there were over a hundred vineyards in the district producing over half of all the wines in Australia.

Unfortunately the dreaded disease phylloxera, the same which destroyed the French vineyards, almost obliterated the Rutherglen vineyards.

Like the French, the Australians imported phylloxera-resistant rootstocks from California but the loss of vineyards due to the disease combined with the devastation of the Depression severely reduced the country's volume but it still retained the reputation for outstanding fortified wines.

Chris Killeen, the sixth generation involved in the Stanton & Killeen vineyards, said that the Rutherglen vineyards' reputation for luscious dessert wines frequently overshadowed the fact that all the vineyards produce a full variety of rich red and lovely, dry white table wines.

Bullers Wineries, a small, family-owned operation, is typical of the district.

Its vineyard Calliope was started in 1921 and was moving into its third generation of owners.

Richard Buller and his wife Valerie operate Calliope while Richard, Jr. operates the larger vineyard at Swan Hill, farther down the River Murray.

The Bullers are easy-to-talk-to-people, genuinely in love with their work. They turned down a million and a half dollars for the properties.

"What would we do? Raise a pack of wasters." Two other sons are joining the operations.

"We have lots of empty bedrooms now. If you come back through, stay with us."

Friendly, comfortable people.

We last visited the All Saints Vineyard and Cellars which began in 1864. The founders built the present multi-turreted building in memory of a castle near their ancestral home in Scotland.

Most of the vineyards offer sampling, on-site buying, and, often, shaded picnic grounds. They generally are closed only on Sundays and holidays.

Note: At one vineyard it was reported that a well-endowed lady had been invited by the proprietor for a private tasting behind the barrels which resulted in not only a personal sip but also a personal pinch.

The wilted crowd was driven across the Murray River to the town of Albury, New South Wales, where we stayed in a pleasant Travelodge and that night went to the Commercial Club.

New South Wales is awash with "private clubs" dominated by slot machines called "pokies" which pay for the reasonably priced drinks and food and the large dance band.

Every table was full at the Commercial Club — and in the "pokie room" every slot machine was occupied.

One thing that father taught me was that slot machines are a no-win proposition and it was only with brute force that I pried a whimpering Lady Navigator off of a twenty-cent gobbler and hauled her off to bed.

The morning brought news that they turned the lights out on the "pokies" at one o'clock but they didn't turn the lights off of the Rutherglen Red troupe until about four a.m. after much room visiting and drinking and a skinny-dipping party. Bodies scattered all over the hotel.

After a fine night's sleep and a walk through Albury's botanical garden we were almost saintly.

One slit-eyed young man confessed that he had had one hour's sleep. Another complained about the loss of his coat.

"You probably left it in a room."

"I was in eight rooms that I remember," he said.

There is a certain don't-give-up spirit about Australian partyers which you must respect . . . at a distance.

By ten-thirty everyone was back on buses, many with a life-saving tin of beer and we were off on a country tour including huge Hume Weir, a major dam, then back into pokie-less Victoria to the Seppelts Vineyard for a barbecue of beef and sausages and salads under the shade of lemon and orange trees.

Pretty.

The Rutherglen vignerons, as hosts, poured a generous splashing of red and white wines. People started to doze off on the grass.

It is hard to believe the trip back on the train.

Jugs of white wine started flowing; the party resumed its full tempo.

Dancing in the party car. A contest in a coach to see how many bodies could fit into one compartment.

The first attempt scored thirty-one. A crushing, sardine effort. A second attempt squeezed in forty bodies. A world's record.

General hilarity everywhere. Much hand holding.

"How many romances begin on an average trip," Greg Driscoll was asked.

"Arf! The disasters often exceed the romances," he answered.

We arrived back at Spencer Street Station, bottle laden, slightly sloshed. Another body was hauled away *flat*.

We appreciated the quote in the Link Tours brochure which summed up the Rutherglen Red:

"Look mate, I bought wine from the wineries, met a beaut girl whom I am taking out next week, won at the pokies and shouted everyone drinks at the bar and came home showing a profit, and some reporter writing a story for a newspaper asks me did I have a good time!"

The Rutherglen Red now runs three weekends a month. Cost about $199. Save $20 by booking a month in advance through Link Tours, 1527 Dandenong Road, Oakleigh, Victoria.

Another beaut, Mate.

The Famous Hunter Valley

One of the first wine producing areas in Australia was in a river valley north of Sydney.

The famous Hunter Valley.

Probably James Busby, familiar to New Zealanders as the first British Resident at the Bay of Islands and drafter of the Treaty of Waitangi, brought grape vines to the Hunter from France, Germany and the Kew Gardens in London in the 1820s.

By 1856 there were almost three hundred acres of vines planted in the Hunter.

By far the most famous winemaker was the immortal Maurice O'Shea, son of an Irish farmer and a French mother. He was sent to France to study winemaking and with his knowledge took over the family vineyard in 1921. O'Shea, more than any other, was responsible for the reputation of the big Hunter Valley wines.

Actually the weather in the Hunter is dismal. When rains are needed before budding and before flowering, it is often parched. When dry weather is desired during the vintage, it often floods.

Hail can and has flattened the vineyards.

Nevertheless, the area has grown from 1,500 acres under vine to 10,000 acres.

The established vineyards of the Lower Hunter near Cessnock are now augmented by new vineyards in the Upper Hunter from Denman to Scone.

And characters like O'Shea are everywhere.

Overseas visitors to Sydney who want to visit the Hunter Valley are fortunate because the vineyards are only three hours away by car and forty-five minutes by airplane.

You can get bus tours out of Sydney which also include the Hunter Valley.

We did an extensive week in the Hunter, first by car, and then later, for the fun of it, by airplane.

Rebel Air is an operation with a DC-3 for charter. Among their suggestions for a group is to take their plane to the Hunter Valley where they will have a bus ready for a wine-tasting tour and a barbecue lunch.

Another exciting option in the Hunter Valley is to inspect the vineyards from the air—specifically from a balloon in the dawn hours followed by a champagne breakfast.

Adventure Travel Centre in Sydney offers several ballooning adventures. The most popular are the Hunter Valley Day Flights from Braxton in the April to November period.

The flights last about one hour and are dependent on the weather. Cost about $95. Contact number is (02) 298 052.

We arrived in the Hunter by car on an early December afternoon. The vineyards were reaching their peak: fully, richly leafed and laden with red or white grapes in thick clusters.

Residences do not mar the Hunter landscape; the gently rolling hills are covered with tidy rows of green vines and an occasional winery. The late afternoon sun threw deep, seductive shadows in the cleavages of green. It was like being enfolded into the arms of a beautiful, full-bosomed woman.

I instinctively gave out a big sigh of rapture as we drove to the top of a rise, to the Elfin Hill Motel and Vineyards, a popular, small establishment.

Once checked in, we made reservations for dinner at Blaxlands Barn Restaurant, also highly recommended. The proprietor, Chris Barnes, was then president of the Hunter Valley Vineyard Association. He was most helpful in arranging appointments and making suggestions.

The first favour he did was to reserve a bottle of Tyrrell's Vintage 1973, Vat I Riesling for dinner.

After the photogenic introduction to the Hunter, the bottle was the perfect follow-up. I can't remember having a better bottle of white wine. Soft, elegant, fully flavoured by the semillon grapes, it turned to gold in the throat.

Our first winery was Tulloch's Glen Elgin managed by J. Y. "Jay" Tulloch, originally a family winery established in 1896 and now owned by Gilbeys.

It was an example of new money being infused into a family operation. As Jay Tulloch led us through the modern winery we could appreciate the major investment required to buy and install the array of new equipment.

Although, like many Hunter Valley wineries, Tulloch's was carrying the load of over-production of red wines, he felt that the demand by customers would settle out at about sixty percent white and forty percent red.

We also learned from Jay that a 'Hunter Riesling' is a semillon and a 'Hunter Hermitage' is a shiraz.

Our first serious course in wine appreciation in the Hunter took place at Tyrrell's Ashman.

Tyrrell's is still a family dominated winery and Murray Tyrrell is well known for being a strong personality in the Hunter Valley. The distinctive Tyrrell wines of international standards are a reflection of his own personality.

Our education was conducted by a tall, intense, young winemaker, Ralph Fowler, whose knowledge was matched by his enthusiasm.

He paced us through seven white wines, rieslings and chardonnays, and then six reds — cabernets, shiraz and a pinot noir which had won a gold medal in a French wine show over a 1969 Clos de Vougeot, a Gevrey-Chambertin and a Cotes de Beaune Village.

"The Vat I you had last night came from an area we call 'the short flat.' All Vat numbers indicate that the wine was produced from a particular part of a vineyard.

"These good wines take care of themselves. Bad wines need a lot of work."

Ralph took us through the winery and showed us part of the original winery which is protected now under a modern shed. Outside the original slab hut of the founders, built in 1858, still stands.

The original grant of land to a Tyrrell goes back to 1858. Murray's uncle, Dan Tyrrell, took over the family vineyards at the age of fourteen and saw seventy-six vintages.

Tyrrell's is popular. On summer weekends the bar in the salesroom will be five and six people deep.

Hungerford Hill is a major tourist-oriented winery attuned to the visitor market and it succeeds in attracting 200,000 people a year.

Reg Mowat, the marketing officer, showed us through the complex establishment with pride.

Besides the modern winery, Hungerford Hill includes a Wine Pavilion where barbecues are served to large, pre-booked group tours, a Farmers' Market selling jams, jellies and honeys of the region, home-made pork pies.

Nearby is a craft centre and art gallery. A kiosk offers ice cream and sandwiches. A stable has over fifteen horses available for short arena or longer trail rides. A recent addition was a greenhouse which also sells hand-made out-door furniture.

A sizeable children's playground constantly expands according to Mr. Mowat because the employees' children appreciate it so much.

There is even an immense, man-made lake in front of the winery which gives a pleasant vista to the visitor, and provides a place for water skiing.

Three half-underground cellars with green-sod roofs are the heart of the Hungerford Hill operation. Two cellars are tasting-sales rooms. One for week-days, one for Sundays.

The third cellar is the Pokolbin Cellars Restaurant, a pleasant place to lunch among ferns and skylights. The black-board French menu changes daily and is most tempting. Because the restaurant is popular, make sure you have reservations.

Reg Drayton, the no-nonsense but genial manager of Drayton's

Bellevue, is a strong believer in vines developing without using fertiliser or irrigated water which, he says, take away from the grapes' ability to develop their own flavour and body.

"Wine is at its best when the grapes are in the vineyard," he said, quoting Brian Walsh at McWilliams.

To prove it, he opened three bottles of his riesling: a 1959, a 1966 still brilliant in colour and a 1977 which had won all kinds of awards.

Drayton is a family operation which started in 1853 and is now in its fourth generation. Half of the winery's twenty-six employees are relatives.

The Rothbury Estate's stunning winery dominates the landscape in the Hunter Valley. Completed in 1972 the striking, angular white structure is a symbol of the boldness, snobbery and imagination which combine to make the Rothbury adventure successful.

The winery is the brainchild of two men: the strong, solid, singular-minded Hunter Valley winemaker, Murray Tyrrell and the flamboyant, brilliant promoter, wine writer, restaurateur from Sydney, Len Evans.

Read a sample of Evan's *leitmotif* in the *Rothbury Pressings*, a Rothbury Estate membership publication headlined: "In Pursuit of Excellence."

"One of the worst features of Australian life is our apparent quest for mediocrity. Egalitarianism is 'in,' elitism is 'out.' Knock down the tall poppies, good old Norm, she's right mate, it'll do me.

"Well, it won't do me."

It takes that kind of mind to develop a marketing programme that enrolls 32,000 members in the Rothbury wine club, members who keep qualifying by buying a dozen bottles of Rothbury wine every year, thereby absorbing seventy percent of the winery's production!

Who else would think of developing a wine-identification status game whereby the amateur taster, progressing through increasingly difficult stages of picking the proper types of wines, the correct vineyards and the correct years thereby earns a white ribbon, then a green ribbon, followed by a red ribbon until he reaches the pinnacle of success, the purple ribbon.

It's not easy. Eighteen tasters qualified for a red ribbon out of one hundred and twenty who tried.

Only fifty people have ever qualified for the purple ribbon.

As you would suppose there are Ribbon Dinners, schools and seminars, a Great Chefs of Australia dinner, books, and a Home Tasting Dozen with a Len Evans sip-along cassette.

Isn't that bloody marvellous?

The Rothbury Estate is not just a gimmick enterprise. Much money and expertise have been spent and applied to develop a product to meet the principals' high standards.

You can visit their tasting room without being a member. But you probably will be a member before you leave.

We joined Brian Walsh at the McWilliams' Mount Pleasant winery for a glass.

Walsh had come to the winery in 1956 to understudy the great Maurice O'Shea. O'Shea died the same year and Walsh took over.

"O'Shea had a fantastic palate, extremely sensitive in judging white wine. Our difficulty in those days was the lack of technical equipment we have today," he said opening a 1970 bottle of Hunter Valley red out of his "library."

"You find that this wine settles with age into a full, round but soft characteristic that is the signature of Hunter Valley wines. Basically," he said, confirming Reg Drayton's quote, "the quality of the wine is determined in the vineyards. We, the winemakers, only enhance or destroy the greatness of the vintage."

The most popular wine in Australia is Lindemans Ben Ean, the namesake of the winery in the Hunter Valley. The white moselle does not come from the winery, however, but is blended in the company's cellars in Sydney.

The specialty of the Lindemans Ben Ean vineyard is a sweet sauterne called Porphyry Sauterne. You can buy a 1956 Porphyry at Lindemans sales room for $40.

Our last appointment in the Hunter Valley was with Jim Roberts of Belbourie, one of the most controversial winemakers in the Hunter.

We were at the small, rock-walled winery promptly at nine, the appointed hour.

No one was there.

Finally, a tractor roared up the hill, a large man with crushed hat, overalls, gum boots, jumped off.

"WhatcanIdoforya?" was the blunt question. It was Jim Roberts. He'd forgotten the appointment.

He'd just returned to the winery to change clothes and get to the airport to see his daughter off. He apologised for being unable to give us more time and never stopped talking while changing clothes behind the bar.

A summation of Roberts had earlier been volunteered by another winemaker: "Jim Roberts is way off the track. You listen to his rambling and you know he's wrong and yet — and yet — every now and then he drops a piece of gold."

Roberts made his own wine his own way. Anaerobic fermentation was his technique. A method where the grapes, in an airtight container and cooled at the bottom with dry ice, were allowed to slowly crush themselves and ferment naturally producing softer wines with more alcohol and less tannic acid.

He designed his own labels (splashes of wild colour crossing each other) and called his wines by original names: Belah, Super Belah, Bungan, Light Bungan.

"Who says you have to call wines certain names? I give the wines names that are part of their character."

He tapped a container that held wine developing for nine months. He siphoned off a glass. "That is going to make the best port you ever taste," he said and took off for the airport.

We hope he wins.

Another character representative of the Hunter Valley comes from another side of the social spectrum.

We didn't meet him in the Hunter but finally found him in Sydney and on the top of the Gazebo Hotel shared a bottle of white wine and the view over the harbour.

I didn't take any notes because Max Lake mesmerises you with his talk about wine, about food, about women, about himself.

He didn't stress his reputation as a surgeon. We found out later that he was one of the finest hand surgeons in Australia.

His ambition to become a winemaker was born, as he tells it, in 1960 when he tasted a 1930 Dalwood Cabernet Sauvignon.

His white head rolls fondly on his large, formally dressed frame at the memory.

"I thought: 'I'd like to be able to make a wine like that.' "

In the early sixties he explored the regions within reach of Sydney and finally found suitable acreage in the Hunter. So began Lakes Folly, the name of his vineyard.

"I put everything into it. Time, energy, money. My God, the money. There was one year of a horrible vintage when it looked like everything was going to come crashing down and I had mental pictures of living in a small cottage and riding a bicycle to the hospital. That was the year I became a winemaker."

A couple of years ago he left the hospital and his medical practice.

"I'd had enough. To stay abreast of modern developments demands long hours of constant study. I've studied enough. Besides I lost my nurse and I was damned if I'd go through the trauma of training another one."

His fifty acres of wines now produce outstanding cabernets, which are his pride, and an excellent fruity chardonnay.

Dr. Max Lake with his pioneering in 1963 led the wave of ambitious, probably over-eager winemakers into the Hunter who didn't have his medical discipline and they failed where he succeeded.

The nicest part about Max Lake, the winemaker, is his larger-than-life enthusiasm . . . about everything.

Tip for the Hunter

If you are serious about exploring the Hunter and want to take, say, a week to give it a good try, the best bet we found for accommodations is The Pokolbin Cabins.

They are big, modern, pre-cut log cabins set well apart in the middle of an extensive treeless field originally prepared to be a vineyard until over-production necessitated an economic alternative.

The three and five bedroom cabins are spacious and clean, completely furnished with everything from linen to crockery. Included in the rural setting is a swimming pool and a tennis court.

There is a weekend rate and a weekly rate. Much better value than a motel. The reservation number is (049) 987 611.

The Old New Wineries of Mudgee

We made a country swing out of Sydney to include the Blue Mountains, the goldfields beyond, the outdoor zoo at Dubbo, the museum at Gulgong and also tucked in a couple of wineries at Mudgee, 277 kilometres northeast of Sydney.

Craigmoor is the oldest existing winery (1858), operated by

continental-charming Cyrille J. van Heyst. We sipped a glass of cool champagne at the van Heyst home preceding a barbecue and watched a classic golden sunset overlooking the green vines. We thought that Jehovah was going to come out of the silk-toned clouds.

At Huntington Estate, one of the newest wineries, we followed at the heels of Bob Roberts, tasting from first one cask and then another, first one bottle then another. Handsome and glamorous enough to make the Lady Navigator blink with pleasure, the owner-manager-winemaker made good wines too.

An Eye Opener at Griffith

The problem with Griffith for the overseas taster is that Griffith in the Riverina District is 637 kilometres southwest of Sydney. For us it was also the week before Christmas.

"If you are going to write about Australian wines, you have to visit Griffith because it produces ten percent of all Australian wines," said a wine promotion manager in Sydney.

"You should first make contact with Gino Vitucci. He is a prominent grape-grower, president of the local viticultural committee and is on our Australian Wine Advisory Board," he said.

Gino Vitucci turned out to be a gumdrop.

Medium height, solidly built, about fifty, Gino was a serious but easy-to-laugh gentleman who took over our lives with the easy assumption of the natural leader, saw that we met the right people, visited the right wineries and were entertained. A great, warm, open-hearted, hard-working Italian grape grower.

Orlando's Wickham Hill Cellars was our first visit where Bernard Hickin, the young winemaker showed us around.

In seven years the winery has gone from a crush of 300 tons annually to 10,000 tons. The operation produces bulk wines, light in flavour, low in cost, to attract the flagon and bag-in-the-box sales.

Leon Wolman, the winemaker at De Bortoli, gave us a tour of the family-owned winery which specialises in sparkling wines.

"The use of the words 'irrigated grapes' has been used in the past as a stigma but today with modern refrigeration and modern techniques we produce quality wines.

"During the Easter Wine Festival, we will have five to six thousand people at the winery every day. Country music, entertainment for the kids. It's wild!"

McWilliam's Hanwood Winery is one of three McWilliams's operations in the district. Together they crush forty percent of the entire local grape production.

Glen McWilliam, the manager, is one of seventeen family members involved today in the largest family-owned wine producing company in Australia.

Glen has seen forty vintages. He is a designer at heart. A technician. He created the immense half-wine-cask sales room at Hanwood and was working on the architectural design for a museum. It would be a gigantic wine bottle.

We were invited to the Vitucci farm for pre-Christmas "after church" drinks. Champagne punch. Beer. Hard liquor. (No one touched hard liquor)

It was an open-hearted, gusty, Italian-type party with friends dropping in, grandchildren running around, adult sons mixing the champagne punch.

The family makes its own salami, cures its own ham into prosciutto, makes its own olives.

"Every year we put up four hundred bottles of tomato sauce and I make eight hundred bottles of wine. Tomorrow night you come to dinner with us at the Italian Catholic Club and I'll bring my wine!"

Gino's wife, Joanna-of-the-smiling-eyes, obviously loved to spoil her family.

"Twice a week she makes me home-made spaghetti," said Gino, "or I don't live."

(He was giving her a new electric pasta-maker for Christmas. Men are all heart.)

She served delicious mini mince pies, fruit cakes, smoked oysters, cookies and cold fried zucchini which we couldn't stop nibbling.

The next night we had an excellent Italian dinner at the Italian Catholic Club with the Vituccis.

Delicate ravioli and scallopini . . . and good talk.

"You know, my father came from the old country." Gino said. "He could have returned many times but he wouldn't. 'I am an Australian,' he would say. He was the most democratic man. When I was fourteen, he took my brother and myself into the bank where we all signed cards making us part of his bank account. 'We are now equal partners,' he told us and shook us each by the hand."

He uncorked a label-less bottle.

"Tell me what it is," he demanded.

I sniffed and rolled it in the glass and peered at the colour, sipped it, bit it, gargled it.

"Tell me what it is!" He was like a bright-eyed, eager boy.

"It is a six-year-old cabernet," I said with authority.

"Hah!" he jumped with delight. "It is my home-made eighteen-month old shiraz. How about *that*!"

A memorable evening.

Bubbles and "Bubbles"

An overseas visitor to Australia is soon aware that the whole country is fizzing. At horse races, in homes, in restaurants, the bottles of "champers" are visible everywhere.

It follows in an increasingly sophisticated wine industry that champagne production is reaching new levels in quality and in volume.

At Seppelts Great Western champagne cellars Dominique Landragin said, "You have to understand that by world-wide standards our annual production of three million litres is a modest figure."

Three million! Ye gods!

"You know there is an annual Australian increase in white wine consumption of ten percent. But the increase of sparkling wine consumption is twenty percent.

"Also there is an increasing appreciation of better wines and a willingness to pay for better quality. That is why I am here. Excellent prospects for the future."

We had stopped off at Great Western, a village in Victoria 217 kilometres west of Melbourne, to take a short look at The House of Seppelts champagne facility, not knowing really what to expect.

Perhaps, we thought, it would be a bottling factory where they made lemonade on Tuesday, sparkling wine on Wednesday and orange crush on Thursday.

Ho-ho-ho. Surprise.

Bill Norton, the company's sales diplomat, turned us over to Dominique, 32, who had been brought out from France by Seppelts to supervise champagne production. Dominique came from a French family with a three hundred year tradition for making champagne.

"You know, of course, that sparkling wine is fermented in bulk as opposed to champagne which is fermented in the bottle," said our French authority.

"Here at Great Western we have two different champagnes: The Imperial Reserve which is stored above ground in two immense refrigerated warehouses and kept under strict temperature control for a minimum of six months.

"Our Great Western Vintage label is aged in underground cellars — called 'drives' because they were dug by ex-miners. Here we have a million and a half bottles of vintage champagne which we will age for a minimum of four years.

He produced five bottles of vintage champagne: two '70s, a '71, a '72 and a '74 for our private blind taste test.

Very serious drinking ... no, not drinking, sipping and spitting out. And instruction: "Look for crispness without too much acid. Proper bubbling collar around the rim of the glass very important. Proper yellow-gold colour."

Our second champagne experience was easier to reach.

In the foothills of Adelaide in the district village of Magill are the Seaview Champagne Cellars, one of the three most important champagne producers in Australia, administered by a congenial giant of a man whose unlikely nickname is "Bubbles."

His real name is Norman Walker and he stands about six feet, four inches and moves like a football player, his massive hands and shoulders a physical contradiction to the delicate task of making one of Australia's outstanding champagnes in the exacting, costly French method.

Bubbles spent four years in the Roseworthy Agricultural College, worked after graduation as a vineyard roustabout, then as a winemaker at Coonawarra and returned to Seaview in 1958 to take over from his father.

"Tell me what you are looking for?" we asked Norm — I didn't dare call him "Bubbles" — as he opened three bottles of Seaview champagnes.

"Look at the bubbles. The fine bubbles indicate proper aging. Smell it. The champagne has a clean nose. You don't want the characteristics of the fruit to dominate. Taste it. Notice that it is delicate without being thin. Crisp. Clean. Not too sweet. Taste it again and then wait. The depth of the flavour stays in the mouth.

"This is Australian champagne. We will never duplicate French champagne because they use different grapes grown in different soil in a different climate."

"Take a bottle with you," he urged.

"Thank you, no," we burped our way gently to the door and went back to the hotel to take a mid-morning nap.

The Rich Barossa

One of the many charms of Adelaide is that the city is in the centre of a major portion of Australia's best wine production.

South is the district of Coonawarra, famous for its red wines. An hour from the city is McLaren Vale, scene of a camel safari and, even closer, Reynella. The two areas comprise the Southern Vales.

To the northeast is the highly productive Riverland and on the same parallel but west, the valley of Clare.

In the foothills of Adelaide the visitor can visit "Bubbles" in his champagne cellars and other near-by wineries.

But an hour's drive from the city — tour buses go three times a week — you can judge for yourself the most famous of the wine districts, the rich Barossa Valley.

The Barossa's popularity is based on its attractive, marketable German heritage . . . the visual appeal of its historic buildings and green scenery . . . and, not least, its acceptance as a leader of quality Australian wines.

A massive festival every odd-numbered year adds to the Barossa's reputation.

The German heritage dates back to 1847 when Johann Gramp first planted vines at Jacob's Creek.

A brigade of German Lutherans followed in search of religious independence and the wine that supported them also supported their churches. There are thirty wineries in the Barossa and about thirty Lutheran churches.

Visually the wineries and the churches are examples of old-world graciousness and old-world reliability.

You have to go to Seppeltsfield, if not to visit the winery, then to drink in the palm-treed elegance of the vast estate.

On the way you'll pass, at Marananga, the perfect German Lutheran Church, meticulously, harmoniously balanced.

Look at the Germanic castle facade of the Kaiser Stuhl Chateau, a classic case of architecture serving the designs of smart marketing.

At Angaston you'll take a photo of the town hall, the Barossa Brauhaus Hotel and, outside the village, the fortress-like Yalumba Winery with flags flying from the blue marble clock-tower.

The Barossa Valley appeals to the stomach as well as the eye. Excellent German picnic foods can be found in butcher shops and bakeries . . . father-to-son recipes . . . sausages and calorie-laden cakes. Try, for a sampler, the *metwurst* at Shultz's Meat Market in Angaston or the *bienenstich* at the Apex Bakery in Tanunda.

David Allnutt, secretary of the Australian Wine Board in Adelaide, a most knowledgeable pointer to wineries, inns and eateries, said not to miss Die Weinstube Restaurant in the Barossa, operated by Horst Boettger. We had a most enjoyable lunch in the Stube.

But the wineries! The wineries!

Our first visit was to Yalumba Winery outside of Angaston. Yalumba is unique in that its heritage is not Germanic but English.

Mike Hall Smith, sixth generation of Smiths at Yalumba, guided us through the winery which was established in 1849 but which had been pre-sold to us as an example of a family-owned operation that was up-to-the-minute-modern in equipment and techniques.

"Heat is the Australian wine industry's biggest problem," Mike explained. "Grapes, like apples, tend to turn colour and change character when exposed to air and heat. We harvest at night with automatic harvesters to beat the heat and prevent spoilage.

"We also crush at night and the *must* goes immediately into modern coolers. We now have completed major refrigeration rooms — not tanks. Yes, like McWilliam's.

"We even have our own nursery where we can graft our own vines from different clones."

Yalumba, best known in the past for its fortified wines, now produces outstanding red wines known as "signature wines" honouring the people in the winery who have built its reputation. A white wine, Pewsey Vale, is a fine riesling which you might find on better restaurant wine lists but is usually sold out.

The Brut de Brut Champagne and the Galway Pipe Port are two other famous products of the million gallons of wine produced annually.

Beneath the winery, the old concrete tanks formerly used for bulk wine storage now hold 15,000 bottles allocated to the "wine museum." These wines date back to 1870. French wines, German wines, California wines, Australian wines comprise what Mike called "the best wine collection in Australia." Annually there is a tasting for two hundred friends, customers, wine writers.

In the large commercial tasting room you can sample the Yalumba wines available for purchase. Bargain of the week was a five gallon French oak cask (Yalumba makes them on property) filled with ten-year old tawny port for $120.

From the clock tower an Italian flag was flying.

"We also make Martini & Rossi vermouth under licence and their representative from Turin is here. If we'd known you were coming we would have flown the American flag too."

We are going back.

Kaiser Stuhl Chateau was designed to enhance the sale of wine. You couldn't have such an impressive building and not have fine wine!

The extensive wine-tasting sales room serves and sells wine to over 100,000 visitors a year.

Below the bar is a cellar banquet room also used for merchandising functions like the rare wine auction of the Barossa Festival.

Kaiser Stuhl is a cooperative created by Barossa grape growers and is a major operation, crushing and processing 34,000 tons of grapes annually. In individual winery sales, Kaiser Stuhl ranks fifth in the nation.

Aggressive marketing is a trademark of the company. An example is Summer Wine, a pop wine, sparkling white with a touch of sweetness which jumped to the leading wine in Queensland almost overnight.

Ian Huntley, the export manager, said that the winery was enjoying increasing sales of cabernet and riesling to Japan, the United States and Canada.

In the cool, gracious office lobby is a memorial: "This plaque commemorates the visit by Her Majesty the Queen, Monday, March 21, 1977."

Kaiser Stuhl goes after everyone.

That night at our motel two bottles of 1971 Kaiser Stuhl Special Reserve Claret were delivered. One black-labelled bottle had in old

English lettering my name and the date of our visit. "The Lady Navigator" and date were inscribed on the other bottle.

We drank mine. She took hers 6,000 miles back home.

Malcolm Seppelt is a drop-out.

He left the security of the family winery to establish on a hilltop within view of the grandiose Seppeltsfield estate, a boutique winery, Gnadenfrei, meaning "Made Free by God" which is apropos of the big company executive who wanted to find a more personal relationship with his own vineyard, his own winemaking ability, his own clients. The winery specialises in red and white table wines.

Aided by his attractive wife, Joylene, they have created a hand-built tasting-room combined with an art gallery which is unique.

Thirty acres of vines are now in production and another fifteen are being prepared.

The couple accepted a change in life-style, leaving behind a family mansion with swimming pool and tennis court in exchange for a mobile home on the hilltop while their lodge-type home is being built.

They radiate the confidence of success created by hard, personal, satisfactory labour.

Gnadenfrei, also the name of a village in upper Silesia, is located just above the classic Lutheran church you took a picture of at Marananga.

We visited Krondorf Winery, a boutique winery in the southern part of the Barossa and chatted with Syd Hueppauff, the general manager.

Not far away is Chateau Yaldara which is known for its antiques and its champagne.

Worth a stop. Worth a sip.

Riverland

If you drove northeast of Adelaide about three hours to Renmark as we did to get a Liba-Liba houseboat, you'd have to sample the Riverland wineries.

Riverland growers who get ten tons per acre compared to Hunter Valley's one-and-a-half to three tons per acre produce a large percentage of Australian grapes.

We called in at Angove's, a family-owned winery which produces a full range of table wines, fortified wines, South Australia's most popular brandy (St. Agnes), and under licence to an English company, Stone's the Original Green Ginger Wine. Also Marko Vermouth, second only to Cinzano in Australia.

John Angove, the fifth generation of Angove vignerons, told us that climate, not irrigation from the Murray River, was the controlling factor in Riverland's successful production.

"Much of the grapes grown in Riverland is controlled by Barossa wineries but not openly acknowledged," he said.

Farther west, outside of Berri, fronting the highway, is a squadron of giant holding tanks advertising the largest single winery and distillery in Australia.

Each 20,000-gallon tank bears a single letter. The line-up reads: "B-E-R-R-I E-S-T-A-T-E-S."

Berri Estates is a cooperative founded in 1918 by local fruit growers to solve over-production of sub-standard fruit by turning it into alcohol.

How they have succeeded!

Pretty Clare

Go north from Adelaide on Highway 1 to Highway 32 to Highway 83 and you'll find yourself in the lovely wine district of Clare.

At Watervale take a side road into the spring-like valley of Quelltaler — which means "spring valley" — where the two-storey stone cellar built a hundred years ago gathers beauty as it grows older.

Try the white wines.

Go farther up the highway to find Sevenhills, the oldest winery in the valley, founded by Jesuits. It is not easy to find. No directional signs on the highway. Deliberately.

We eventually tracked down Sevenhills, named after the seven hills of Rome, and Brother John May, an ecclesiastic in blue smock and beret and gum boots, with a beautiful soul and intense blue eyes in a serene face that looked fifteen years younger than his true years.

He showed us with pride the sheds of the new winery built with in-house labour. He is the only member of the Order in the winery.

Altar wines are sold around the world and the remaining selection of wines are sold out to the public year after year.

"Without any highway signs," he said with a sigh, "we still get 15,000 visitors a year."

Between visiting Sevenhills and the Stanley Wine Company, we lunched at an artsy-craftsy spot off the highway near the Mitchell winery.

Called Kilikanoon or The Cottage, it is an old, charming, vine-covered house with a dozen new pine tables inside a cool, flagstoned corner facing hen houses and vineyards and roving sheep. The restaurant is run by Molly and Ian Bennetts, an artist couple — potters and weavers. The chilled cucumber yoghurt soup was almost as smashing as the hand-knit black wool ski sweater we bought.

Here is Molly's Cucumber Yoghurt Soup:
Peeled and liquefied cucumbers (remove seeds if old)
Fair bit of mint
Pressed garlic
Pepper and salt
3 Tbs. oil
3 Tbs. vinegar
1 cup of water
1 cup of pineapple juice
1 cup of yoghurt
Blend and garnish with paprika and chopped chives or green onion tops.
Optional: a dash of sugar. A dash of soy sauce.

Stanley Wine Company just outside of the village of Clare is managed by Nick Knappstein, the granddaddy of Clare Valley winemakers and an easy-to-talk to, easy-to-like gentleman who was as relaxed as he was knowledgeable.

Nick Knappstein personified the many men we meet fleetingly during our wine tour who we wanted to have as personal friends.

The closely held family winery began to receive multiple buy-out offers in the wine boom of the sixties and, faced with future management and tax problems, an offer was accepted from H. J. Heinz which took over total control in 1976.

"I completed fifty vintages in 1978," said genial Nick. "It was enough. With the turn over to Heinz there has been an infusion of capital, lots of it. Our storage capacity alone has more than trebled.

"Out of the 12,000 tons of grapes crushed in the Clare Valley, Stanely Wine crushes over 8,000 tons."

The Best Reds in Australia

We were curious why Coonawarra with the reputation for producing the noblest red wines — "the Bordeaux of Australia" — received so little attention in Australian promotional literature.

A three-day trip southeast almost into Victoria showed us why. There is so little there.

Nine wineries in a nine-mile strip of red dirt called "terra rosa" comprise Coonawarra.

Great wine districts usually attract outstanding restaurants. Not at Coonawarra. Or colourful inns. Not at Coonawarra.

If you are a serious wine buff, go. You'll enjoy Colin Kidd at Lindemans and Eric Brand at Laira and perhaps you can ride on an automatic harvester with Owen Redman as we did through the Redbank vineyards.

Otherwise, buy the Coonawarra wines in Adelaide and enjoy them at your leisure. The wineries, even in hard times, sell out every year.

Oh, yes, we can recommend the Naracoorte Golf Club course. Excellent.

And we can tell you that at the Greenline Motel you can get eggs and lamb chops for breakfast for $1.90!

The Dromedary Lurch and Sip Safari

You can fly to Hunter Valley from Sydney on Rebel Air for a one day wine tasting. You can go to Rutherglen on a weekend excursion by rail from Melbourne. You can cruise up the Swan River in Perth to taste the grape for a day. All great fun.

But the biggest giggle is to go on a day wine tour out of Adelaide through McLaren Vale — by camel.

During the cool season between November and April Transcontinental Safaris operate camel tours in the Flinders Range north of Adelaide.

During the hot season Rex Ellis, the owner, takes the camels to Kangaroo Island south of Adelaide for day treks through "The Ravine" and to McLaren Vale for day treks through the vineyards.

The camel safari at $40 including a picnic lunch and a huge jug of wine, of course, was a "best buy" nominee.

The tragedy of the day, however, was that there was only one camel left and I had to go alone. Even worse was to find that I had as company seven lovely young ladies from Adelaide. Well, sometimes you just have bad days, as I told the Lady Navigator that night.

Less than an hour's drive from Adelaide is the Reynella district of the Southern Vales and beyond Reynella is McLaren Vale, a Garden-of-Eden valley of vineyards and fruit trees.

I found my way through the little village and out to Blewitt Springs and in a pasture-corral was Ian Collett, a movie-handsome young man, saddling up five camels.

Soon after I arrived two cars disgorged this mob of giggly young things and between cautious introductions, etc, we all managed to ask questions of Ian.

Camels, contrary to reputation, are gentle, non-smelly, non-spitting, non-halitosis animals.

"Ibna" means go ahead.

"Hosh" — sit down.

"Ooroo" — stop.

The camels were five to fifteen years old and each was valued at about $1,500.

Does anybody ever fall off? Yes, occasionally. The apprehension rose fifty degrees.

You get on when the camel is down. The camel puts its long back legs up first tilting you way forward and then rises to its front knees — jerk one — and then its feet — jerk two. You descend in the same manner. Jerk, jerk, plop.

Each camel's saddle was a two-person saddle, one behind the other. I rode singly without a saddle but with a comfortable sheepskin thrown between the two canvas saddle bags carrying the picnic lunch and with a saddle-horn around which I could wrap my legs. It was the best seat on the tour.

Our mounting and departure was a ten-minute routine of gasping, shrieking and wild laughter. Hilarious.

Eventually we were single-filing down the road, all roped together. Khartoum, the oldest camel in front to act as an anchor example. Chaluk, the youngest and silliest followed and then my camel, Ghandi, with Natasha and Gij trailing.

It was a gorgeous, sunny day. The vineyards were in the midst of the harvest and many vines were still heavy with unplucked grapes and it was a joy to rock and lurch from a ten-foot high platform among the green rows of leaves and grapes. In the far distance we could see the ocean.

Our due hour at the corral was nine o'clock and we left at ten and returned at five, covering ten miles, during which we visited four wineries out of the forty in the Southern Vales. Amery's (Kay Brothers), a family-owned winery on a hilltop with marvellous views was the first stop where I had a glass with "Cud" Cuthbert Kay, son of the founder, who recently turned the winemaking over to his son, Colin.

We rode across the hills to Coriole Winery, small, fifty-five acres, mostly red wines made in concrete tanks and there had a pleasant sip with Mrs. Mark Lloyd, wife of the winemaker-owner.

On camel and away to d'Arenberg Winery which crushes less than four hundred tons, non-irrigated grapes. Strong on riesling and shiraz.

In the shade of the trees at d'Arenberg, Ian spread cover for us to sit around. We drank a jug of Kay White and nibbled on chicken, salad, buttered French bread and, as a contrast, sipped a cup of tea. My harem posed around me for a picture which later proved to the Lady Navigator how hard I had worked.

Our last stop was at The Settlement Wine Co. where the ladies tried sweet champagne — terrible — and bought inexpensive bottles of it. Mr. Berlingieri from Northern Italy looked like the fiercest character out of Oliver Twist and I couldn't work up the nerve to ask him a question.

The hour ride back to our Square One was relaxing. Ghandi and I were soulmates by this time.

Carol on the camel behind me giggled from the time we started until the time we finished. Non-stop.

"How was the safari?" asked the Lady Navigator.

"It was one big laugh." And it was.

Kay Brothers Amery Winery was so enjoyable I took the Lady Navigator there on the way south and we had a chance to meet young Colin Kay, a graduate of Roseworthy who serves on their advisory board.

I asked him how he was able to compete as a small winery with a requirement of expensive equipment to provide refrigeration and oxidation control and he maintained that it is a matter of quickness — of control which you have when you live closely with your wines.

"Look," he said, "my house is only a hundred yards away from the maturation tanks and kegs. When I wake up in the middle of the night I come down here and just sniff around."

Colin, like his father, has the eager eyes of a born winemaker. They both agreed that the prettiest time at McLaren Vale is July and August when the almond trees are abloom with pink and white blossoms and for visitors they recommend the Bushing Festival in October, an English inheritance from an older time when a bush or ivy was put over the pub door to announce that the new wine was available.

With a bottle of their excellent light luncheon wine, cinsaut, a sample of a cabernet and riesling we retired to The Barn in McLaren Vale where we had one of the best luncheons in Australia.

The setting at The Barn is indoors with an outdoors feeling. Big skylight over a courtyard. Hanging ferns everywhere. You order your lunch at the bar and sip a glass of "tap" champagne. Go to the cellar room next door and pick out your wine from the best restaurant selection we ever found too.

We had a delicious home-made pâté, giant mushroom caps stuffed with garlicky ground meat and baked with a cheese top. I had veal chops which had been spread with a vegetable puree, crumbed, deep fried. Fantastic.

A touch of dessert. Negritas, chocolate mousse on a bed of crumbled chocolate cookies with a brandy base and a cream top. Four-star restaurant.

Old Wine and New Bottles in Western Australia

You can visit the first wine cellar in Australia, scratched out of the earth in the early 1830's, at Olive Farm, just outside of Perth . . . and taste Gold Medal wines while you are there.

The Swan River wine centre, now crushing 5,000 tons of grapes a year, is being crowded by suburbs, factories and wealthy medical men who want land to raise thoroughbred horses and have the money to buy acreage.

The primary expansion district for Western Australian wineries is on the southwest coastline, two hours from Perth, at Margaret River. In less than ten years, more than a dozen vineyards and half-a-dozen new wineries have sprung up. The area has a frost-free climate, copious sunshine and evenly spread rain.

Remembering our first bottle of Houghton White Burgundy at Alice

Springs, we particularly wanted to visit the Houghton winery in the Swan River Valley. That wine was more consistently found on restaurant menus than any other and we used it as a barometer for classifying restaurant mark-ups on food and beverage. (Low $5.50. High $9.)

Also because Houghton is owned by Thomas Hardy & Sons, a major family-owned Australian company with wineries throughout the country, it gaves us a chance to talk with a family member, Bill Hardy, twenty-nine, the senior winemaker.

We found Bill Hardy at Hardy's Valencia Winery, a personable, happy young man with lots of infectious bounce.

"We have sixty acres here at Valencia, another two hundred acres at a new property at Gingin called Moodah Brook Estates.

"Hardy's will crush about half the entire Swan River grape production.

"Our most popular wine is the Houghton White Burgundy. To meet the demand we bottle fifty thousand cases a year and seventy-five percent of that goes out of state."

Bill Hardy studied two years at the Institute of Oenology at Bordeaux, worked three years as a winemaker in McLaren Vale and went to Perth in 1976.

Son of the chairman of the board, nephew of Jim Hardy who skippered an early Australia entry in the America Cup, Bill Hardy feels the challenge to improve the Hardy line of wines and is sensitive to the response of the public and the medals won by the wines at the annual wine shows.

Both the Valencia and Houghton properties are showcases of good merchandising. Great places to visit.

The son of the man who created the Houghton White Burgundy, Dorham Mann, works for Sandalford Winery, the second major winery of the Swan River. Jack Mann retired from Houghton's in 1972, the same year that his son, raised in the craft, became the winemaker at Sandalford.

"The operation is still small enough so that I know what is happening in the vineyard, what condition the grapes are in, when we should crush. There are only two men besides myself in the winery supervising the crushing, the maturation, the blending, the bottling.

"I like being responsible for everything that happens from the vine to the bottle."

Dorham, naturally, has his own personal pride in the Sandalford White Burgundy.

"In the earliest book on viticulture in Western Australia the verdelho grape got high marks. The verdelho has been resurrected in the Swan River and I think it is one of our most successful wines with a beautiful aromatic character that grows on the palate with a good measure of finesse. In cooler regions like the Margaret River where we have a major investment in new vineyards, this aromatic characteristic will be enhanced."

We sampled the verdelho, the white burgundy, the chenin blanc, the gewürtztraminer, the rosé, a zinfandel, the cabernet, the shiraz and a 1976 spaltese "with the noble rot."

We then joined the passengers on the cruise boat, *Miss Sandalford*, in a large dining room and enjoyed a bit of lunch with a glass — or was it two? — of cabernet.

Most of the small wineries in the Swan Valley are owned by Dalmatians, typified by Westfield Winery, owned and managed by John Kosovich, who was born in the family-owned winery, rebuilt it with his own hands and now produces outstanding cabernet sauvignon.

Floating to the Vineyards and Floating Home

The wine flows faster than the river water on a Swan River cruise to the vineyards.

Perhaps that's why there were only two seats left on the Friday tour we had picked . . . during an off season.

Popular? Oh, yes, popular with every visitor who goes to Perth and very popular with the local populace.

"Take a trip during the week days," advised a friend. "The local boys on a weekend sometimes get a bit rowdy. During a recent trip one of the cruise captains had two ribs broken."

You have a choice of daily cruises between the *Miss Sandalford* and the *Lady Houghton*.

Both offer air-conditioned luxury, free wine, a good lunch, winery tours, sing-alongs and a chance to meet new friends. The more the wine flows the more friends you meet.

The price for both cruises is the same: $25.

The only difference is the *Miss Sandalford* visits the historic Tranby House while the *Lady Houghton* tour offers a brief horse show at the Valencia winery with Juan Carmona and his performing Andulusian Abra horses.

Having lunched with Dorham Mann in the Parmelian Room at the Sandalford winery with a *Miss Sandalford* cruise crowd, we picked the *Lady Houghton*.

We were at the jetty at the bottom of Barrack Street promptly at ten. Our reserved seats were separated so we found a padded seat together on the open front deck. It was a sparkling day and our open air perches proved the best seats on the boat.

Tea and coffee were served at the departure and we were soon off upstream for a leisurely two-hour cruise passing the Gloucester Park Racecourse, the Belmont Racecourse and the Ascot Racecourse.

By ten-thirty wine was being poured — riesling, rosé and moselle — and it continued with steady frequency until we left the boat to bus our way to the Valencia vineyards.

As we passed waterfront houses and apartments the captain announced the sale prices which drew gasps of incredulity from the passengers but which we, from Hawaii where property is truly sky-high, thought quite reasonable.

Sharks do come up the Swan after small river fish and shark nets for swimming are a common sight. Eight-foot sharks had been sighted three weeks before. The threat didn't seem to bother a waterski meet in progress on an upper part of the river.

We passed the Guildford Grammar School and in the distance could see the tower top of the Guildford Hotel.

Dockside buses waited to take the passengers the short distance to the Valencia Winery where a tour was conducted, a tasting of a cross-section of the Hardy wines and liqueurs offered and the outdoor horse show performed. All quite pleasant — and well organised.

Then we were bused to the Houghton Winery and led through cask-lined cellars to the luncheon cellar where there was an ample cold lunch of chicken, ham, salads. Four white wines on the table and one red. "We always have to throw away the untouched red wine," said the hostess.

We touched it. All of it.

After lunch, there was more tasting, this time in the sales room where half of the passengers purchased take-home bottles.

(Bill Hardy had told me during my earlier visit that the winery usually averages two to four busloads of visitors a day and together with the passengers on the boat there are as many as two hundred people for lunch. The number of visitors per day ranges from fifty to five hundred people. The winery averages $30,000 a month in retail sales.)

The luncheon hostess, in a short speech, said, "We'd like you to buy and drink Valencia-Houghton wines but if not ours, just as important, drink Western Australian wines. Ask for them in your restaurants and wine shops. Restaurants and stores will only stock what sells."

Free wine continued to flow downstream in the same manner as it did upstream. The bar offered other drinks for sale and many Australians had gone back to their traditional drink, beer.

Part of our mob was made up of women of the Fremantle Bowling Club, average age sixty-five. By the time we returned to the dock at Perth all of the members were dancing to Greek music in the aisles.

We made quite a sight and sound spectacle while landing.

"Louder," urged the captain and the disembarking passengers of the *Miss Sandalford* turned to gape at us in envy. . . just as the captain had intended.

The body profile of many Australian men includes a sizeable mid-section protrusion lovingly built on glass after glass of beer and wine. After our six-month stint in Australia, after devoting self-sacrificing research into the country's beverages, I returned home with a physical souvenir resembling an indiscreet pregnancy.

Indeed on my first day to the tennis courts my dear partner asked sweetly, "Who did it?"

It took six weeks of tea and dry toast and grapefruit to rid myself of the Australian bump.

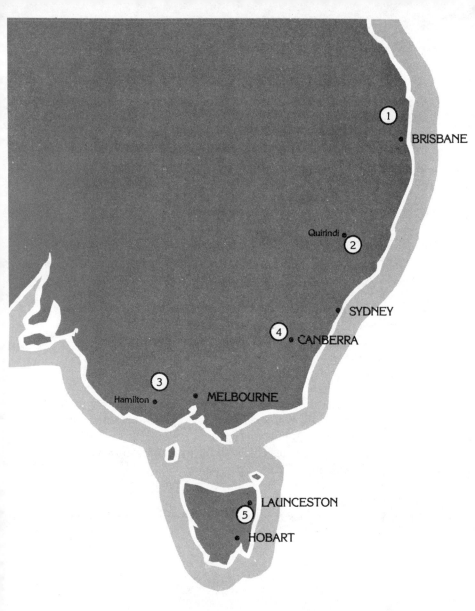

FARM STAYS

1. "RATHBURNIE"
2. "KARANILLA"
3. "GLENISLA"
4. "TRALEE"
5. "PLEASANT BANKS"

10. Sampling the Country: Station and Farm Holidays

In our first book, *How to Get Lost and Found in New Zealand*, we recounted our experience of staying at one farm, Linden Downs, outside of Masterton.

Not only was our visit most enjoyable but the subsequent reports we received from overseas readers were so enthusiastic about their getting to know a farm family and taking part in the rural life that we decided to expand the theme in Australia. After all if the book was to centre around The Country, what better focus could we have than a farm or station holiday?

You have to be careful in Australia. You don't want to rent a miner's cabin or the sheep-shearers' cabins in the off season . . . you don't want a youth camp with barracks.

We once found what sounded like an ideal farm outside of Orange in New South Wales and we had a weekend free so we called for a booking. "Yes, we can take you . . . but you should know we have twenty-two boys here also!"

What is desirable is a farm or station where you stay at the homestead, where not more than six people can be accommodated, where you eat homestead food with the family and where there are other amenities that interest you in particular: horseback riding, gemstone hunting, swimming, bird watching, fishing, etc.

A Queensland Farm

We stopped by the Queensland Government Tourist Bureau in Brisbane on our way north and picked up a directory of station and farm holidays — several states have something similar — and it was apparent that within five hundred kilometres of Brisbane the selection was rather thin.

However, we marked a property called "Rathburnie" and wrote down a telephone number — which we promptly lost — thinking we would give it a try on our way back from the Sunshine Coast.

113

It was one of those funny mistakes that turns out to be accidentally pleasant.

Finding Rathburnie was an adventure in itself. We went swinging through small towns to smaller towns, asking at post offices and taking off again, until we finally found the combination general store-post office that made up the entire township of Linville.

Another eleven kilometres farther, we came to a formidable wooden sign created in the style of state parks: RATHBURNIE . . . FAUNA SANCTUARY ENVIRONMENTAL ESTATE.

My!

We turned into a tree-lined lane and were met by a pack of yapping kelpies. Across the lawn an older man was strolling back from his mail/newspaper box.

I introduced myself and explained that we had lost his telephone number and enquired if there were room for us?

He seemed rather puzzled by the request and said we should talk to his wife.

At the door of the homestead the wife also seemed nonplussed but invited us to come inside and have a cup of tea.

Over tea and biscuits we learned about our hosts. The family name was Burnett. His name was Graham and her name was Valmai.

The 1,700-acre farm on the upper reaches of the Brisbane River supported four hundred head of Aberdeen Angus cattle.

His great grandfather came to Australia in 1860 from England. Another branch of the family went to America and became major property owners in California. (Peter Burnett, the first governor of California under the American flag probably was his relative.)

With all of the social conversation was the niggling question, could we stay?

We showed the Burnetts our pamphlet of farm stays in Queensland.

Upon closer examination it became clear from the brochure that the rental accommodation at Rathburnie was a farmhand's cottage!

Clunk.

It was now late in the day and we were miles out in The Country.

Yes, it was a problem, all agreed. Hmmm, hmmm, well! Yes, well, indeed.

Valmai announced we could stay. (We had passed inspection.) She wouldn't accept any money but we could make a donation to their favourite environmental fund.

The homestead was most comfortable. The Burnetts were doing

over one wing but we stayed in a pleasant backroom with tea-making facilities and a plateful of biscuits and fruit.

Graham Burnett had a cause.

During the last twelve years he had come to believe that the standard practice of burning off the property annually and topdressing the ground with oil-based fertilisers was wrong.

He supported the theory that the pasture was better off when using natural humus, turning the organic material of dead leaves and grass back onto the ground.

Before dinner he took us for a long ride around his property to show us the results of his theory.

Side by side with his neighbour's property, it was very evident that his pastures were fuller, lusher, greener.

It was a peaceful time of day and he was a man in touch with his land and his livestock.

As dusk settled in, he spotted a "pretty-faced" wallaby in the distance, pointed out birds, talked about the various trees on the property.

Graham apologised because he moved rather stiffly but Valmai explained later that her husband, in riding horses over many years, had survived a broken shoulder, a crushed chest and four concussions.

We had a sherry before dinner and a bottle of white wine with an excellent dinner. Angus beef curry as a first course. Salad as a second course. Chicken tetrazzini with fresh field mushrooms. Fruit and ice cream for dessert.

The Burnetts enjoyed travelling, especially when it included an environmental programme. They had toured America's western national parks the year before.

He had always wanted to return to Austria where he had been a prisoner of war during World War II. He had been taken when the Allied destroyers which were to rescue them off a Greek peninsula turned around, leaving the troops behind. Graham was a prisoner of war from the 29th of April, 1941, until war's end. He speaks German well.

One custom at Rathburnie which we were to encounter in other farm stays was that the mailman doubles as a country courier.

He would bring meat from Moore, bread from Kilcoy, groceries from Linville.

"Bring four bags of cement" could be the order. The charge was only cents per parcel but it was part of the mailman's remuneration.

Valmai gave us a suggested route the next day which would take us through the Bunya Mountains National Park, down onto the Darling Downs, a famous wheat-belt of Australia, and into Toowoomba, the "garden city" of 74,000, then south to a mountain resort and to the Queensland-New South Wales border.

"Over the border you are on your own", she said. "But if any of your readers should follow your footsteps to Queensland (and telephone 075-848140 beforehand – mind!) perhaps we may be able to offer them an en-suite room in the 'new' north wing and a warm welcome to our Sunshine State. We have enjoyed your visit with us – even if it was unexpected."

A New South Wales Farm

Our second farm stay was in northeastern New South Wales.

We had checked into the regional tourist office in the country-music town of Tamworth. From a most helpful tourist officer we learned that "Karanilla," a host-farm outside of Quirindi, fifty miles to the south, had received many praising letters from visitors. We made contact by telephone and were told we could be accommodated for a couple of days.

The owner of the farm was to pick up clients from Sydney at the Quirindi railroad station at one-thirty. If we could meet him there, he could lead us to the farm.

A tall, grey-haired man with the squared shoulders of a practised horseman introduced himself as Bob Crossing at the appointed place and time. He collected his other guests, a mother and teen-aged daughter, and we departed for Karanilla, Aboriginal for 'cool water in high places.'

Crossing shares an entire valley with another grazier – mountain to mountain – a picturesque spring scene of trees and green grass. At the junction of the two properties an old icebox served as mailbox and depository for all the mailman delivered extras. We crossed a meandering creek, drove through stands of river oak and apple box and eucalyptus to the comfortable homestead of the 3,000-acre spread which supported about 1,000 head of cattle.

The homestead was framed with a gracious wide porch, topped with a sloping, corrugated roof to catch rainwater. At the door was a charming woman, Di Crossing, the hostess.

The homestead had grown around a family.

As a bachelor Bob Crossing had acquired the property and around the original two rooms he had added on the bedrooms, kitchen, bathrooms, living rooms and porches as children came into the family.

Children had to have occupations besides chasing cattle on horses and he built a clay tennis court and beside it a swimming pool, night-lighted, with a fern grotto and dressing room at one end.

As the children grew up and disappeared so did the cattle market. In 1972 cattlemen were having a hard time covering the cost of getting steers to the stockyards.

With empty bedrooms many holiday farms came into being in 1972.

The first year that the Crossings went into the tourist business they had fifty guests. Not bad.

Now they have two hundred and fifty guests annually — most of them repeat visitors. The cattle market has bounced back and economically they don't have to be in the holiday farm market but the extra income is handy and it is a hedge against the historic, roller-coaster cattle market cycles.

Probably, just as important, the guest business brings the outside world to the farm and people like Bob and Di thrive on the stimulation of different people from different places.

The key to success on a holiday farm is to make the visitor a member of the family, immediately, automatically. The guest, in turn, must take on duties as part of the family. Help with the dishes. Set the table. Don't take too much time in one of the two bathrooms.

The first thing we did after being ensconced in a double bedroom, was to have tea and scones and a chat around the kitchen table.

Despite the heat of the afternoon, we changed into tennis gear to play three rousing sets of tennis with our hosts, breaking after the second set for a cooling swim in the pool and finishing the third set in swim suits.

We relaxed around the pool after tennis, napped briefly, and when it was nearly dusk went to the stables where Bob had saddled horses for himself, the teenager and for us.

We couldn't remember the last time we had been riding, the farm stay preceding our horse safari in Victoria.

"I watch to see how a guest gets on a horse. If they mount from the head side, I know they have had some experience. If they mount from the rear of the horse where they can get kicked, I know they need help," said Bob.

We needed help.

However, our animals were just of the right temperament and spirit to take the inexperienced and pretty soon we were walking peacefully in the shadow of the mountain, saving the horses from the sun, and wending our way upwards.

Bob pointed out a stray wallaby on the hill and then a buck kangaroo which, startled from its evening feeding, pronged off into the bush.

We chased up a whole family of kangaroos at full gallop, hand on the reins, hand on the pommel, heart in the mouth, arms flapping, legs flapping, hind-end bouncing. Exciting. Magnificent.

The surrounding rolling hills were still green with spring grass and it looked like the foothills of California. Vistas? As we climbed on easy slopes higher and higher to the top we could see fifty miles to the west. We dismounted to absorb the view. It was now twilight and the last bit of sun disappeared. The shadows started to deepen . . . and then lighten from an almost full moon.

We descended the mountain slowly but when we reached the level valley, Bob led us into a gallop again, flying in the light of the moon. The former nervousness was replaced by the whiz-bang thrill of it all. Absolutely exhilarating.

It brought back long-forgotten memories of – of what? A childhood experience in Prescott, Arizona? A John Wayne movie? No matter. It was now and it was wonderful . . . country saddle magic at its best.

Dinner was preceded by a whisky and accompanied with one glass of wine. Country-done roast chicken and vegetables and Karanilla Home Made Ice Cream, a Di Crossing specialty. Here is how she made it . . . by the gallon.

Karanilla Ice Cream

Make stiff meringue of eight egg whites and half a cup of sugar in a plastic one gallon container.

In a bowl whip two cups of whole cream. Add two egg yolks and mix.

Flavour with crushed strawberries or two tablespoons of instant coffee or two teaspoons of vanilla.

Pour cream mixture over meringue and fold together gently.

Put in freezer. No need to remix. Will not crystallise.

After dinner there was parlour conversation until ten which was "tea" time again and then bed. Bone weary. Still weary from our river-raft trip. Horse weary.

The next morning we joined Bob in the kitchen. He had taken the teen-age girl for her first milking experience and now was skimming the thick cream off the previous day's milk which had been refrigerated overnight. What cream to pour over your fruit and cornflakes for breakfast. (I think the barn-fresh, butterfat-rich, yellow cream was the real difference in the ice cream.)

One of the many attractive virtues of our hosts was their ability to swing in time and activity according to the wishes of their guests.

Riding, fishing, exploring, gemstone hunting ... or just sleeping ... whatever the guest wanted to do could be fitted in.

Or the Crossings would take charge and lay on a programme.

The first morning, after breakfast, we went on a fresh-water, cray-catching expedition in a section of the creek running below the homestead.

At the creek's edge we were divided into two teams. Team A on one side of the water. Team B on the other side.

Fresh meat was tied to a string, the string to a tree twig, the twig stuck in the mudbank and you then waited.

When the line twitched, the trick was to lift the twig slowly, slide a net down and under the line and gently scoop in the tiny cray.

Over the morning we caught a small bucketful which became an excellent appetiser mixed with a cocktail sauce for dinner that night.

After our fishing expedition Di showed us her collection of sea fossils taken from a nearby creek shelf which four hundred million years ago was the shoreline of the ocean.

Within the space of fifty yards she found seashells encased in hardened mud which covered periods of time of a mere eighty million years. A time probably before the surface of the earth was pushed up, forming the Great Dividing Range.

She takes guests interested in such fossils to her "lode" — and she has a difficult time dragging them away.

That afternoon friends of the Crossings came from Quirindi and we played tennis and swam and in the late afternoon competed in bitter, raging, bitchy, smashing games of croquet. I kept ending up in the rose bushes.

After another excellent homestead dinner — and more ice cream — deep, country-induced sleep came quickly again.

The mornings in Australia are special for the song of birds at dawn. The flute sound of the mountain magpie ... the thrush's melodious whistling ... the laughing hoot of the kookaburra. What a way to wake up.

We packed slowly. The Crossings were to take us for a bit of fossicking into the foothills of the western slope of the Great Dividing Range.

We pulled out of Karanilla reluctantly. First class spot.

A Victoria Farm

In Victoria we had another first-class experience about three hundred kilometres west of Melbourne at a working sheep station called "Glenisla."

Glenisla was first taken up as a run in 1843 and 90,000 of the original 100,000 acres of Glenisla were bought by Charles Carter in 1860 along with 28,000 sheep, 500 cattle and some horses.

Samuel, the eldest son, designed the present homestead and had it built in 1873. It was a showpiece homestead.

The thick walls were built of stone quarried from a mountain two miles away. The fireplaces were of imported Carrara marble from Italy. The interior walls were finished of brick hand-made on the site. A huge underground 40,000-gallon tank was built under the flagstone-tiled centre courtyard to ensure ample fresh water for household purposes.

It is all still there.

Over a period of time, the station shrank in size and prosperity and it was all gone by 1922. The grand homestead at one time was used as a horse stable; its parlour a storeroom for hay.

Eric and Evie Barber bought Glenisla in 1970 and in a true sense the homestead came back home. Evie Barber is a direct descendant of Charles Carter.

They have restored the property with loving care and excellent taste. It is now a National Trust building.

We arrived on the property after lunch and drove through the grove of huge eucalyptus trees the quarter of a mile to the home, circled the front of the house through fruit trees and stopped.

Eric Barber, slight, nearing fifty but looking thirty, a full head of brown hair, came out to meet us. A fifth generation farmer, he had been raised on property in the same valley.

Evie, fair of hair and blue of eyes, with just a hint of roundness in face and figure, joined him. She was sixth generation. They took us into the house with quiet pride. We later found that this was the third homestead they had restored.

The two front rooms were lounges and both boasted restored Carrara marble fireplaces and moulded ceilings and cornices created by an Italian craftsman. He carved the designs of wood, cast them in wax, filled the wax with plaster of Paris and then melted the wax away. In 1873 in the middle of the then Outback.

The beams in the house were constructed of huge Oregon pines, a workable softwood lacking in Australia and transported to the homestead from Melbourne by bullock teams.

Behind the two lounges were a dining room and a modernised kitchen on one side, a master bedroom and two small bedrooms on the other side.

Flanking the gracious, flagstone courtyard were two wings of the same soft yellow sandstone block. Three guestrooms and a bath were in one wing. A guest suite with "fridge" and "facilities" was under construction in what once was the homestead kitchen.

The guest accommodation can comfortably provide for eight to ten visitors.

Completing the courtyard square was a storage building.

Adjacent to the new kitchen in the main building was a small room which served, until 1970, as a country post office and telephone exchange. The old plug-in equipment was still there.

Behind the homestead proper, stables of split logs and bark had been restored by Eric. Handsome.

To the side was a modern corrugated metal sheep-shearing shed and behind the shed and stables were corrals for several horses and one randy ram.

One third of Glenisla's visitors came from overseas. (Guests who don't arrive by car arrive by train, plane or bus in Hamilton, forty kilometres south, and are picked up and returned by Eric without charge.)

Many of the overseas visitors are botanists attracted by the famous flora of the Grampian Mountains or by the Aboriginal paintings, the only such paintings in Victoria.

Others come, as do the city people from Melbourne, Sydney and

Adelaide, just to enjoy the peaceful, other-world of the solid, sensible existence of a working sheep station.

Glenisla now has 12,000 acres under lease and own almost 1,000 acres outright supporting 2,000 to 3,000 head of sheep.

The first afternoon Eric drove us around part of the property. In the first paddock he spotted seven emus peacefully grazing. We got out of the car, crossed the fence and crept closer . . . and closer . . . and closer . . . until we were within a hundred yards and only then did the giant ostrich-like bird start to amble off.

Along the road we later saw white cockatoos, green parrots, ibis, and a flight of black ducks as they v-planed across the sky and circled a nearby swamp.

We cut across a pasture on a faint trail and raised a mob of sleeping kangaroos . . . and then another . . . and we gave pursuit in the car as they scattered in all directions like wound-up, spring-engined stuffed dolls.

From a rocky outcrop in the middle of the valley which serves as a fire-watch ranger station, we could see the peaceful valley in all directions. The cleared sections of land contained red gum trees which were recognised by the pioneers as a signal of good sheep-grazing land.

The settlers would come to this hill to watch for fires of nomadic Aborigines who, protein-starved, learned to appreciate the taste of mutton and they developed at the same time a tendency to *borrow* a few sheep for food. (The Aborigines would herd the sheep into a hidden valley and break their front legs so they couldn't wander, then eat them at will.)

"It is said that the sheep grown in the shadow of the Grampian Mountains produce the finest Merino wool in the world," Eric said.

He pulled out a sample of wool he had reserved for a centenary neighbourhood show. He parted the grey exterior to reveal the snow-white downy wool underneath.

"It is a source of personal satisfaction for a farmer to get the top price for his wool." Eric graded his own wool into four grades, not counting the "bits and pieces." The prices ranged from $2.65 to $3.95 a kilo at the time of our visit. The average value of the wool from one Merino sheep came to about $18 for five kilos.

He employed only two shearers.

"You have to be able, in case of an emergency, to do everything yourself."

That night we had a drink before dinner — beer or sherry or whisky — then beef stew, peas, potatoes, baked pumpkin — Australians are very big on pumpkin — and bread. Excellent stew.

The sideboard displayed four kinds of dessert. All with cream and whipped cream.

Coffee was served in the garden as the evening sun was setting . . . a showboat display of brilliant colours.

Being summer the last light did not disappear until almost ten o'clock and with the dark we went to bed. Another farm sleep.

I am nearly always the first up. In slippers and Japanese-Hawaiian kimono I leaned on the fence at the edge of the lawn and watched the dawn touch the Grampians, its soft light slowly flooding over the purple hills and spilling over the bleached blond pastures. When dawn kissed the tops of the stately eucalyptus trees, the birds sang.

A lady once replied to my enthralment of Australian sunrises that she found them cold, almost forbidding with austerity. She preferred the warmth of the sunsets.

I found the dawns pure, virginal, unspoiled. A fresh dawn gives promise of the potential of a new day to be carved out without yesterday's mistakes. And it unfolds like a flower, from grey to pink to yellow to gold, whispering, "Here I come. You'd better be ready for me!" Then, curtain up. Sunshine!

Trixi, the black Shetland pony, came to the corral fence and was disappointed that I hadn't come bearing apple or sugar or a hunk of bread and I promised to do better the next day. And did.

The house came awake with much bustling of tea-making and coffee-making and getting ready for a bush breakfast. We eventually all piled into three cars and were off up the paved road and then onto a gravel road and through a couple of miles of bush until we came to picnic grounds known as Red Rock, a quiet pond with ranger-built stone barbecues.

Normally, the place abounds with wild birds but a Melbourne family was camping in the area — how did they ever find this hidden oasis? — and the birds had dispersed.

Orange juice, home-made granola, bacon and eggs, toast and billy tea made up breakfast. Very satisfactory out in the bush with the smell of fireplace smoke.

After breakfast Evie took one car and the dirty dishes and the left-over food and returned to the homestead. We proceeded through the bush to the foot of the Grampian Mountains to one of thirty-three known locations of Aboriginal cliff or cave paintings in the mountains.

Eric had started his hobby of locating ancient Aboriginal wall art at the age fifteen and had found half a dozen of the recorded thirty-three.

At one time four men knew all the locations but one man died of cancer, two went with heart attacks and Eric was the last source. He was now teaching his sons the thirty-three locations . . . and they had begun to take up the hunt for more paintings.

Our destination was the Cave of Hands. We walked a white sand path several hundred yards until we reached a massive outcropping of huge rocks and around the corner came to a sheltered overhang of rock, formerly a cave. Across the face of the rock were hands. Small hands. Children's hands. The hands of women. The hands of men.

The outlined hands were probably made, Eric said, by placing the hand against the rocks and then spewing through the mouth a mixture of ochre from bark and clay mixed with possum oil.

What did the hands signify? No one knows. The settlers didn't care to know and the Aborigines didn't care to tell. And now there are no members of the tribe left to tell.

What is known is that there are undisclosed burial caves in the area and perhaps . . . perhaps . . . the hands are those of the deceased.

Only one old man has seen the hidden burial caves but he has said, "Let them lie there in peace. The white man will only spoil it."

Indeed the front of the Cave of Hands is protected by a strong wire fence. The wall face is scarred by bullet holes and air-can sprayed hand prints and "Johnny Loves Lucy" graffiti.

The morning of our arrival — this is painful to even write — Eric had chased away a car-load of young men who were taking potshots at the helpless emus with shotguns. On our first drive we had found half a beer bottle shattered by bullets standing upright in the middle of the road ready to slash any on-rushing car tyre. Nearby were empty 30-30 rifle cartridges.

Later, on the edge of a swamp we could see the carcass of a grey kangaroo the same brave young men had slaughtered.

They are everywhere in the world.

That afternoon we went with Eric to check on sheep.

A mob of sheep establish a "camp" under tree shade and stay there during the hot periods of day. When it starts to cool they go out and graze again.

The back seat of the car was full of bright-faced border collies. Three of them.

"One dog would be enough," said Eric, "but the others would get their feelings hurt if I didn't take them."

At the first paddock we chased up a big, old kangaroo which went pronging over the fields with its trampoline mechanism. The dogs were hanging out the window whimpering and whining, eager to join the chase. The kangaroo showed no signs of panic and when we had come within a football field of it the animal pressed an extra spring button and sailed over a four-foot fence like it wasn't there.

Later, at the end of that pasture the dogs herded some two hundred sheep together in a tight circle and Eric inspected each one closely for any drooping head or runny eye or limping.

He culled out one large ram — there are two rams for every two hundred sheep — and caught the animal by a hind leg and easily flipped it into a sitting position in front of him where it rested perfectly immobile.

As he had in the woolshed, he parted the grey wool to the lovely, snow-white Merino fleece underneath.

Holiday farms are principally working farms and the majority of income must be derived from the farm.

We were Eric and Evie's hobby. The sheep were their livelihood.

That night Eric showed coloured slides of some of the spring flowers we had missed — wrong season — and Aboriginal paintings we hadn't seen.

The next morning, packed again, we left behind new friends.

You make new friends so fast in The Country.

Western Australian Station Stays

Western Australia like South Australia has farm-holiday facilities which consist primarily of quarters on a station, shearers' cottages where you cook your own food and do your own thing which is not what the overseas visitor wants to experience.

What the overseas visitor wants is the experience of staying on a homestead with the family, eating home-cooked meals, taking part in the working life of the sheep raising, riding horses, collecting rocks, visiting old mines . . . getting to know the Country.

Western Australia, as most states do, publishes a "Farm and Outback Station Accommodation Guide" to homesteads that currently offer rooms or cottages, listing dining arrangements and the various types of recreational options available.

The popularity of the program has led many new stations to become host farms. The program has now spread through almost every district of the state. Write for the latest guide to Western Australian Government Travel Centre, Perth, 722 Hay Street 6000.

A One-Day Farm Visit

If you can't tuck in an overnight farm stay, you should take advantage of a day visit to a farm. Many are made available in packaged tours from principal cities.

We had the good fortune of being included in a farm visit outside Canberra.

Our farm was "Tralee," a sheep station owned by Bernard Morrison, which was opened to visitors in 1972.

For a man who owns 3,500 acres, runs 3,000 sheep and 300 head of cattle, you couldn't find a more gregarious host, a man who is in love with his property and in love with the hobby of showing it off.

First, the visitor is shown the working sheep dog in action ... a marvel of an animal: thinking, moving, driving sheep.

Secondly, you are shown how to shear sheep ... first with the old-fashioned, hand-powered shears ... and then a contrasting demonstration with the modern power shears.

A hearty barbecue lunch follows at Tralee Tavern, a spacious room built especially for entertaining visiting groups. Hefty barbecued steaks, salad, jugs of white and red wine.

Host Bernard Morrison, in his standard garb of a deer-stalker's hat, tweed jacket and red trousers presents a memorable picture and a non-stop flowing account of life at Tralee.

Since opening the station he has entertained over 150,000 visitors.

During that time he has demonstrated the art of throwing a boomerang to the thousands of guests and always repeats a standard offer. If a boomerang doesn't return to him properly, he will turn the station over to a pretty visitor.

He still owns the station.

If you only have one chance to go to The Country, go to a farm.

A Tasmanian Farm

Our farm stay in Tasmania was an entirely different experience.

We stayed at the homestead-manor-mansion of "Pleasant Banks" within a few kilometres of Launceston Airport and enjoyed not a ride-the-horse, shear-the-sheep farm stay but rather a weekend on a country estate where all was quiet, all genteel.

The sizeable, two-storey homestead was built in 1838 of brick and nails made on the property and was now governed by Margaret Foster, (she was a Lawrence, you know) a porcelain-pretty aristocratic lady in her seventies who held her head in the chin-tilted manner of the born-proud.

John Foster, Margaret's husband, now gone, acquired the property in 1929 to continue his maternal great-great grandfather's line of Saxon-Merino sheep.

In the large dining room full of English oak furniture is a framed notice dated 26 July, 1821 advertising a mansion for sale in Yorkshire, England:

ARMSTEAD

Property of the late
John Foster, Esquire, deceased
Stone built Mansion
Seven good Bed Rooms
Five good Servants' Rooms
(etc.)
with an excellent Pew
in Giggleswick Church
(etc.)
water running through the Yard
which is conveyed by Pipes into
the Kitchen, Brewhouse and Laundry
(etc.)
— with two good Farm-Houses with
suitable Farm Buildings,
upon the Estate, at convenient
distances, and nearly out of
sight of the Mansion.

When the estate was sold, the oak furniture came out from Armstead with widow Foster and her sons to Tasmania.

In the parlour at Pleasant Banks is a seventeenth century bookcase cabinet of carved wood which came over with the Leakes, another part of the Foster family, who had extensive trading with Hamburg when they lived in the Old Country.

The Leake family brought the first Saxon-Merino sheep to Australia from Germany, duty free, early in the eighties.

The treasures of the house, an accumulation of three original Tasmanian settlers — the Leakes, the Fosters and the Lawrences who also received extensive original land grants — were shown to us with reserved pride by Margaret.

Indeed the unique attraction of Pleasant Banks, in addition to Lady Margaret to whom I was now a kneeling admirer, was the intriguing collection of antique furnishings:

* The Hallway painting of 1888 showing Mount Byron
* The Royal Engineer brick made in 1818
* The George II silver whistle-tankard. (You whistled into it when it was empty.)
* The royal purple glass finger bowls.
* The wine holders made in the shape of silver chariots.
* The oil painting portrait thought to be an unsigned Constable
* The carved blackwood fireplace mantel and side columns by Robert Prenzel
* The walking stick souvenir left by Harry Lauder
* The photograph of the gentry in top hats and much lace on the way to the races in a giant coach pulled by four matched horses
* The coat of arms of Admiral Leake

Each farm stay we experienced was unique, unique in its personality, unique in its setting which was one of the great appeals of Pleasant Banks.

Our bedroom, for example, was about thirty-by-twenty feet and was furnished with a canopied bed, antique furniture and a recently installed private bath.

Our cost per couple, including bed and breakfast — farmyard eggs with deep yellow yokes — and dinner was $40 a day, the average price for a farm holiday.

Although Pleasant Banks didn't offer conducted tours or farmyard activities, its own charm was enough.

In the vicinity were other mansions to visit.

Evandale, an historical village, is just up the road with its several attractive pioneer buildings including a nineteenth century Anglican Church on one side of the main thoroughfare and a Uniting Church on the other.

We asked Margaret Foster, "Was this area settled by the Scots? So many place names are Scottish."

"Oh, yes, the Camerons and the Mackinnons were all over on that side," she waved her hand imperiously towards the mountain Ben Lomond. "*We* were on this side."

"Is that why there is an Anglican Church on one side of the road in Evandale and what must have been a Presbyterian Church on the opposite side?"

"Certainly," she replied. "But the Uniting Church! Can you imagine the Presbyterians of yesterday kneeling down with the Methodists today! *Hah.*"

Oh, she was a delight, our *chatelaine*.

Ten minutes south of Evandale is Clarendon House, a superb Georgian structure restored and refurbished at great expense by the National Trust.

Franklin House, another charming Georgian homestead, built the same year as Pleasant Banks, is just a few miles north.

To the west of Launceston is Entally House, for reasons we don't understand, run by the Wildlife Service. Entally House is an excellent example of a self-contained colonial complex where everything was grown, made and repaired on the farm. Nursery. Chapel. Blacksmith shop. Servants' quarters.

The antiques at Entally are simply exquisite. Even the kitchen table is a treasure.

To the north of Launceston is Bell Bay where alumina is smelted into aluminium. (We saw the bauxite come out of the ground in Weipa on Cape York, saw the alumina plant at Gladstone and now we saw the final stage of aluminium processing at Bell Bay — a three-stage process taking place over a distance of about 2,500 miles.)

In the pioneer town of George Town, The Grove, 1832, is the oldest remaining home in the village which once flirted with the importance of being the capital of Northern Van Diemen's land. But George Town was passed because of the lack of water.

Inspection of the house for a modest fee is supervised by ladies dressed as servants of the Colonial period.

Our guide, Ruth Clarke, who looked and obviously enjoyed playing the servant wench, was dressed in black shoulder-to-ankle with white apron and white bonnet.

She lifted her skirt rather daringly to exhibit black and white pantaloons with white lace on the leg bottoms.

Interesting restored home where the pride of the house is reflected in the staff.

From the four-bedroom second floor a steep, narrow staircase leads to the third floor sleeping quarters of the female convict servants who were locked up at night.

The male convict servants were locked up in separate quarters in back of the house.

Help was hard to keep even in those days.

Tough Talk About Flies and Strikes and Things

The overseas visitor to Australia has to be aware that the country, like all destination areas, has unique, aggravating problems.

Case in point: leaving tranquil Tasmania turned into a semi-nightmare.

We had planned to spend four more days in Tasmania exploring the beautiful western coast, to boat up the Gordon River, to visit the central plateau if possible.

Instead we were informed that a ferry pilots' strike was imminent and that we should get our car to Bell Bay immediately, or wait an extra week.

Plans were cancelled for the western tour, car driven to Bell Bay, taxi back to Launceston airport ($32), fly to Melbourne and . . . wait and wait for the Green Pony now stuck in Bell Bay by the strike. We cancelled and rescheduled repeatedly until ultimately we had to ship ourselves and car by rail to Adelaide to catch up with our on-going itinerary.

That's the point. Visitors to Australia will find that strikes are of plague proportions.

The visitor has to be flexible. Ready to carry own bags (hotel strike). Change itinerary (airline strike). Stay longer (petrol strike). Stay in room (electric strike). Walk (public transport strike).

The strikes, "industrial actions" is the gloss-over term, are designed to hit when it hurts the most, no matter who is in the way — during Christmas shopping time, during farm harvest time, during vacation time. The "screw you" attitude of the unions is matched only by the phlegmatic "roll-me-over-do-it-again" acceptance of the Australian general public.

There are other negatives.

The flies top the list. Are there flies? Yes, millions and millions of them. Bush flies, blow flies, house flies, fly-up-your-nose flies. If flies really bother you, don't go to The Country. And stay indoors in the cities.

A Chinese school teacher was widely quoted in Australia when she said that in her country the solution would be simple. Every person would be given an assignment to kill ten flies a day. Of course in China there are 900,000,000 people.

Australians were not born to be servants.

The history of the country is anything but servile.

You don't come off the farm and make a great waitress or bartender or reception clerk.

The overseas visitor will find gracious, genuine hospitality in homes and private clubs but won't find, with exceptions of course, a high standard of service in public places.

A final negative.

When you leave Australia, you will be charged a $20 "departure tax." We find it surprising.

Why spend millions of dollars enticing visitors to come to Australia and then give them an economic kick in the pants as they are going out the door?

Kind Talk About Information

While we are putting the boot in, as the Australians say, we should also share our pleasure as overseas visitors at the vast amount of information available.

State tourist offices are located in every metropolitan centre with helpful personnel and informative literature where you can find the latest tourist news and also book tours and accommodations.

The printed information on the whole is excellent.

One small example. Our drive across the Nullarbor Plain was engrossing because the strip map published by the Western Australia

Tourist Office fed us fascinating material as we rolled down the highway. What to look for. Where to stop. What to see. History. Geography. All inclusive in readable, abbreviated form.

The newspapers, radio and television in Australia are second to none. The national newspaper is *The Australian*, a business oriented publication but with outstanding national and international content. A stable of fine writers.

The Weekend Australian on Saturdays was our favourite reading.

The *Canberra Times* and the *Mercury Hobart* are examples of smaller newspapers which are anything but provincial, crammed with news.

Television across the board is of a high standard.

Two brothers, Mike Willesee and Terry Willesee, have separate television programs. Each has a distinct talent for coming into your living room, sitting on a stool and talking to you.

Sixty Minutes, a weekly television news show is just as good as the American show it is based on and is done on a tenth of the budget.

Our favourite radio was Radio Two and its classical music format. Thank you, thank you, thank you.

11. The Big Four

Early in our Australian adventure we surveyed travel experts who told us that overseas visitors come to Australia to see (1) the Sydney Opera House, (2) the Great Barrier Reef and (3) Ayers Rock.

Our own survey among visitors brought forth a constant remark: "The War Memorial in Canberra! We could have spent days there."

We've added the Australian War Memorial in Canberra.

The book is about The Country . . . but when such major attractions are in cities, they can't be ignored. The Sydney Opera House, for example, is visited by forty percent of overseas visitors.

The Sydney Opera House

It's hard to remember that the Sydney Opera House, now the graceful symbol of Australia, was once a joke everywhere in the world.

Estimated originally to cost $7 million, the final figure ballooned to $102 million.

Tee hee hee, said the cynics.

Would it ever open? From the first concept in the early 1950's, the planning, the architectural competition, the initial construction, the building dragged on and on.

The foundation alone took four years. The shell roofs, the famous "sails" of the building, required one million Swedish tiles to be set by hand. Time: six years. The interiors, the promenade, the approaches: another six years.

In the nineteenth year the Sydney Opera House was finished. Queen Elizabeth officially opened the complex on October 20, 1973.

Since then the ugly duckling has turned into a queen of her own domain.

Situated at the end of Bennelong Point overlooking the harbour under the shadow of the Sydney Bridge, the marriage of the location on the isolated point surrounded by water and the free-flowing shell design of the roof structure, unlike anything else in the world, is visually, spectacularly successful.

The best part of the Sydney Opera House story is that it also functions with equal spectacular success.

The "Opera House" is a misnomer. Actually it was always intended

133

to be a performing arts centre with an opera theatre, concert hall, drama theatre, cinema and supporting restaurants and bars.

There is always action within and without its buildings and the events — be it opera, symphony or a play — are almost always sold out . . . and that is a problem for visitors.

On Sundays the stages are dark but there is promenade action galore — all free. Puppets. Rock concerts. Dance groups. Action.

You can take guided tours of the complex most days.

You will inspect the Concert Hall seating 2,690.

The Opera Theatre seating 1,547.

The Drama Theatre seating 544.

You will learn that the international competition design for the complex was won in 1957 by Danish architect Jørn Utzon who resigned from the project in 1966.

That "Opera House Lotteries" raised the money to keep the project going until the finish. (The Opera House Lotteries were so successful that they still continue but the money goes into general state funds.)

The building covers four and a half acres and is 200 yards long by 120 yards wide.

The highest point above sea level is 221 feet.

Et cetera.

The Opera House and the Concert Hall are carpetless to prevent the absorption of sound and late comers are not admitted but must wait for an intermission but may watch the performance on black and white television sets in the lobby.

There is a back stage tour. Every Sunday. $4.

In 1979 the Concert Hall announced the completion of the largest mechanical action pipe organ in the world (10,000 pipes).

Designed and built by Ronald Sharpe the organ cost $1.2 million and took four years to complete.

Ronald Sharpe is almost always tinkering with his love child as he was when we toured the complex.

"Ronald, are you there?" shouted Jane, our guide, into the upper reaches of the hall.

An acknowledgement was returned.

"Play us a tune," yelled Jane.

Negative acknowledgement returned.

"He can't play," confided Jane.

The firmest recommendation we make to overseas visitors is to see your local travel agent early and sign up for "An Evening at the Sydney Opera House" which includes a guided tour — but with a small group, not a horde — a dinner with wine at the Bennelong Restaurant which is the posh restaurant in the complex and a guaranteed "best available" seat in the opera, symphony or play that you choose.

Seats are reserved in blocks by the operators of the "evening" package.

It is possible that you can contact the Tourism Marketing Section at the Sydney Opera House on arrival for tickets but it is better to make your reservations before leaving home. The Sydney Opera House, Box 4274 GPO, Sydney 2001.

We took the tour, dining before the Australian Ballet's performance of "Don Quixote." The whole exercise gets first class marks. The combined tour-dinner-performance is a neat way to put it all together.

We later also saw Joan Sutherland, Australia's heroine, in a Verdi Opera. What a glorious, God-blessed voice.

Hard to get in?

Not long ago all the performances of famous New Zealand opera star, Kiri Te Kanawa, who can't perform in her home country because there is no worthy opera house, sold out immediately.

She was persuaded to give one extra performance with the understanding that the first call for tickets would go to New Zealanders.

Over 1,000 New Zealanders flew to Sydney for the occasion.

It was wildly successful, the promoter told us.

"The only small lapse was that we gave everyone streamers and daffodils to throw on stage at the end of the evening. Marvellous. At the curtain calls the house was filled with streamers. But no flowers were thrown to the diva. Where were the flowers?

"Well, when the people left it was obvious. The little old ladies were clutching their daffodils to their breasts. It was their souvenir of a treasured evening. They weren't about to surrender their daffodils."

Hard for a visitor to get back to the hotel?

Yes! Unless you reserve your "Evening" through Ansett Airlines which includes a bus to and from your hotel.

Or reserve a taxi.

There is no taxi stand with waiting cabs. At the corner of the stage door entrance is a yellow phone marked "Taxi." If you get to the phone before the mob, you can get a cab without too long a wait.

The Great Barrier Reef

After constant media exposure from childhood *Boy's Life* to adulthood's *National Geographic* a visit to the Great Barrier Reef was a dream come true.

But where to start?

That is where the education began.

The Reef is an immense thing, the largest such reef in the world.

It extends over 2,000 kilometres from New Guinea halfway down the coast of Australia. In places it extends over 300 kilometres out to sea.

There is a near reef, a middle reef and a far reef. To really get into the fantastic coral and the schools of fish requires either chartering a dive boat or going to a deserted island on one of the outer reefs.

Among the twenty resort islands only two, Green Island off of Cairns and Heron Island off of Gladstone, are technically part of the reef. The others are continental islands and although many are surrounded by coral and fish they aren't part of the Great Barrier Reef.

We immediately headed for Heron Island.

To reach Gladstone meant a night flight from Sydney to Brisbane 800 kilometers—and a morning flight from Brisbane to Gladstone another 500 kilometers—and a twenty-minute helicopter flight to Heron Island. The daily helicopter trips cost $185.

The launch goes five times a week and cost $85. I preferred the thirty-minute chopper ride avoiding the possibility of getting seasick.

The aircraft has room for six passengers and one pilot and is equipped with an electronic triggered float device. If an emergency forced the helicopter down on water, it would settle onto its own rubber raft and float indefinitely. We liked that.

Our four fellow passengers were fishing buddies from Sydney and they were hyped during our short flight on sight of frequent schools of fish.

Heron Island, even from a low-flying helicopter, appeared small. We could see the blue-water passage through the coral for the mainland launch and for the island's fleet of boats for fishing and diving.

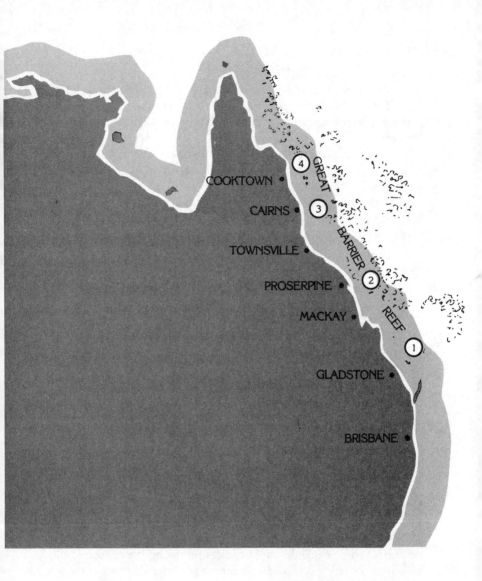

COOKTOWN •

CAIRNS •

TOWNSVILLE •

PROSERPINE •

MACKAY •

GLADSTONE •

BRISBANE •

GREAT BARRIER REEF

THE GREAT BARRIER REEF

1. HERON ISLAND   3. GREEN ISLAND
2. HAYMAN ISLAND   4. LIZARD ISLAND

Heron Island covers a little more than seventeen hectares, or forty acres. Part of the island is reserved as the Heron Island National Park and the visitor shares the white sand cay with scientists from the Heron Island Research Station.

The overseas visitors who make up more than half of the island's annual clientele — predominantly American, German and Japanese with only a smattering of New Zealanders — are attracted by the island's total environment, not only the reef but the birds and the fish and the general ecology.

Initially scuba diving and snorkelling would appear to be the most popular activities but that is because they are the most visible. Actually, the largest number of visitors are there to enjoy the reef and nature walks and to visit the marine station.

The island is a haven for birds: heron, noddy tern, banded rail, muttonbirds, silver-eye finch, seagulls.

Films are shown which give visitors a closer understanding about the environment in which they are vacationing.

Heron Island accommodates two hundred visitors in bungalows and motel-like cottages equipped with overhead fans, small refrigerators and tea-coffee making facilities.

A heavily used tennis court provides one activity and a heavily used bar provides another. Evenings there are costume parties, bingo, shipboard-type horseracing, et cetera on a weekly rotating basis because most vacationers stay a week which we wish we could have done.

The meals at Heron Island are quite pleasant. A combination buffet-served breakfast. Buffet lunch. Served dinner. Decent wine list.

We had tablemate bonuses, having as company an Australian doctor and his wife who knew about diving and shared their enthusiasm with us. (We enjoy our fellow Americans but we don't want to go half way around the world to eat with them. Good marks to the management for inter-mixing.)

"People who go down for the first time come up absolutely stunned by the beauty of it all. The dive boat stops at the first giant coralhead where the crew feed the fish every day. When you go down you literally have to part the fish with your hands to see where you are going," the doctor said.

We couldn't wait. The Great Barrier Reef. We signed up for snorkelling the next morning.

The next morning the wind blew.

It blew hard and it blew from the wrong direction. White-caps dotted yesterday's placid blue water. Damn, damn, damn.

The diving instructor said it was okay for experienced scuba divers but the surface was too rough for snorkellers. Damn again.

Fortunately even in such weather you can get in the water.

During low tide the surrounding reef surfaces, and you can carefully pick your way over the coral to ocean pools bordering the reef.

The resort provides excellent maps showing where the pools are to be found. Also old tennis shoes for reef walking and walking sticks are provided for those who want to go out on the reef but didn't bring their own gear.

At low tide we headed out over the reef with diving masks to find the Blue Pool on our map.

Three snorkellers were diving around the Blue Pool where there was easy access to the deep water.

Shedding the sun-protective shirt but keeping on the tennis shoes, I slipped on the mask and slid into the water without waiting. (Waiting begets niggly doubts. "Go Now" is the Cowards' Club motto.)

The pool was a small inlet in the reef with canyon walls of coral. The water was blue and it deepened in colour as it fell away into the ocean.

I ventured towards the deeper water and was somewhat startled when one of the swimmers, dressed in a vermilion wet suit, swam straight at me and stretched out an arm for a handshake.

"That's downright country-Texas friendly," I thought.

The diver turned out to be a lady from Dallas. One companion, female, was in the apparel business, and the other, male, was a prominent surgeon. With a gold ear-ring. You meet all kinds of things underwater.

Including dangerous fish. One of the Dallas contingent found a five-inch fish which was fastened to a coral ledge blending perfectly into the coral in colour and texture. A stone fish. Its spine has a spike which can result in almost instant death. They don't attack but watch where you step.

We stumbled our way back to the beach at the first sign that the tide was turning. You don't want to be caught on the reef during an incoming tide.

The Lady Navigator slipped and sat down heavily and for two

weeks she sat on one cheek and had daily applications of antiseptic on the other. Coral cuts are not funny even on your derriere.

The next morning we had a chat with the young manager of the island resort which was founded by a family as a resort in 1938. The majority of the stock is presently owned by P & O Lines.

"In 1920 the island was a haven for turtles but then the turtle population was slaughtered for meat and shell. It was decimated within three years.

"Now the island is a turtle sanctuary and the turtles have come back. The island tags 70,000 hatchlings a year. The mother turtle lays a clutch of eggs every four to six weeks, goes out to sea and comes back and repeats the performance probably four times, laying up to a hundred eggs on each visit.

"Turtle viewing goes from November through May.

"Heron Island's turtle conservation is so successful that it is now one of the three biggest turtle rookeries in the world."

The glass bottom boat at Heron Island is a major attraction. The fish swarm at the sound of the motor and it wouldn't be an exaggeration to say that five hundred *sizeable* fish – not the little blue damsels or butterfly fish – show up for the feeding. The passengers are enthralled.

That night at dinner the doctor and his wife were bubbling about their diving even in the rough water.

"The fish are so tame and so used to being fed that you can feed them by hand. Harry and Fang are two moray eels which are pets and even they are fed by hand," the doctor said.

Harry and Fang? Pets like in tigers?

When the doctor was young and without funds and in medical school, he entered into a contract with the government whereby the government paid his school costs and a minimum subsistence allowance for two years in exchange for three years service as a clinic doctor in a small country town where he was the only doctor. He had to do everything.

He told a couple of stories which were unself-consciously revealing of the Australian character.

Once the doctor had to perform an emergency caesarean section and the only blood type available that matched the woman's was his own.

He had the nurse take his matching blood and with the plasma sack hanging beside him he performed the operation successfully.

"I was a bit woozy at the time," he said.

The doctor told another story of a cowboy who broke his arm on the first day of a three-week muster, the gathering of the cattle from the range to send to market.

The stockman came into the clinic at the end of the three weeks with the arm strapped to his chest. The bone sticking out of the arm. Black. Smelly.

Why didn't he come in when it happened?

Oh, he couldn't leave his mates with all that work to be done.

Yes, they saved the arm.

Hayman Island

To reach Hayman Island from Heron Island involved helicopter, rental car, jet aircraft and another helicopter. Simple.

One benefit was stopping overnight in Rockhampton, an important Queensland cattle centre where the railroad cattle cars that go down the middle of town often stop traffic for considerable lengths of time.

The streets are wide and there has been an obvious effort to repaint and refurbish the business fronts. (Lots of saddle stores.)

The old Colonial Hotel is now called the Heritage Terrace and its elaborate ironwork that laces the balconies is absolutely first rate in the late golden afternoon sunset.

An old warehouse has been converted into a crafts and cultural centre. Its huge doors and open beam ceilings provide just-right ambience for potters, musicians, little theatre, the junior symphony and art gallery.

Another mark-of-pride in the community is the new Pilbeam Theatre, built at the cost of three and a half million dollars, combining an 800-seat complex with an air-conditioned art gallery.

We visited the new art gallery and came away impressed with its collection. Much fine talent. A frequent subject of the Australian artist is the sombre, sometimes stark landscape of Outback Australia. The lonely station house. The barren river. Humour is evident too, and boldness. Strength. Good collection.

Where did the money come from to purchase such art work?

Mayor Rex Pilbeam, sometimes referred to as "Sexy Rexy," an

acknowledged character, put the suggestive arm on citizens to sub-scribe to the collectors fund. The price tag of $2,000 included a name inscription on the bronze tablet. There were sixty names listed when we visited.

Strong mayor.

I called his office but he was home ill.

Stories about him were so colourful I chanced a call to his residence. The voice of death answered. The mayor.

He hadn't had a vacation in twenty-five years and now he had the Russian flu. He sounded like a dead Russian.

He perked up only when we said we had been by the Pilbeam Theatre and found it magnificent.

"Yes, isn't it," he said.

Among the locals the theatre is referred to as "The Rex."

Queenslanders' reputation is for white, right and might.

Aborigines are not a subject among painters, for example.

Yet, north of Rockhampton, at Yeppoon, Mr. Iwasaki from Japan had just bought twenty-two kilometres of beachfront to build a Jap-anese destination resort.

It sounded out of character.

"He had megabucks," we were told. "That made it right."

Hayman Island is probably the most popular, sophisticated island resort on the GBR.

"It is the island of smiles. Cheerful service is the motto. No tipping. The only palm you will see will be on a coconut tree," the manager, Andre Maestracci, said.

The Royal Hayman Hotel can accommodate 400 visitors and is serviced by 200 employees. There are two swimming pools, two tennis courts, one bowling green and one railroad station.

What?

Yes, the long jetty and the helicopter are connected to the hotel by a tiny railroad that takes you and your luggage to the centre of the complex. Fun.

The beach — at low tide — is huge. The hotel runs a fleet of boats including cruise and fishing boats and small putt-putts with outboard motors which you can hire for about $20 a day and go off — within a boundaried area full of private islands and private beaches — to do your own thing. That would have been first on our priority list but for the wind from the wrong direction. Instead we opted for a day cruise to other Whitsunday Passage islands.

The manager encouraged his guests to see the other islands. We understand why. They didn't compare with Hayman.

"When passengers come back, they tell other guests what they saw. It creates a certain smug satisfaction."

Our cruise ship venture started with an early barbecue lunch opposite the tiny railroad station and among tame parrots so glorious in colour they looked painted. Then by rail to the jetty, we boarded a 100-foot white ship to the south end of Hook Island — not what you'd call smooth water — to an underwater observatory.

First we had a small side trip in a glass-bottom boat to view the coral and then to the observatory where we could see more coral and fish in a natural setting.

Mushroom coral, staghorn coral, stalked coral, brain coral, slipper coral, branching coral, soft coral, foliaceous coral, horny coral.

From Hook Island we crossed the Whitsunday Passage to South Molle and to West Molle now known as Daydream Island, which had a combination of Hawaiian-Mexican, you-name-it-you-can-have-it motifs. It swarmed with an army of day-trippers and is not designed at all for an overseas visitor.

Hamilton Island, ten minutes away by boat from Hayman is a major new development with its own air strip.

Nature walks, snorkelling, bird watching and reef walking are among other activities on Hayman's one thousand acres. At low tide you can see beautiful coral formations, shells and trepang. Trepang is a sea cucumber. It looks like a gigantic slug. In other days in the South Seas the trepang was harvested, smoked and sold to China and was known as *beche-de-mer*.

Hayman is popular. The thirty-year old resort owned by Ansett Hotels runs an eighty-seven percent occupancy even during a season when there have been seven hurricane warnings. You must have reservations.

Green Island

Cairns is a summer resort town and when it is winter in the south and cold, rain-drenched visitors seek warmth and sun, Cairns overflows. Many motels and rental flats. Bus tours, railroad tours, river tours and day tours to Green Island are part of the activities.

A trip to Green Island is considered a "must" because it is *on* the Barrier Reef only twenty-four kilometres from the city.

We took Graham Gordon's twin-hulled *Coral Seatel* to the island, a boat designed to be more comfortable in waters that can become rough without warning. Couldn't help noticing the abundance of seasick bags.

It was a sun-sparkling day and we enjoyed a pleasant cold buffet during the crossing made more comfortable with a cold beer bar.

Green Island is a true coral cay and good for the standard glassbottom boat tour and for the beginning snorkeller.

"The southern diver might be content with the near reef," sniffs one 'put-down' piece of local propaganda, "but . . . ."

There are guestroom accommodations but you have to live through the hordes of day trippers who descend on the island. They swarm the beaches — public toilets and showers are provided — the restaurant, a snack shop, gift shop and bar.

An underwater observatory, a marineland and a reef film theatre also keep the crowds coming. Tickets are purchasable on the *Seatel*. We bought them all.

The observatory, opened in 1954 as the world's first, is superior to the Hook Island observatory. More viewing room and better underwater life and descriptive graphics.

A nice touch is the roll of paper towelling at each window which you use to wipe off the mist caused by the human breathing on the cold glass.

Lots of good fish and coral. When the boat docks, don't go stand in an entry line at the observatory. Go back later in the afternoon when you can have it to yourself.

We walked around the island in much less than an hour and the most interesting sight was a buxom, red-headed, red-shirted young lady whose shirt front said. "OK, America, show us yours."

The Lady Navigator then made a negative remark about my questionable taste and I pointed out that the spirit of competition made the world bigger and better and she said that if competition made what I just saw bigger and better . . . and this nattering went on until we put on masks and took a dive in the Coral Sea.

It was not much. Obviously we were at the wrong place at the wrong time and didn't see exotic coral or fish in our wind-protected beach. Nice beach though.

Before returning to the mainland the ship's crew fed schools of fish at the dock.

Through the mass of little fish nudged a larger, darker shadow.

"It's the pet grouper," said an often-returned Brisbane friend. "Watch it."

A crewman put a fishhead on a string and the shadow suddenly became a huge head and — snap — the fist-sized morsel of fish disappeared in a monstrous mouth. A flash of a curved belly carried the grouper back into the green depth.

The performance was repeated half a dozen times.

"There has never been a case of a shark attack on the Barrier Reef," my friend said. "But the grouper has strong territorial feelings and is considered more dangerous to divers than a shark. You get too close to his cave and you are history."

One of two other interesting islands in the Barrier Reef category is Dunk Island to the south of Cairns which we were scheduled to visit and then dropped because of too tight scheduling. It is operated by TAA, the airline, and has been the object of heavy investing.

The literature photography is beautiful and copy promises such things as "secluded but sophisticated" . . . "hideaway for the discerning."

It has the usual aquatic attractions plus a six-hole golf course.

The other island, north of Cairns, is Lizard Island, the jewel which we visited during our Cape York tour. A superior spot.

I would go back to Cairns on my knees just to eat fish . . . with a touch of white Australian riesling on the side, please.

Other people would crawl back to Cairns to catch the fish.

It is famous as the biggest city closest to the immense black marlin which weigh in at half a ton.

The season is November and December and if you haven't reserved your boat, forget it unless you luck into a cancellation.

Fishing, however, is almost year-round for sailfish, mackerel, wahoo, bonito and dolphin.

To get the big fish you have to go to the drop-off of the Barrier Reef which means you really have to have a "mother-ship" to use as a floating hotel or a large enough cruiser to stay out in the fishing grounds.

The most attractive craft we saw was the new 82-foot *Coral Reeftel*, a sister ship of the Green Island commuting boat but designed for unlimited sea stays with eight private, twin-berth cabins, air-conditioning, a large lounge-stateroom, bar, stereo, TV, diving equipment. Fully carpeted? Of course, of course, of course. They don't want you to get your feet dirty!

It does take a spot of money.

I asked the cost for the ship and its two launches for deep-sea fishing or diving, fully provisioned including the bar, and wine with meals, everything. One week.

The tab would be about $10,000. But if you divide the cost by sixteen people and it isn't too bad.

Another must-do activity in Cairns is the historic Kuranda Railroad. The ride from Cairns to Kuranda on top of the agriculturally rich Atherton Tablelands is a delight.

The Big Red

We were 128 kilometers out when the dark hump of Ayers Rock first appeared on the horizon. It was a welcome visual change because the Great Victoria Desert below offered a limitless expanse of flat, empty land.

As we flew closer to the famous monolithic rock it became more and more a rust-red.

The plane made one pass around the gravel airstrip—now replaced by a new airport with a paved runway—and landed. Chris, a young Malibu-blond-type Australian, drove us to The Chalet, then located about two miles from the old airport.

At that time there were four motels scattered around the Rock offering limited accommodations and minimum standards although there was always a bar with cold beer.

Wisely, the government designed a modern resort area near the new airport—Yulara Village—to offer first class as well as moderate accommodations and camping facilities.

The year 1984 marked the end of the four motel era with the opening of a 100-room Four Seasons hotel and a new Sheraton Ayers

Rock with 250 rooms.

When completed, the resort will take care of 6,000 visitors a day . . . 4,000 in campsites and 2,000 in hotels and motels.

A new air terminal is part of the new sealed airstrip. Fire station, post office, school, water bores are part of the master plan.

The necessary infrastructure is being completed with government funds. Private accommodation and service facilities will be financed and managed by private enterprises.

The former teeth-rattling highway from Alice Springs has been completely paved, making the drive a lot easier, faster and much more desirable, and the option of alternative accommodations more feasible.

Ayers Rock, known to the Aborigines as "Uluru," has gained world-wide fame because of its very physical size and majesty . . . because of its dramatic, photographic changes in colour . . . because of its rich history in Aboriginal "dreamtime" history.

It's big. No photograph prepared us for its overwhelming physical presence . . . over one thousand feet high . . . five miles around. Probably because it is singular, bald, without landmarks, there is nothing to compare it to.

You also shrink in size when you realise that this huge sandstone rock is only the peak that continues below the surface more than a mile.

About 600 million years ago this vast plain was an inland sea. Some deposits of sandstone were so durable, like Ayers Rock and the Olgas, that they resisted the gradual erosion of the lake-bed and remained monuments to time.

On the side of Ayers Rock facing the old airstrip is the outline of a huge skull and what look like details of a brain are in fact levels of erosion.

"The Brain" was one of the first sights of our Sunset Tour which began with a circle around the Rock including parts sacred to the heritage of the Aboriginal tribes.

We saw the Ininti Waterhole, then the Initiation Area closed to the public where bloodmarkings from initiations and secret paintings are still visible within the sacred grounds. We saw Mother Nature's Digging Stick. Visited Kantju Gorge.

At Maggie Springs, a permanent waterhole on the south side of the Rock, we inspected Aboriginal paintings at close hand and heard from Chris the legend of the magic springs.

Before taking off to the west to view the sunset on the rock we paused at the point where you can climb to the summit . . . and looked up . . . and up . . . and wondered if we should really do that the next morning at dawn as we had intended.

About three kilometres west of Ayers Rock, on a dirt road called "Sunset Boulevard," is a small rise where everybody goes to watch the changing colours. A large parking area for a dozen or more tour buses, caravans and cars is a sign of the popularity of the evening event.

Everyone at sunset has a camera and takes shot after shot after shot of the gradually changing colours of the sun rays on Ayers Rock. It is dramatic.

The muted colour of mid-day changes to light red, to burnt red, to orange and finally to brown or many variations of purple depending upon the cloud cover which can reflect and enhance the colour-the-rock show.

Click, click, click.

Actually there is another beautiful shot and that is the sunset itself with the multiple humps of the Olga Mountains silhouetted on the horizon.

At the sunset we had a lovely "small-world" coincidence. There was *Anna*, our Bill King truck-bus of The Kimberley Safari and nearby was Don Nayler, certainly the best tour driver in Australia, and Viv, the cook. Happy rendezvous then and later over "tinnies" at the hotel.

The next morning we witnessed the "birth" of Ayers Rock. The hotel being in the east was perfectly positioned for the sun-rise photographic ritual. The first rays gave fire to the massive sandstone, turning it from a soft pink to a fire engine red.

Click, click, click.

At six o'clock we took off for the dawn patrol effort to climb Ayers Rock.

"Have you ever climbed Ayers Rock?" we asked Chris.

"Never."

"Why not?"

"I don't have to prove anything."

At the foot of the starting point are four plaques dedicated to the memory of people who have died on the Rock. Not necessarily fallen to their deaths but died. Dead.

Surprisingly on such a beautiful morning the winds were exceedingly strong.

"Thermals," said Chris, "created by the sun hitting the rock."

At the gradual slope at the bottom we started off confidently. We enjoy physical exertion.

After the first couple of hundred yards there is a hand-rail chain anchored by iron pylons. You can hold it for safety or pull yourself up or let yourself down the Rock.

We proceeded up a few hundred yards and the wind was blowing a mini-gale.

Now breathing heavily. Up a couple of hundred yards more on a steep incline to an easier graduation and we sat down to talk the situation over.

Ahead of us the steepest incline — it looked straight up — with a clear fall-off on each side. People descending told us that beyond this portion there was only a white line. No chain. Big winds.

"We don't have to do this," we said. And we didn't.

We sat there high up on the Rock enjoying the spectacular view and the fresh wind, locked firmly around the chain, chatting with climbers as they went up and came down.

"Take you long? Did you find it worthwhile? How was the scenery? You're bleeding on your left knee."

We descended in time to catch the bus back to the hotel sipping at our box breakfast frozen orange juice.

After lunch we took the tour out to the Olgas, a bunched together jumble of high rocks dominated by Mt. Olga which is nearly a thousand feet higher than Ayers Rock.

The Olgas, named after a Russian grand duchess, is different in composition from Ayers Rock being made of a combination of pebbles and boulders held together with sandstone.

There is vegetation on the sides and on top. Rabbits and dingos are part of the scenery.

From the west side of the Olgas we could see clearly outlined the separate mountains: Ghee, Walpa separated from Mt. Olga by the Olga Gorge and then Leru.

We came across a third rock in the national park: Derek Roff, the Northern Territory Park and Wildlife Commissioner's senior ranger.

A white-haired, white-bearded, goliath-like English-born gentleman who spent twenty years in Kenya before coming to Ayers Rock where he had been for twelve years. He talked about climbing the Rock, about the Aborigines, about the government's $60 million future development of the Rock which had already begun with construction of a new airport.

"Climbing the Rock isn't dangerous," Derek said. "If you do what you are advised to do: stay on the white line, don't chase a blown-off hat, don't go off trying to take a special picture from a new angle, you'll be all right.

"We had one woman who didn't obey the rules and took a bad fall. She broke an arm in three places, broke her teeth and badly scratched her face. We reached her, however, and got her back on the trail and were guiding her down. The word had gotten out and there was a mob at the bottom watching the rescue.

"During the descent, she sat down all of a sudden and started to cry. 'What's the matter?' we wanted to know.

" 'All of those people down there have cameras and I don't have any teeth!'

"So I sent a bloke down ahead and he asked the spectators to put away their cameras and they did.

"Another time a magistrate from Sydney suffered a heart attack on top. He was a huge fellow who must have weighed eighteen stone (252 pounds) and we had a devil of a time getting him down. There was no airstrip at the Rock in those days and they had to drive him almost five hundred kilometres to Alice Springs. I never, never thought he'd survive.

"A couple of weeks later here he was again. Came back to get his car. 'You know, I want to thank you. That was close, wasn't it? I should know. It was my fifth heart attack.' "

Roff was silent for a moment reflecting and then continued.

"To the Aborigines, despite the visual dominance of the Rock, it was not the most important thing on the landscape. A small hill or a bush could be more important to his family.

"In the so-called 'dreamtime' of the Aborigines — the dawn of time in their mythology before the earth was born — each rock, animal, plant and place had a significant role in their personal lives.

"In a totemic society each family had a blood relationship with these objects. They were the most important things. Not the Rock.

"The Rock was important because it was a sign of dependable water. If an Aboriginal was within many miles of 'Uluru' and could see its top on the horizon, no matter what the drought conditions, he knew he was safe because 'Uluru' had water.

"You may look out on this country and see it as a harsh, hard country. But the Aboriginal sees it as a storehouse of food and water ... it might be grubs or ants or moisture from a bush ... but it is all here and in his 'walkabouts' he knows from the stories passed down from generation to generation exactly what and where he can find food and drink.

"In their processes of passing on knowledge through initiations they have retained much of their culture.

"I have been accepted by the Aborigines to a limited degree — it will always be limited — and I've participated or been present at minor rituals but some things I'll never be told because it is none of my business. Or it doesn't belong to them.

"For instance, I knew vaguely a legend about a cat. When I inquired about the legend, I was told, 'Oh, it doesn't belong to us. It belongs to so-and-so who lives way away. He could tell you.'

"So I took one of the members of the local tribe and we went to visit so-and-so some hundred miles away.

"He knew who I was. He knew what ceremonies I had attended and I was eligible in his mind to know the legend of the cat. He told me right away without any compunction.

"Although he wasn't of our local tribe, the traditional trading routes of long ago led to the trading of songs and to the trading of cultures. I was just part of that trading custom."

The increasing popularity of Ayers Rock and the Olgas—60,000 visitors annually — with its impending disturbance of the ecology led to the far-reaching plan to create Yulara Village, the new, centralised visitors' centre half way between the two attractions.

The resulting improvements make first-rate tours possible.

Airlines of Northern Australia, flyin F-28 jets, offers full-day excursions from Alice Springs to Ayers Rock, bringing the Rock to even more visitors every year.

That means you would miss the sunset and the sunrise, two of the most dramatic viewing time . . . but better than not seeing it at all.

Other tours are overnight packages including guided trips to the Olgas and Ayers Rock.

A third option, which we would find very tempting, is a fly-drive package permitting you to take a four-hour drive one way through this awesome land and then jet the other direction.

If you are into ballooning, check out Adventure Travel Center for two-day, five-day and 16-day (wow!) balloon safaris out of Alice Springs.

A vignette.

On our last evening I took a late afternoon tour of the other facilities with Chris. We stopped by the Red Sands Motel, the camping area, the Visitors' Centre, the Inland Motel, the tour bus camping area and finally the Uluru Motel where we stopped for a refreshment.

The construction workers who were completing the airstrip were quartered at the hotel. A rough, thirsty, bored to-the-danger-point mob.

A couple of evenings before they converted the pool table into a golf driving tee and tee-ed off the cue ball with the pool stick causing a bit of damage to walls and windows. Tough people.

Suddenly through the door walked a Japanese poetess, Kazuko Shiraishi, dressed in Japanese pyjamas and a spectacular silken headdress she had picked up on an invitational speaking tour of Egypt. (Kazuko's forte is to read her erotic poetry to a rock music background. She gets invited everywhere!)

She floated up to the bar in a whisper of perfume . . . the bodies parted miraculously before her . . . and she ordered a lemonade.

In this knock-'em-down, kick-'em-in-the-head society there was stunned silence.

I remember distinctly one worker who wore a gold ring through his nose and whose mouth looked like it would remain open for the rest of his life just staring in complete disbelief.

And the magic of the moment was sustained — and sustained — until she daintily finished her lemonade and drifted out the door.

Exquisite.

The Australian War Memorial

My daughters would give the Australian War Memorial a wide berth. Wars are obscene. Memorials to war are a glorification of wars.

On the surface I would agree with them but would add that wars have always been one of mankind's hobbies and to ignore wars would be ignoring a facet of the human being's existence.

Also, I would point out to the young ladies, that the Australian War Memorial is dedicated first to the memory of those Australian men and women who have died in war . . . and 102,000 names without glorification of rank or title are inscribed in bronze in the Commemoration Gallery's Roll of Honour.

There is no glorification of war suggested anywhere.

To a city of 250,000 more than 2,500,000 visitors come every year . . . and a third of the visitors stay with friends or relatives.

With a small national population of 14,000,000 you can be certain practically all of the visiting Australians to Canberra have a name dear to the family memorialised in brass on the Roll of Honour.

From the spreading, new building of the Australian Parliament, you look across Lake Burley Griffin, up the three-kilometre tree-lined Anzac Parade to the impressive two-storey Byzantine building with a copper-sheathed roof. The Australian War Memorial, set handsomely in twelve hectares of lawn, is backdropped by Mount Ainslie.

A worthy building in a worthy setting.

From the exterior you can look into the Commemorative Stone and Pool. The arcaded cloisters at each side hold the list of those who died during combat.

Beyond is the Hall of Memory, dedicated to World War II, where the entire wall surface was executed with glass mosaics — over six million pieces — and the work was done by Napier Wallace, a gunner who lost his right arm at the shoulder in World War I!

The commemoration feature is a major element of the War Memorial. The second feature, unseen by most visitors, is the library containing an incredible storehouse of war documentation . . . printed, taped, photographs and motion picture. The film footage alone would stretch three times across the country.

The third feature is that which captures the imagination of the overseas visitor. The Exhibition Gallery.

What you find as a visitor are absorbing relics which are, in truth, symbols of dramatic pages in Australian war history.

For example, let me give you just a smattering of relics I jotted in my notebook.

Item: a bullet-riddled life raft. It is the only remaining object left from the sunken *H.M.A.S. Sydney,* lost with 645 hands in its battle off Western Australia on 19 November, 1941.

Item: an ingeniously rigged rifle fixed in position to fire manless, automatically to cover the retreat at Gallipoli, buying precious escape time.

Item: a pith helmet pierced by the nose cap of a Turkish shell. The helmet was worn by Major T. H. Darley of the 9th Light Horse Regiment who was unscathed.

Item: a photograph of the Australian Camel Corps at Magdaha on 23 December 1916. Who remembers that Australian "Light Horse" brigades were once mounted on camels?

Item: in Aeroplane Hall a wicker basket used to carry balloon observers in World War I. The observers, easy prey for enemy aircraft, had the first parachutes. When they were forced to bail out they became members of the "Caterpillar Club" so called because the silk of the parachute came from the caterpillar.

Item: dominating the same room full of aircraft is a Lancaster Bomber: "G for George" which flew more missions than any other aircraft in the R.A.F. command. A rotation of 208 airmen spent 664 hours flying the bomber to 90 targets . . . over seven hours per mission.

Item: a Japanese surrender flag carried by Lt. Gen. Adachi at Wewak on 13 September 1945.

Item: a training aeroplane built in 1912 used officially for engine-starting practice. Used, unofficially, for short hops. The sister aeroplane of the model shown was written off when, during a short illegal hop, it failed to clear a telephone line.

Item: the Shellal Mosaic, a mosaic floor from a sixth century Byzantine church uncovered by soldiers digging a trench in the desert between Jerusalem and Egypt. Volunteer Australian and New Zealand soldiers sweated fourteen days in intense heat to uncover the nine by six metre mosaic.

Item: the joystick from the triplane and the deerskin flying boots of Baron Manfred von Richthofen, the famous commander of Red Baron's Flying Circus, who was shot down by Australian bullets while chasing a British Sopwith Camel at ground level behind Allied lines. (He was buried with full military honours by the No. 3 Squadron of the Australian Flying Corps.)

There are over 30,000 relic items in the collection! Funny, tragic, inspiring.

Important elements of the Exhibition Gallery are the dioramas, scale models of action battle scenes capturing the essence of the scenery, the smoke, the carnage, the conditions of life.

Pioneered by the Australian War Memorial, a single diorama can take a sculptor and an artist a full year to complete.

There are sixty-eight dioramas in the galleries depicting field scenes from both World Wars, Korea and Vietnam.

The Memorial is also a treasured depository of Australian art — some 12,000 paintings, sketches, sculptures and cartoons are part of the collected works. About 1,200 are on display at one time including Sir William Dobell's *The Billy Boy*, my favourite painting in Australia.

Near the exit of the ground floor Exhibition Gallery, almost as an afterthought, is a portrait of General Douglas MacArthur, once the great hero of Australia who said, "Old soldiers don't die. They just fade away."

In Canberra they are remembered.

GOLD & GEMSTONE

1. THUNDER EGG FARM
2. "THE FOSSICKER'S WAY"
3. BEECHWORTH
4. BENDIGO-BALLARAT
5. COOBER PEDY
6. KALGOORLIE

12. The Great Gold and Gemstone Hunt

Australia is rich.

Beneath the surface of the continent the grinding pressures of earth formations and intense heat over millions of years have produced billionaire quantities of desirable minerals: copper, tin, iron, silicate, coal, bauxite, uranium and titanium ores, oil, nickel, silver . . . and gold.

Gold! The first discoveries of sprinklings of gold were suppressed for fear that a gold-rush might remove farmers and convicts and workers from their jobs and disturb the agrarian economy.

But when Edward Hammond Hargraves returned to New South Wales from the goldfields of California with a memory of similarities of gold-bearing country around Bathurst and found payable gold in 1851, the lid came off.

Gold in the next fifty years would be found in every state of Australia. Gold brought prosperity . . . over nine hundred million pounds sterling was brought out of the ground before 1916.

Gold brought waves of immigrants from Europe and from California pumping fresh blood into the nation in place of the convict labour dominant in New South Wales and Tasmania.

But that was not all that lay beneath the ground. There were sultan treasuries of precious gemstones. The brilliant, multicoloured opal, the queen of Australian jewels, and sapphires, emeralds, topaz, ruby, tourmaline, amethyst, turquoise.

In addition, a hush-hush discovery of diamonds — rumoured to be a treasure trove — is reported in The Kimberley.

With a tradition dating back to the 1850's when it was possible for a miner to find a rich nugget practically staring at him from the surface of a dry stream, this rummaging profession — or hobby — of going into the bush and turning over rocks, picking at cliff faces and shovelling creek beds has been called "fossicking."

Visitors to Australia are welcome to try their luck. A real gold nugget. A precious opal. A woman-warming sapphire. They are all just over there. "Where it is? There it is," the saying goes.

We arrived in Australia at a time of a gold-buying boom. The price

157

for gold quadrupled within a space of a few months . . . and with it a marked increase in fossicking.

The buying and selling of metal detectors became a major industry. A travel consultant, himself an avid fossicker, reported a six months wait for a premium $750 metal detector.

"I have a garage full of rocks," he confessed. He also had his own rock cutter and rock polisher and his idea of the ideal vacation was to take pick and shovel into the bush fossicking for two weeks.

He was not after gold or precious jewels. He just had a great hunger for pretty rocks, an enthusiasm embraced by the Lady Navigator.

Our return home from voyages abroad are frequently weighted by large or small, flat or round, rough or smooth mountain rocks, river rocks . . . all of which get piled in hidden heaps in cupboard corners.

To her Australia was Mecca. Unlike the travel advisor rock-hound, she didn't want to find a pretty stone. She wanted to find the mother lode and considered our first experience in the field in Queensland as strictly a warm-up.

We drove south from Noosa Heads, crossed the Pacific Highway, and three kilometres inland between North Arm and Eumundi, arrived at Thunder Egg Farm.

Thunder Egg Farm consisted of a farmhouse, a large shed in back which housed various gemstone exhibits including those for sale. Alongside the building was another shed where rough stones were being washed, polished and mounted.

A gate to a mountain track led to the thunder egg dig-and-pick area.

Tom Dickinson, a fossicker for fourteen years and the proprietor of the farm, explained the thunder egg to us.

Shaped somewhat like an egg, the centre contains thousands of layers of multi-coloured gemstone, mostly agate, in a wild assortment of abstract shapes. A star, a flower or even the map of Australia may be revealed when the egg is sliced in half.

The Aboriginals believed the stones dropped from the sky during fierce thunderstorms. Another theory was that thunder eggs were ejected from volcanoes.

Geologists now believe that the shell, called rhyolite, is formed during a lava flow, then over millions of years agate, quartz, amethyst or other substances seep down into the shell in a solution of silica, building layer upon layer until it is full.

The thunder egg farmer said, "There are only four locations known in Australia: Agate Creek up north where you need a black tracker and a four-wheel-drive vehicle, Tamborine Mountain, Mount Hay and here at Thunder Egg Farm."

By this time the Lady Navigator was jumping with the joy of the prospects: "Let's go look for eggs! Let's go look for eggs!"

But first we paid $5 for a "Fossick Permit" entitling us to "One level bucket or part thereof" on the same day. Mr. Dickinson handed us two buckets and two picks and drew a prospectors' map of where he thought we could find thunder eggs.

Up the mountain we went to a digging site against a small cliff face which had been chewed out by a tractor. Here we started to chip away.

The first lesson you learn about fossicking, at the beginning of summer especially, is that it is very hard work. Clawing at a clay surface under a bright sun, pulling down the dirt, separating it from rocks is fatiguing in the first ten minutes.

We found a few rocks, slightly egg shaped, but nothing gigantic nor conclusive, certainly not convincing. We clawed away here and there in the area for the best part of an hour until we were absolutely exhausted.

Dejectedly, we took a dozen specimens down the hill to Mr. Dickinson and shamefully presented them.

"Oh, yes, you have something here!"

The whole world came alive.

"We'll put them under the saw and see what we have."

He turned his machine on and slowly split the first rock, washed the two halves and showed us the surfaces. Beautiful! The thinnest layers of softly coloured agate in various hues settled into a butterfly motif in the centre. A thrill.

Every stone turned out to be a genuine agate thunder egg and we wouldn't let go of one of them.

We had the "farm yard" to ourselves that day but during the summer holidays two or three hundred families swarm the mountain. "Cars will be parked half a mile down on the road in another month," Farmer Dickinson said.

A visitors book contained names, addresses and comments. One read: "A mug's game but well worth while." Indeed.

Hunting for Gemstones

In the northeastern part of New South Wales in the New England region about 150 kilometres in from the coast is a diamond-shaped area called "The Fossicker's Way."

The district's promotional brochure is enough to make the greedy heart pick up speed. "Some of the best fossicking specimens," it reads, "have been collected by people who have pulled up by the roadside to have a rest or inspect their car."

Just south of the Fossicker's Way there is a sign in the hills pleading "Don't Dig Up The Streets." And what does the sign encourage people to do? Right. Dig up the streets.

At Glen Innes we stopped at the Total Service Station and talked to Frank Cheshire, the owner and tourist information chief for the area who was an authority on gems. He brought out a tray of sapphires which he explained are bought by the ounce in the rough and by the carat after being cut.

He said that the Thais come to the area, buy gems and take them back to their country where the stones are cut and sold back to the Australians. "An Australian-cut stone," he said, "takes more time and costs more money but it will be perfectly symmetrical whereas the Thai-cut sapphire most likely will be lopsided."

He showed us white, blue and pink topaz. He had a piece of quartz cut to look like topaz.

All of the gemstones had been found in the area.

You can get a map at Glen Innes which shows twenty-four gem-stone areas.

Three of the privately owned lands allow fossickers to dig for a small fee. You have to have your own pick and shovels and sand sifters.

Number twelve, unnamed on the map, was to the north of town, Dunvegan to the west and Clunemore in Shannon Vale to the east — the direction of our travels later in the day. Clunemore, we decided, was to be our mother lode.

The way you dig for sapphires — because that is what we settled on finding — is to find a creek bed, dig down through the gravel until you find clay, chunk the clay into a sieve, wash it down until only the rocky remains are left. Amidst the pebbles you will find the gem-stones to create pure envy-hate among your neighbours.

We not only didn't find a sapphire, we couldn't even find Clunemore.

For sixty kilometres we circled Shannon Vale in search of Clunemore and the owners, the McCabes.

"Scotch ancestry, they are," said our tourist authority. "If you are in luck Mr. McCabe might play his bagpipes for you."

No dig, no jewels, no bagpipes.

Our fortunes improved with our farm hosts at Quirindi who took us up into the foothills of the Great Dividing Range, above the former gold town of Nundle.

From a dirt road where we parked our car in the shade, we strolled down a mountain path lined with woods, until we reached an open cut of marble. Professional rock hunters had blasted open the mountainside and had hauled away truck-loads of stones.

We were looking for chrysoprase, a semi-precious gem akin to jade. The idea is to find a clear stone of apple green colour without other minerals running through it.

For an hour we turned over rocks, stooped, picked up pieces, squinted at them thoughtfully, edited, threw away.

The Lady Navigator found a fist-sized chunk which she showed later to a rock-hound in Melbourne who judged it worth cutting and polishing.

The stone from Nundle is now one of the Lady Navigator's most prized corner cupboard possessions.

The mineral map of Nundle lists twelve different kinds of minerals and stones to be found in the area including sapphires and gold.

It is all still there.

How About Gold Panning?

A month later in the foothills of the Snowy Mountains in the upper corner of Victoria, we stayed in the historic town of Beechworth.

As a result of that stay I have in front of me a strip of honest gold. Real gold, Gold we found.

Of course the tiny-tiny particles of gold are so small they could only be picked up with a band-aid. To be generous one could say that the gold is visible but not measurable.

We were taken several miles below Beechworth to a small creek where once a thriving gold digging community, Woolshed Falls, supported 8,000 miners. Today it is an empty field.

At the junction of a road with the creek, we waded in ankle-deep water equipped with shallow pans the size of large skillets.

A shovelful of creek bottom matter — rocks, gravel, clay — was dumped into each pan.

The trick was to wash out the rocks and clay with a circular motion allowing the rich lode of heavier gold to sink to the bottom. When only a teaspoon of fine sand was left, we could detect among the black traces of tin, the minute specks of gold.

Eight of us worked the creek-bed for an hour and a half and put all of our findings onto the single, glittering band-aid which I have in front of me.

Beechworth may not have produced much material gold for us but it was rich in colour and history. In 1852 gold was found just under the bridge that now crosses into town and in ten years the miners won over 150 tons of the precious metal.

One ostentatious political candidate even shod his horse with gold ... and was elected.

In Beechworth at the height of the digging there were 40,000 miners including 5,000 Chinese who had their own joss house, restaurants, hotels and opium dens on the hill overlooking town.

Beechworth has many lovely architectural gems — thirty-four buildings in the National Trust — left over from the Victorian period. We had dinner at Tanswell's Commercial Hotel, a pub restored in 1962 to its original splendour. A pleasant French restaurant. The next night we dined at the Georgian Opera House-cum-Regency Restaurant.

Tom Thumb, the famous thirty-one-inch midget, once played the opera house and left behind a pair of boots which are immortalised in the Burke Museum across the street.

Beechworth boasts a carriage museum, a rock museum, a gaol museum, a slab cottage museum and the old powder magazine (powder needed for mining was centrally stored). For my money, the first rate attraction is the Burke Museum.

Robert O'Hara Burke once served as superintendent of police in Beechworth. A handsome, dashing, commanding figure he led an 1861 expedition, well-funded (50,000 pounds sterling) with William

John Wills to find the first south to north passage across the continent. They succeeded but died of starvation on the return trip.

Considerable space is given in the museum to its gold history, to a re-created "street" of Victorian times with wall-sized, historic murals, to Ned Kelly, the notorious bushranger who was a native son.

One of the town's attractions is "Ned Kelly's Cell" in the old gaol. He was charged, incorrectly according to his present-day supporters, with beating up a Chinese man, tried and found guilty in the Beechworth courthouse. He was jailed in a solitary cell for three months without so much as a change of clothing. He was sixteen years old.

The wrong, according to his supporters, turned him against the law and he and his brother Dan and two others became the "Kelly Gang" famous for taking over police stations, telegraph communications, removing the contents of banks and gold treasuries. The signature of the gang was armoured helmets and vests that looked like they were made out of old hot water heaters.

Unfortunately during one of their escapades a policeman was killed and later Ned Kelly was shot, captured, nursed back to health so he could be hanged which occurred in Melbourne in November, 1880. He was twenty-six.

The Beechworth area offers an interesting microcosm of gold history.

When gold was discovered in 1852, the metal was taken out with pick and shovel and simple gold pans like we had used. When gold stopped in 1956, it was being extracted with a mammoth floating dredge, the largest in the world. It stands there still outside of Wangaratta, alone in a muddy pond, slowly rusting away.

Richer Gold Finds

I have a more formidable sample of gold in front of me in a glass vial filled with water. Painted black on one side so you can better see the gold flakes inside is a fairly respectable pile of precious metal. It is measurable.

On the outside of the vial is imprinted, in gold letters naturally, "Gold Panned in Red Hill Gully, Sovereign Hill, Ballarat."

When the government of Victoria heard of the gold exploitation in New South Wales, they were properly concerned that their population would leave for the northern goldfields and they quickly became involved in the hunt offering sizeable rewards for payable gold finds.

If anything, the effort worked too well.

Rich findings of gold were discovered in a stretch of land running south from Bendigo through Castlemaine to Ballarat, a distance of one hundred kilometres.

Gold hungry novices abandoned cottages, businesses, farms and schools. But new bodies flooded the state. The population of Victoria increased from 71,000 in 1850 to 267,000 four years later and by 1859 was over a half a million!

The entire Bendigo-Ballarat district still is a living exhibit of those golden days of Victoria.

In Bendigo you can stay, as we did, at the Welcome Stranger Motel, visit the Central Deborah Gold Mine which goes down seventeen levels and take the "Talking Tram" tour through the city on weekends, the last of Bendigo's municipal street car lines.

In the lobby of the motel is a replica of the "Welcome Stranger" nugget, the largest such nugget found in the world, which had a gross weight of 2,520 ounces. Its net weight after being cleaned was 2,284 ounces. (The gold taken out of the washed off material weighed almost two pounds and it was estimated that the discoverers probably knocked off another pound of bits to give to friends as souvenirs!)

The two miners were Richard Oates and John Deason and it was reported that the nugget was unearthed by a rut made by their cart.

In the lobby is also a picture of Mr. and Mrs. John Deason looking very staid . . . and prosperous.

In Bendigo you should stand in awe of the Shannon Hotel, now a government-owned building with an unknown future, which is a monument to Victorian taste. A jewel in its own right.

South of Bendigo in Castlemaine visit the Market Hall, a classic structure, appearing as a Greek building erected only yesterday. It was built in 1862 and is now an excellent museum with well-done audio-visual presentations. First rate. Robert O'Hara Burke was also a superintendent of police in Castlemaine in 1858, three years before the successful but fatal expedition.

Ballarat is the undisputed star of Australian gold-mining towns.

With a population around 60,000, it is the largest inland city in Victoria, about the same size when it was ballooned by miners who came to dig in the richest alluvial deposit in the world.

Eleven years before the finding of the "Welcome Stranger" at Bendigo, the "Welcome" nugget had been dug out of Red Hill at Ballarat. The almost solid gold chunk weighed 2,195 ounces.

As part of our research of the Red Hill Gully, we expected to find something just a bit smaller. After all we had paid a 20¢ licence fee which included a gold pan. The result of a half an hour's work — and we suspect a bit of planting by the management — is in the vial in front of me.

Red Hill Gully is part of the Sovereign Hill Gold Mining Township recreated by the Ballarat Historical Association.

Everything this association has accomplished is superb. Sovereign Hill, for example, is a fascinating, live, educational reproduction of the step-by-step methods of extracting gold over a fifty year period of development.

The first method was by gold panning in the hilly creek that cascades through Red Hill Gully.

You, and the children, can pan for gold. Ninety-five percent of the panners find "colour."

As the alluvial gold from streams disappeared, mine shafts were dug.

Means of extracting the gold became more sophisticated progressing through cradles, where the rock and muck were washed away by hand, to mill ponds where a horse circling around a pond harnessed to a rake performed the same function.

Finally, the dirt ran out and gold-bearing quartz had to be broken up first with giant wheels and then with giant hammers.

The shafts went deeper and deeper. Wind was diverted down the shafts by the use of sails, adapted from ships, to ventilate the mines.

At each new depth, the dangers multiplied.

A miner had to have a mate. It was a job impossible to do alone. His life depended upon the man on top who wound the windlass, who lowered the bucket or "kibble" . . . a carelessly kicked rock could kill the miner below.

The mining partners slept in the same miserable conditions together. Got drunk together. Made or lost a fortune together.

It would be interesting to know just how much of today's still dominant Australian "matesmanship" goes back to the inherited blood brotherships of the mining days.

The Red Hill Gully is a fine example of the days of alluvial gold mining. One appreciation comes through clearly. In the rough and tough times of the early miners only the strong survived.

When the alluvial gold ran out and the mine shafts no longer produced payable metal, the third phase of mining came into being.

Next to Red Gully is a recreated typical quartz mining operation which existed in Ballarat from 1860 to 1918.

Here gold-bearing reefs of quartz were dug out of the ground, stamped to powder and the gold extracted. It took money and machinery, engineering and science. The day of the individual gold miner was essentially over.

Above the ground you can look over steam-powered engines and compressors, stamping batteries to crush the gold-bearing quartz, vibrating machines to separate the gold from the tailings.

Below ground, in airy, well-lighted tunnels, you are shown the progression of quartz mining from small parties of men using manpower and primitive tools to present day blasting and diamond drilling.

In digging one of the exhibit tunnels, workers broke into a real previously mined tunnel where you can see how pioneers followed a reef of gold through the earth and hollowed out what must have been a major find.

Above Red Hill Gully and the Mining Museum is the Sovereign Hill Gold Mining Township. The Main Street of the township is lined with recreated shops of the 1850's. If the buildings look relatively new, remember that in 1850 they were new.

Everything is functional. The Apothecary Shop sells soap and other good smellies. Dilges' Blacksmith's makes horseshoes for the carriage horses which are hitched up for rides down Main Street and through the Gully. The Red Hill Photographic Rooms takes mid-century costume pictures. The Ballarat Times prints posters.

Confectionery shop, bakery, tinsmith, foundry, joss house, school house, furniture factory, dressmaker, shirtmaker, they all function.

Up the street next to the United States Hotel, the Victorian Theatre gives week-end performances.

The Victorian Theatre replaced the Adelphi Theatre which along with the original United States Hotel was destroyed by fire in 1855, killing one of the three American partners. The new theatre was opened on February 16, 1856 with a performance by the infamous Lola Montez whose "Spider Dance" blew the moralists right out of their church pews.

Lola Montez was born in Limerick, Ireland as Maria Dolores Eliza Rosanna Gilbert in 1818 which meant at the time of her appearance she was a mature thirty-eight.

She had seen a bit of track first as a courtesan and then upon graduation as the mistress to Ludwig of Bavaria.

Lola Montez was a pale-skinned, black-haired wench with wild, laughing blue eyes coupled with a cupid mouth. She was a sexy sensation.

The editor and founder of the Ballarat Times, Henry Seekamp, himself a fiery personality, incurred the Lola Montez wrath when he accused her of immoral conduct. She responded by horsewhipping him through the bar of the United States Hotel.

The entire Sovereign Hill operation is top-notch. Well planned, well run. But the best is yet to come.

Across the parking lot is another Ballarat Historical Park Association accomplishment: The Gold Museum.

It is magnificent.

Phase I of the three-part project has already been completed.

The handsomely modern, low-lying building contains an exhibit lobby known as the Buckland Gallery and in the interior — there is a modest entry fee — the remarkable Jessica and Paul Simon Gold Pavilion.

Paul Simon's passion was finding gold and collecting gold coins. He believed the history of mankind could be told by his collection and after his death in 1972 his widow, Jessica, and the Ballarat Historical Park Association began the fulfilment of his ideas.

It is beautifully done ... dramatically displayed and lighted ... and invaluable in content. Simon's gold collection alone, before the gold boom, was estimated to be worth around three and a half million dollars.

The story the museum tells starts in Mesopotamia and moves through the early Greek civilisations, the gold treasures of Africa, the ancient treasures of Latin America, the Medieval and Renaissance periods of European history.

One exhibit — number three of thirteen — has in the centre of the room a relief map which shows forty-four gold-bearing creeks in the Ballarat district where Paul Simon and his friend, Jim Jones, explored for gold. By pressing a button on a drum-shaped exhibit case a light shines on the sample ounce of gold taken from the area which also is indicated by a red light on the relief map.

Around the circular ceiling eighteen slide projectors unfold a ten-minute presentation on the Saga of Gold.

The whole pavilion is of such calibre.

The glamorous coins of history (actual coins, not duplicates, are shown): the ducat, the piece of eight, the Roman denarius, the sovereign and the silver penny of William the Conqueror.

Unfolding along with the sample coins is the history of the hunt for gold in different countries — Australia, Great Britain, Europe, the Middle East, the Americas, India and Africa, South Africa — and in different eras.

I really want to stand on my typewriter and applaud the whole operation — the Sovereign Hill Township, Red Hill Gully, the Mining Museum, the Gold Museum — and especially the staff and membership of the Ballarat Historical Park Society, a non-profit organisation which has only been in business since 1966.

What great imagination has brought to life such great exhibits . . . obviously with great effort.

Interestingly, of the 400,000 people who visit the area every year, about ten percent are overseas visitors. Someone has the good word. Alone . . . by itself . . . Ballarat is deserving of a trip from overseas.

In early March the city holds a Begonia Festival . . . a perfect time to go. Don't miss the lovely pubs and the Victorian architecture in the city while you are there.

The City of Opals

Coober Pedy invites exaggeration.

Over ninety per cent of Australia's fiery opals come from Coober Pedy.

Fortunes have been made in Coober Pedy in the space of a few months' time.

Luxurious homes are built underground to avoid the heat. Even a church has been built underground.

All true.

The other side of the story is that Coober Pedy is isolated in the most desolate part of Australia, six hundred kilometres northwest of Adelaide, reached only by a tough, dusty road or by air.

Approaching the Coober Pedy gravel airstrip on Opal Airlines from Adelaide, the surrounding countryside looked like an abandoned battlefield: pits, trenches, bomb craters, all clearly delineated by outlines of white earth.

We were hustled into a dusty bus and driven the few miles into town. The legendary village didn't look much better at ground level.

Every car and truck (all speeding) left rooster tails of dust which settled on shacks above the ground many of which had strange, giant pieces of equipment parked in the yard.

The bald, treeless centre of town had a cluster of stores, a post office, a Greek restaurant, a Chinese restaurant and the Opal Inn Motel-Hotel whose sidewalk directory listed room numbers for Hong Kong opal buyers.

Our room, in the newest wing, was somewhat distinctive by four-letter words written in dust on its window.

The bus driver, Tom Campagna, said he'd be back for us after lunch to go touring. After he had left we looked at each other with mutual why-did-we-book-ourselves-into-this-hole-for-two-days expressions.

Depressing.

What you do under these circumstances is to laugh, make yourself a cup of tea and wash the windows.

We did.

From then on Coober Pedy, meaning "white man digging" in Aborigine language, began to take on rare characteristics. It is the damndest town in the world.

Consider the population. When the full work force of miners — all working for themselves — returns to Coober Pedy after the summer hot spell the population is close to 5,000. During the post-war boom the miners were predominantly Italian who built the Italian Club for after-mining socialising. Now the population is mostly Greek (forty per cent) and Yugoslavians (thirty per cent) and Greek and Croatian clubs have sprung up.

When the first opals were discovered on top of the ground after World War I, it brought an influx of miners. Civilisation centred around a post office and a store. But life was hard. Camel trains brought the only water.

It was not until 1919 that the first Model T Ford reached Coober Pedy. The car was called "Wilful Murder." A second car was named "Sudden Death."

The mine field declined over the depression years. By 1940 there were only thirty-four men left, mostly pensioners scratching at the earth.

In the post-war II period new interest was shown in opals which was reflected in soaring prices particularly in overseas markets. New mining techniques made financially possible by more rewarding prices brought the new boom to Coober Pedy after the rich "Eight Mile" field was discovered by an Aboriginal stockman in 1946.

How do you mine for opal?

It depends on how much money you have.

Everyone must buy a prospecting licence, $10 a year.

You find a place which you think might hold opals ... and you find a "trace."

You can peg off only a maximum of fifty square metres ... and you register the location of your claim within thirty days after pegging. You have fourteen days to post your registration number on your pegs.

Only one claim can be registered at a time and not more than four adjoining claims can be amalgamated for working. Opal mining is basically an individual operation.

Now you and your partner — you never work solitary in the opal fields — pick and shovel straight down hauling gravel to the surface with a hand winch and you wash the tailings for a glint of opal. Tough work but you don't have any money. And you dig deeper and deeper and deeper. If you haven't found a productive trace below ninety feet you give up because the old stream beds holding opals don't exist below that level.

But let's say you have money.

Ah ... now you hire, or you own, a giant auger like a telephone pole digger to drill the test bore and bring up samples.

You find a "trace."

You hire a Caldwell driller which can sink a three-foot diameter shaft from surface to ninety feet in a single day. You find a vein of opal. You widen the first tunnel to ten feet square and at the productive level you bore a horizontal shaft with a miniature tractor; its rotating blade in the front takes out the white soil. A spotlight on the tractor catches any tell-tale glitter of opal which is carefully removed.

A second vertical tunnel supplies air and a blower pumps fresh air into the workings while a giant suction machine evacuates the remains of dirt to the surface piling it into white mullock heaps.

A faster and cheaper method for shallow opal is open cut mining. You lease a giant bulldozer whose owner will work for a sizeable percentage of the find, remove all the dirt from the top down to the level of opal. The remains of dirt must stay within the registered claim thereby reducing the potential of the mine. There is also a risk of destroying the opal in the process of finding it.

Is opal mining dangerous in itself? Yes.

Six weeks before our arrival three miners were trapped in a tunnel weakened by an unseasonable rain. They had gone back to work the water-logged silica sand too soon. Two of the bodies had been flown back to Greece.

In 1978 nine people were killed.

About once or twice a year they lose a tourist! Signs on all roads leading to the mines warn the visitor to watch for abandoned shafts. The shafts plummet straight down. A careless step could ruin your whole day.

Tom Campagna picked us up in a passenger car — we were his entire "tour group" that day — and we rattled out of town over a corrugated road, the "highway" which we soon left for a barely discernible trail into the bush.

Italian-born Tom and his wife Pat from Alice Springs had an above-ground home in the middle of Coober Pedy, a large bus, a small airport bus and an assortment of cars for hire.

Tom also had a claim staked in the Olympic Field south of Coober Pedy which he thought would bring him riches and his wife thought would bring him nothing more than a backache.

He said in Coober Pedy there was no political entity. No town council.

There was a school built with South Australian government money, a police station, a branch of the Mines Department, a hospital.

A "Progress Association" had raised funds to build a town hall and the association also owned the town's drive-in theatre. Profits were directed into community projects.

The need for a $6,000 ambulance was met in one night's pass-the-hat collection.

A strong community spirit exists in Coober Pedy.

We passed a barely discernible racetrack where Tom said "the Kentucky Derby" was run the first week of October.

"But where do the horses come from?"

"Oh, around," he waved his arms in a vast manner which took in several million empty acres.

We toured the diggings. It was mid-afternoon and no one was working. During summer months, if you haven't made enough money to go on vacation, you go to work at three in the morning and quit at ten a.m. If you are working underground, the temperature won't change but above ground where somebody is manning the equipment temperatures soar to over 120° Fahrenheit.

Around us were heaps of mullock ten to fifteen feet high.

Inside of those piles of white chalky waste were overlooked opals.

The looking, scratching, digging process through mullock is called "noodling" and for a half an hour we noodled.

And found opals. Flecks of opal. Tiny pieces of opal. Pale, not-glittering, not-flashing opal but junk which is called "potch."

Legally you should have permission to noodle on a claimed mine but it didn't seem to be of consequence.

Later we were to see Aboriginal families noodling the mullock piles with sieves. "There'll be nothing left there," Tom said.

Also we saw professional noodle machines in which the debris is conveyed through a black lighted darkroom where an operator can easily spot the colour.

The strangest sight, however, was a man in the distance walking with his arms out in front of him.

"Look, he has iron rods in his hands, you know, like you find water?"

"You mean divining rods?"

"Yes. Some people believe they can find opal with iron rods. The rod will bend when it passes over opal. It makes most people laugh. Watch now, he'll put away the rods so we won't know what he is doing. See!"

The opal searcher tucked the rods along the side of his trousers and looked the other direction.

We drove out to The Breakaways, the edge of the Stuart Ranges, which from the cliff height looks across to the start of the Never-Never land, a painted desert of varying colours. In the distance we could see the faint straight line of the "dingo fence" which goes from sea to sea.

At the foot of this escarpment the first opals were found in alluvial bedstreams in 1915 ... bedstreams which now go underneath the cliff and are found "inland" at different levels.

Back in town we visited the site of the mineral probably more precious than opal: the town's water supply.

Bore water, heavy with salt, at one time was desalinated through a slow, lugubrious, solar evaporation process. Pure water was rationed to fifty gallons per person every two weeks.

Now bore water is processed by osmosis filters. It takes three gallons of bore water to make one gallon of fresh water. The excess water is used for fire control, toilets and the making of concrete.

We visited Umoona Opal Mine with the museum above ground and an actual former mine underground, both fascinating.

We went to the home of Faye Nayler, sister of our Kimberley tour driver, who has been a successful opal miner buyer and seller and has a luxurious underground home with carpets and indoor pool — *cold* water in the pool. An indoor fireplace was faced with jasper stones.

We visited the underground church of St. Peter and St. Paul where a side altar is made of petrified and opalised mussels and petrified wood and stones of jasper.

The Lady Navigator went "noodling" in opal shops. Very interesting. Very expensive. Read the chapter on shopping.

I sought out Sgt. Dave Habich of the police force to talk about the characteristics of Coober Pedy.

"Coober Pedy has become domesticated in the last six years. Most of the men are now married and have their wives here. Our school now teaches five hundred children.

"We have the occasional drunk or disorderly charge but we are like any other small town with a juvenile problem. Kids in cars. That kind of thing.

"The town sticks together. There is an identity.

"A good rain can isolate Coober Pedy for four days at a time. No TV. No newspaper. We have to get along."

We asked about stories we had read of gunfights in the opal fields. Hijacking. Robberies, that kind of thing.

"Well, the 'night shifters' or 'ratters' still exist and we get about a dozen incidents a year: pirate miners going out at night to work someone else's claim. Many cases probably are not reported because the informer could find his machinery filled with sand, putting him out of business. To protect their interests some people live on a claim or hire someone to stay out there at night.

"Our biggest concern is for the tourists. We'll have a thousand tour buses through here in a year and every year one or two people drop down an old mine and the miners' rescue squad has to go out and find the body."

Our nearby Chinese neighbours from Hong Kong work in their permanently rented ground-floor motel units, their doors open at night inviting sellers, bent over cutting and polishing machines, cleaning up the opals they have bought during the day.

If you have $100,000 worth of opals to sell, that little man hunched over the desk will buy the stones from you . . . in cash. No receipt. No paper. No taxes.

The annual value of opal out of Coober Pedy is estimated between $12 million and $18 million. No one knows for sure.

The dramatic spotlight on the night-time table also catches the outline of a steel safe in the corner anchored in concrete.

A cooking pot is on the floor near the safe connected by an electronic embryo cord to the bathroom electric outlet.

The Chinese opal buyer cooks his own rice, makes his own tea.

Beautiful, Coober Pedy is not.

Fascinating, multi-coloured, like the opal? Yes, it is.

Gold! Gold! Gold! Go West, Young Man!

Little news items in the daily press tend to fan the hidden flames of greed.

A schoolgirl on the way to country school kicking over rocks finds a $2,000 nugget.

A metal detector dealer decided to put his stock of metal detectors to work and finds two fist-sized nuggets.

Another digger claims $9,200 worth of gold on a two weeks' vacation.

A nugget weighing almost ten pounds is found by a Perth butcher "somewhere out of Kalgoorlie" and insured for $160,000.

A grazier and an orchardist, part-time prospectors, unearth a thirteen pound nugget in the same area where the first payable gold was found in Australia in 1851 by Edward Hargrave. The orchardist uses the nugget for a doorstop for eight weeks and finally brings it to Sydney "in my truck with a load of apples."

When we finished driving the Nullarbor Plain and turned north at Norseman to Kalgoorlie we were heading for one of the former richest goldfields in Australia and because of today's gold prices the site of a born-again gold-mining industry. Kalgoorlie is also the target area of starry-eyed week-end prospectors with the golden chance of striking it rich.

It was Easter weekend and we had four days to spend in Kalgoorlie. What could be more perfect? An Easter Egg Hunt where we would really be looking for a *golden egg*.

Kalgoorlie is a most satisfactory gold town.

While it is in the heart of gold ghost towns, Kalgoorlie itself is still very much alive with a major gold mine still operating. Multi-million dollar investments have been approved to bring former marginal gold mines back into production.

The main street, Hannan Street, is an architectural delight, lined with ornate buildings constructed at the turn of the century when money came in large chunks . . . frequently.

For example, the Palace Hotel at the corner of Hannan Street and Maritana was built of granite taken from nearby quarries in 1897. It was considered the most luxurious hotel outside of Perth.

The furniture alone, shipped all the way from Melbourne, cost a fabulous $40,000.

The Palace had its own electric plant, its own fresh water system with water piped to the bathrooms!

An imported chef presided in the kitchen and six live turtles were on display in the vestibule to advertise the fact that there was nothing "mock" about the turtle soup on the menu.

Across the street the more photogenic gingerbread Exchange Hotel was built three years later in early English and Gothic style.

Down the street, named in his honour, is the statue of Paddy Hannan who discovered the first gold in Kalgoorlie. Born in Quin, the tiny village in County Clare, Ireland he went to Australia when he was twenty to work the fields as a miner and prospector at Ballarat and then New Zealand and, ultimately, throughout Australia.

Despite much government encouragement, the western part of the continent had proven almost valueless until 1886 when gold was found north in The Kimberley. Two thousand miners at one time worked at places like Halls Creek.

For ten years thereafter new finds followed a line which ran south from The Kimberley to Norseman at the edge of the Nullarbor. Sensational finds were made at Bayley's, later known as Coolgardie, just west of Kalgoorlie and then at Kanowna and Londonderry, north of Kalgoorlie.

Later, however, when miners following Hannan's discovery broke through the crust of ground at Kalgoorlie and its sister village Boulder, they found a dazzling depository of gold in an area about one mile square. "The Golden Mile" reached a peak annual production worth $180 million by today's market standards.

How it boomed.

In 1903 Kalgoorlie and Boulder had a combined population of 30,000 serviced by ninety-three hotels, eight breweries and five newspapers.

The State's population almost quadrupled (from 53,250 to 193,000) in a space of ten years in the 1890's.

The traditional vices of gold-rush times, gambling and prostitution, flourished then ... and still remain. The illegal "Two-Up," a coin-matching game, goes on in the backroom of a quiet club on Hannan Street seven nights of the week ... except on Miners' Paydays four times a month.

On Hay Street, one block west of Hannan, between Lane and Lionel in a block of cubicles, ladies of the evening work the oldest profession.

Both diversions have been a traditional part of the community since there was a community and are taken for granted as a normal part of the social scene.

Visitors wanting to appreciate gold-mining techniques and the difficulties of gold-mining can tour above and below the ground at the Hainault Gold Mine.

The mine was in production for over seventy years, finally closing in 1968.

In 1972 two young men, Ian Moffett and Doug Daws, bought the mine and opened it to the public.

Without charge you can visit the above ground plant: change

rooms, the boiler room, the gold room where the gold was poured into ingots, the assay room, etc. All the authentic buildings and equipment of a working mine.

The best part, however, is the tour underground; the fee is nominal. From the moment you select a hard helmet and enter the elevator to descend two hundred feet below the ground you feel transformed into a miner. The cage can drop at a rate of 1,200 feet a minute or faster depending upon the mood of the driver. There are ten levels, or drives, of the mine shaft. Each drive goes off horizontally following the veins of ore.

At the elevator level the miner hangs up his "crib," his box lunch ... and a safety device. If he doesn't come back for his lunch, his co-workers know there is a problem and go looking for him.

The underground tours are conducted by ex-miners.

Our portly, burly, big-handed, gentle guide showed us in a walking tour how mining progressed from hand and chisel digging to pneumatic drilling — "if the silicosis didn't kill you the noise would" — to modern-day diamond drilling.

Thirty holes are bored by the diamond drills in a pattern on a tunnel wall and exploded by nitropril in a sequence to shatter the rock from the face where it is loaded into cars on rails, taken to the shaft, brought to the surface and the quartz is "stamped" into fine particles from which the gold is extracted on sheets of mercury.

It formerly took two men a minimum of three to four shifts to make the same cut that is made today with one man, one diamond drill, in one shift.

Lighting progressed from candles (three per day per man) to smelly carbide lamps to electric torches.

Wages changed too. From a squeaky minimum living wage, miners still employed today make $200 a shift. Not all actually "mine." Workers underground include men laying rails (platers), timberers, pipers, ventilators, surveyors, scalers ... and a city of technicians.

At one point in the tour our guide stopped at a gaping hole in the earth and tossed in an empty tin ... and it clunked away into the dark ... farther away ... fainter ... fainter until the last distant tinkle.

The mine workings go a mile down.

The tour of the Hainault Gold Mine underground is Kalgoorlie's best attraction. It deserves the Sir David Brand Award it received for the 1973 outstanding contribution to tourism.

The mine attracts 40,000 visitors a year and provides a memorable experience for each one of them.

Enough of this viewing and gawking and listening.

Let's get out there and get the Golden Egg!

We signed up for an Easter Sunday afternoon Gold Detector Tour. "*Any gold you find is yours*"... providing you have a current Miners Right obtainable from the Mines Department for fifty cents which, of course, wasn't open on Sunday. Never mind. With our huge find we would work it out.

Also, on the Sunday tour was a scheduled trip on the Loop Line Railway... a community-run railroad which once hauled passengers and freight in a loop line from Kalgoorlie to Boulder; distance: three miles.

"Where it is, there it is," hooted our driver.

It wasn't there that Sunday.

We have been on many disastrous tours but this promised from the outset to be a Five-Star-Nothing-Is-Going-To-Work Tour.

1. Tour left late.
2. At the Loop Line terminal: "Can't get on," says the driver. "It's filled." He buys an ice cream cone.
3. "I've split me Daks," says the bus driver. (He's ripped his trousers.) He drives home with one hand, holding ice cream cone in other hand. Dashes inside. Comes outside with trousers in one hand, ice cream cone in other.
4. Drive out to the goldfields. Goldminer who was to show us how to work a stake — he makes $100 a day according to the driver — has gone home.
5. Visit former gold town of Kanowna. Population 12,000 (the driver says 45,000). Formerly held a hospital, race track, tennis club, courthouse, post office, a railroad station. Today there is nothing left. *Nothing*. Driver has old time photographs of how the gold town used to look. "Damn. Brought the wrong photographs."
6. We go prospecting. The bus driver has *four* metal detectors for the *ten* passengers. Demonstrates briefly how the machines work. No instruction about where to look. Goes back into bus and goes to sleep.
7. Lady Navigator and I get a metal detector and go sweeping left

and right into the country. Big buzzing sound. Dug up top to old tin can. Big buzzing sound. Found empty 303 rifle cartridge.
8. Went home without Golden Easter Egg.
There was one good thing about the trip. The driver didn't ask for a tip.

If the Metal Detector tour on Sunday was unproductive it didn't matter. We had found gold on Saturday when we met the Mayor of Kalgoorlie at the beautiful Town Hall. Our scheduled short chat lasted an hour and a half.

Mayor Ray Finlayson, sixty-two, doesn't have a grey hair. Although he doesn't look like a man who gets much exercise, he gets a lot of work for an official who has been mayor since 1976, has never had a day off and doesn't get paid.

"In 1976 when most of the mines closed letting seven hundred and fifty wage-earning miners go, we were in trouble. There had to be a lot of help on both sides of the fence, from union and from management. Leadership. Guidance.

"From 1976 to 1979 we faced three bad years and we had to get the people, the land people, the store owners, the bankers together.

"We had to change from being a wage-earning community to a service and supply centre.

"I got the bankers together — you know they didn't even know each other! — and I said, 'Who are the first people that needy businesses turn to when they are in trouble? To you, the bankers. You have to be optimistic. If you aren't, you'll spread gloom. We have to borrow money to create jobs.'

"Hotels were to be specialists in their attention to tourists. We promoted ourselves on a regional basis. 'The Heart of Gold.' From Esperance to Laverton. 'Come to Kalgoorlie on your way to . . .' That was and is our theme.

"I got the prime minister and the big businesses together. 'Look,' I said, 'you are going to spend $300 million mining nickel at Agnew. We want part of it to flow through Kalgoorlie.' Charlie came through magnificently." (Sir Charles Court, the premier).

"So did the companies. I'd get a call and the man would say, 'Hey, Ray, so-and-so's tender on that contract is too high. He won't get it.'

" 'What would it take to get it?' He'd mention a figure and then I'd call the service contractor. I would never tell him what was wrong and what the proper figure had to be on his contract bid, but he'd get the message and he'd end up with the contract. More money for Kalgoorlie.

"We're safe now. We have two of the largest nickel provinces in the world at Kambalda and at Agnew ... probably four hundred kilometres of ore. Nickel you have to have for making steel.

"Gold is going back into production. We have it all. Black opals have been found outside Coolgardie. Diamonds in The Kimberley. You know the scarcest mineral? Water. Now we have enough water too; piped up from Perth.

"We'll double our population in ten years. We're home."

The mayor spoke in such a quiet tone, pleasantly, directly. No showboating. No political bragging. We felt free to ask him a couple of delicate questions.

"You have the reputation of being a controversial mayor," I said. "That is difficult to understand talking to you."

"Oh, well." His eyes sparkled at remembered incidents. "My job has been to sell the community. I'd enter into the most controversial issues. Make the most outlandish statements just to get the name Kalgoorlie in front of people."

"Name one incident," we urged.

"I could name twenty. There was the time that the state administration tried to pass a Miners Act which was a bad act in my opinion so I had a flat-bed wagon pulled into the middle of town and advertised a public debate on the bill and invited the premier and his minister of mines to come. Of course Charlie didn't show up and on television I tore a copy of the act in two and threw the pieces into the crowd. Oh, it was a scene. Charlie has never forgiven me.

"They used to say, 'The bugger is never off of the bloody television.' But it was a deliberate campaign to make sure that Kalgoorlie wasn't forgotten. We could have become a ghost town. Now our future is assured for the next hundred years. We aren't just a gold town anymore but a multi-mineral service centre."

What about the gambling and the girls?

"Two-Up is the fairest gambling game that has ever been invented. It is particularly well controlled. There is a balance, you know, of common sense and the spirit of acceptance on the part of the community. That is the determining factor."

And the girls?

"Same thing. Bringing these madams into court is hypocritical. The government is willing to take their taxes. If they come into my court — I'm also a justice of the peace — I fine them $5 if I fine them anything and let them go. I'm too busy to waste government time and energy.

"I think our system is better than city massage parlours. If anything, I'd rather see the girls in better buildings with better prophylactic facilities.

"You know, the few of them that I have met are interesting people."

Easter evening I went to the Two-Up game in the back room of the United Nations Club. It was in full swing.

(There is a second "recognised" game out in the bush on the road to Menzies. About three miles out turn off the track at the forty-gallon drum. You'll find it.)

The only no-no's are (1) no betting on pay day, (2) no drinking and (3) no women.

Looking like a ground-level snooker table, a solid rectangle of men grouped around a fifteen by ten-foot piece of felt framed by a foot-high railing which kept the tossed coins in the playing area.

A bench around the rectangle provided seating for one line of men. A second line of men stood behind the benches.

Overhead lights, just like on a pool table, gave a theatrical touch to the action. A line of string was stretched taut at the level of the lights.

Two-Up is a simple match game.

Two coins are tossed high enough to clear the overhead string from a small wooden paddle. The paddle prevents manual manipulation. You win if you back 'heads' and 'heads' shows on both coins. Same with tails. If the coins don't match, there is no play. Toss again.

A ring master controls the game.

Most of the bets were $20 and over made by the men on the benches. The mood in the room and in the crowd was electric and the explosive involvement of the participants was accented by a surprising amount of money changing hands in a short period of time.

It was not a place for beginners and I took my tuition money — untouched — back into the Easter night.

On the way to the motel I detoured through the "action" block of Hay Street.

The doors were open and the red lights were casting a forbidden glow over the ladies who were standing, sitting, lounging . . . waiting for the trade just as they had in Galilee two thousand years ago.

Peace on earth.

Since our visit, the traditional game of two-up, according to a Western Australia official, has been "descriminalised." Two kilometers due north of Kalgoorlie is the tiny town of Broken Arrow. There you can find a legitimate, no-arrest game of two-up.

Also the official reported that Hay Street is still operational and Mona, the famous madame, is still in command.

13. Let's Have a Party! Festival Time

It's easy to understand that a country as large as Australia populated for so long by so few people would be eager to initiate any excuse for a get-together.

Being exuberant by nature the Australians have year-around celebrations for one cause or another in every section of the country. It's party time!

Here are a few:

The Sheer Nonsense Festivals

A unique, piquant humour often lies sub-surface in the Australian character.

The Henley-on-Todd event in Alice Springs puts this quaint trait squarely out in the open.

Where else would you mimic the famous English crew races at Henley-on-Thames in Oxfordshire than on the barren Todd River, dry-gulched ninety-nine percent of the year, which "runs" through the middle of Alice Springs.

C.W. West Lau, a Dutchman by family origin, was the first "admiral" of the now-famous spoof event.

"It started one year in Rotary. We were thinking of fresh ways to raise money and have a bit of fun when the Henley-on-Thames came into the conversation and it was suggested that we have a similar event in Alice Springs." The fact that the River Todd was always dry didn't bother the lads from Rotary. They made "boats" out of boat frames which were put around two-man crews, four-man crews, eight-man crews and the crews ran from one point of the dry river to another. Great sport.

"The first year," said West Lau, "only four hundred people showed up. It was a bloody disaster. But everyone got a little drunk and they ran the races and said to each other, 'Thank God that's over.'

"Then the next year they thought they would try it again. Well, Henley-on-Todd caught the eye of the press and the event just took

FESTIVALS

1. HENLEY-ON-TODD
2. BEER CAN REGATTA
3. ADELAIDE FESTIVAL
4. BAROSSA VALLEY
5. JACARANDA
   FESTIVAL
6. AUSTRALIAN
   COUNTRY MUSIC
   AWARDS
7. NARIEL CREEK
   FESTIVAL

off from there. B.B.C. sent a television camera team. Famous journalists from around the world started to show up. The publicity was astounding.

"A university in America, seriously, wanted to send over a rowing team. Yale, if memory serves me. 'Wait,' we said, 'this is a joke.'

"Now it is incredible. Schools all over Australia train for the event. This year there will be fifty teams. Thousands and thousands of spectators come. Not a bed in town.

"Oh, now, we have lots of events. We duplicate life surfing events on the dry sand. We have a greased pole contest. A Miss Henley contest. To get rid of the kids during the judging for Miss Henley we have an airplane fly over a nearby pasture and drop a sheaf of cards. If a kid gets a card with a number on it, he gets a free ice cream. Actually they all get a free ice cream; we just want to get them out of the way.

"Last year we split about $12,000 in profits among various charities.

"A couple of years ago we had a terrible emergency. It rained. There was water in the river. But we got hold of a contractor, a Rotarian, who bought in equipment to shove the river around and create enough dry land to permit us to hold the races. Close. Very close."

The Henley-on-Todd August event is preceded on the Alice Springs calendar of events by the Bangtail Muster Rodeo and followed by the Lions Club Annual Camel Races.

Darwin, capital of the Northern Territory, not to be outdone, stages an annual Regatta like no other regatta in the world.

Darwinites are known for their prowess in drinking beer. The "Darwin Stubby" for example, is the size of a large fire extinguisher.

But you won't find a thrown-away beer can anywhere in Darwin. Collecting beer cans, the symbol of modern day sloppiness, is a year-around anti-litter occupation because of the Beer Can Regatta.

Rowing boats, rafts, power boats, "yachts" are made out of disposable "tinnies" and floated in the harbour during the Queen's Day celebration.

You just have to assume that the winners get free beer.

Not to be forgotten in the nonsense category is an Australian World Gum Boot Throwing Championship.

Another is the National Cow Chip Throwing Competition. According to a documentary film we saw, texture is all important. Nothing worse than a wet chip. It was said in the film that "America has the record now but we've got the men and we certainly have the cow chips."

The Glorious Adelaide Festival

Another kind of Australian festival is the art and cultural category and certainly the oldest, largest and most expensive ($3 million!) is the Adelaide Festival, held every even-number year.

It is dazzling.

Brilliant and daring in concept, the Adelaide Festival is several steps above anything else in Australia.

In 1960 the Adelaide Festival moved its axis to a modern Festival Centre built between the railroad station and the Torrens River in the middle of the city. Events spread from there throughout the city.

Over a three-week period in March some sixty-plus groups — local, national, international — give multiple performances of opera, ballet, plays, films.

It is huge, permeating every corner of Adelaide.

(We are not writing about cities but Adelaide must be a favourite cosmopolitan spot for every overseas visitor. The city combines country charm and city sophistication in an appealingly balanced degree. We found ourselves making excuses to sneak back to Adelaide on weekends from remote corners of South Australia not only to take in the festival events but also enjoy the city for itself. Outstanding restaurants. The Rundle Mall has to be the most successful shopping and social mall in the country. Great fruit stands. The Torrens River and the green core of parks and river which make up the visual centre of the city is as urban planners would have it — a gift of far-seeing forefathers.)

We had the good fortune to see the East Berlin ballet company of the Komishce Oper, Berlin, perform an entirely new version of *Swan Lake*, defrocked of gossamer and feathers and recast into a mythical dance drama of a spiritual and political struggle. Meticulous dancing such as you would expect from the Germans. Simple sets. Fantastic costumes. A provocative experience.

Cultural Culinary Note:
After the ballet we stopped at the pie cart across the street from the hotel and had a famous "Adelaide Floater."

The dish is a meat pie swimming in hot pea soup. If you can keep your eyes closed while eating it, the concoction tastes quite good.

Even more provocative was *Conversation of the Birds* by Peter Brook's Paris-based Centre for International Theatre Creations which was performed in an old quarry during a freezing night. Magic. Simple theatre magic.

Peter Brook is probably the most revered director in the Western World today and the fact that the Adelaide Festival brought the director and his troupe was accolade enough.

As part of the Festival, he gave two public interviews, one of which we attended. More magic. To watch this soft-mannered, polite man is to feel his inbred intensity and intelligence. It was quite an experience to hear him take each question ... pause on it ... turn it ... and regardless of the question's value convert it into a thoughtful theatre essay.

Staging a happening as big as the Adelaide Festival invites criticism, as it should.

The director resigned or was fired and walked off with cigarette holder atilt firing potshots at the city's "provincialism."

The press, much of it from other urban areas and perhaps just tinged with a bit of jealousy, flayed several productions as "failures" thereby insinuating that the entire festival was a bomb.

Nonsense.

All artistic directors want to be given a pot full of money and complete authority on how it is going to be spent, as much as anything to please their own artistic vanities without subjecting their programmes to the people who put up the money. Unrealistic.

And in a programme as broad and as ambitious as the Adelaide Festival there are no "failures" ... there are only disappointments.

Many of the international productions appear at the Festival first, then disperse around Australian cities playing the rest of the country so, in fact, it is a national festival and one which we heartily enjoyed.

First rate.

Wine Festivals

The Barossa Valley Vintage Festival, an hour north of Adelaide, is the best example of an industrial festival.

Most major wine producing areas have an annual vintage party of one sort or another but the Barossa, held in odd-numbered years, is a major week-long April event.

With its strong German heritage there is an easy theme to follow. Very photogenic with lederhosen and peasant skirts and Teutonic bonnets and hats and oom-pah-pah music.

A rare wine auction with a charity as the beneficiary is held in the basement of the Kaiser Stuhl Chateau.

Food and tasting and fun combined into a gay package including dances, picnics, dinners . . . and wine, wine, wine.

Flower Festivals

The first flower festival in Australia was at Grafton where an early (1870) seed merchant was responsible for planting the jacaranda tree — not just one but a solid line of jacarandas down one street. That led to other avenues being planted with the flowering tree.

We saw the last of the October and November blossoming and it turned the city into a glorious mauve-to-purple arboretum.

The Jacaranda Festival is held the last week of October and *everyone* gets involved. (The Jacaranda Queen attends over seventy functions.)

There are school displays, kiddies in tableaux with crepe paper costumes, parades, an Olympics; the streets are decorated from Bacon Street to Sea Park amid the blossoming of four thousand trees.

Darwin also has a Bougainvillea Festival in July but the city freely admits that the blossoming of the plant is just incidental to the real purpose of getting together and having *fun*. Maybe drink a little beer.

Music Festivals

Music festivals are another common denominator in getting together in Australia.

Tamworth in the New England district of New South Wales boasts the largest country music get-together in the nation for the "Australian Country Music Awards," a January event attended by an astonishing number of visitors.

It is not just a country-style hoe-down but a very professional award event which is used as a standard of excellence — and promotion — throughout the industry.

Music is traditional, progressive, gospel, bluegrass, steel guitar.

The organisers import international country singing stars for guest appearances. Songwriters' meetings, national banjo pickers' championship, a steel guitar convention, charity concerts, square dancing, barbecues . . . it is all there.

Highlight of the long weekend is the Gold Banjo presentation to the winners who also get their names immortalised in brass on the Hall of Fame Cornerstone.

The Country Music Awards is organised and proudly professional. The Nariel Creek Annual Black & White Folk Festival, by contrast, is described in its own literature as "non-political, non-religious, non-profit-making."

Nariel Creek is a thirty-kilometre long farming valley eight kilometres south of Corryong.

Corryong in turn is a tiny town just inside the border of Victoria tucked under the shadow of the Snowy Mountains. In fact Corryong's claim to fame is that its cemetery holds the hero of Banjo Paterson's famous poem, *The Man from Snowy River:*

"He hails from Snowy River, up Kosciusko's side, where
the hills are twice as steep and twice as rough."

The festival is an informal gathering of *anyone* who wants to perform. The programme reads:

"Where Folk Singers, Musicians, Dancers, Poets, Reciters, Tall Story-Tellers, etc. from all Australian States and Overseas, meet and compare their individual Arts."

Why the venue of a creek-side camping ground?

During a folk dance gathering in Corryong, the local dancers were joined by campers vacationing in tents at Nariel Creek. The next night the local people were invited out to the camp site and an informal country music dance party was held with great success. It quickly became a tradition.

We attended the New Year Festival—there is a second festival during the Labour Day weekend in March—starting with the launching event, a Country Dance at the Memorial Hall. Admission, fifty cents. The music was provided by a piano, half a dozen concertinas and a drum.

Waltzes, reels, colonial dances. A junior group of sub-teenage concertina players took over at intermission and they were replaced in turn by a country western group playing square dance music.

The hall and dance floor became more and more crowded and soon a hundred or so dancers were stomping their feet and clapping their hands in thunderous, dust-raising, wall-shaking time. The joy of dancing shone on their faces.

Costumes ranged from the colonists' swallow-tailed coats and dirndl skirts to today's denims, vests with muslin shirts, see-through blouses without bras, ballet slippers and bare feet. (Signs everywhere said "shoes must be worn.")

The scene the next night at Nariel Creek camping ground, New Year's Eve, was night life at its loosest.

The dance area was a large patch of lawn strung loosely with a few coloured lights around the perimeter; the area was at first covered with picnickers and imbibers. Mostly imbibers.

A hot food stand at the edge of the danceground was run by Rotary on a fourteen-hour stint. (Breakfast: bacon and eggs, $2. Tea: steak and tomatoes, $2.50.)

By ten p.m. the feasting was over and a country band mounted the rickety wooden stand and music time was underway. In less than a half hour the danceground was crowded — there had to have been five hundred dancers vying for a foot of grass. They had come from all over Australia to dance to the folk music beside Nariel Creek.

Children ran in and out among the dancers. Romping dogs ran after the children, tipping them over occasionally.

One very inebriated couple tumbled and fell on the dance lawn and stayed down kissing fervently, only stopping when the music stopped and finally rose slowly and staggered off in the dark direction of the creek bank.

The general costume motif was overalls and gum boots, T-shirts and scraps of cottons, and bits and pieces of colours and patterns.

A remarkable scene.

We went back the next afternoon to attend the Picnic Concert.

According to our informal guide, Keith Tregalgis, the three-hundred pound councilman (non-paid) who also runs the only remaining motion picture operation in northeast Victoria, there were about one thousand tents at the camping grounds.

(Keith also drives the school bus, repairs cars and washing machines. He replaced a burned out fuse in the Green Pony, gave us an extra replacement and refused compensation, finally agreeing to take fifty cents, the cost of the fuses.)

During the musicale of the afternoon Mrs. Klippel, a sweet featured lady whose deceased husband founded the festival, motioned me up to the stage where she was strumming a small wash board in time to the country music.

"Doesn't everybody seem to be having a good time?" she beamed.

Yes, everyone was having a good time.

A bit of skinny-dipping was going on farther up creek and one wondered if the scent of smoke in the air didn't have a touch of sweetness to it.

"It's 1980," said Keith, "not 1934.

"Drugs? We don't ask. We only look for decent behaviour. We just don't want the police telling everybody what to do."

An unusual admirable tolerance towards visitors with funny long hair and strange clothes from a small, conservative town.

Ethnic Festivals are a post-war development in Australia.

We went to the Glendi Greek Festival in Adelaide in March (the Italian Festival is in October) and enjoyed an evening of Grecian music and food and dances and drink. Have you ever tried ouzo and coke?

The agricultural shows are festivals in themselves and are major annual events in every major city.

The Royal Sydney Easter Show is a week-long affair and is the bell-ringer of all the shows.

HORSE RACES

1. THE MELBOURNE CUP
2. HANGING ROCK
3. GREAT WESTERN
4. THE HOBART CUP
5. KALGOORLIE CUP
6. THE GREAT EASTERN STEEPLECHASE
7. BIRDSVILLE

14. Following the Bangtails

The Australians' penchant for getting out in the open extends to risking their health and wealth at the hundreds of racetracks spread across the nation where over 3,000 race meetings for horses are run annually.

Of course you have to excuse the hordes of horse lovers who crowd into the off-course, government-regulated betting shops (TAB) you see in every Australian city, town and village.

These outdoorsmen are inside because they are susceptible to sunburn.

Savour this: in training in Australia are 30,000 — repeat, 30,000 — race horses.

The annual cost of keeping, feeding, training, paying vet bills, jockey bills, entry fees amounts to an average $5,000 per nag.

The total annual prize money is $50 million.

It works out then that the average winner would be $1,600. Take away the lopsided winnings of the big stake and Cup races won by a handful of champions and it becomes painfully obvious that owning a race horse is a very "iffy" proposition indeed.

The fact discourages absolutely no one in this land of gamblers.

They clamour all over each other to pay $40,000 to $100,000 for yearlings at the leading horse sales in Australia and New Zealand.

The Melbourne Cup

At two-forty on the first Tuesday afternoon of November the sporting world stands still.

All eyes, ears and pocketbooks open towards Flemington Racecourse.

It is the hour of the Melbourne Cup, the most famous horserace south of the equator . . . and the richest.

The first races in Melbourne were held on March 6th and 7th, 1838 on a track laid out between the present North Melbourne and Spencer Street Stations under the auspices of the new Melbourne Race Club.

Bullock carts served as grandstands and the weighing in was done with a butcher's scale.

Wagers were made in bottles of rum and one successful and inebriated punter wandered into the River Yarra and drowned.

In 1861 a second racing society in Melbourne, the Victorian Turf Club, inaugurated a new prestige race which they called The Melbourne Cup.

The steward on the Air New Zealand plane leaned into my ear just before the arrival in Melbourne and said, "Red Nose."

The fever of The Cup is hot-on-hot.

Everybody touts a sure horse.

The steward on the airplane (Red Nose), the taxi driver (Panamint), the bellboy (Earthquake McGoon), the waiter (Warri Symbol).

Fortunately we had a chance to go straight to The Source.

The day before the Cup is the Parade of Studs, a day for visitors to go to the leading stud farms around Melbourne. Miriam McMillan, our godmother from the Victorian Government Tourist office, took us to Stockwell Stud Farm, a splendid 1,000-acre property less than an hour out of Melbourne where three stallions worth more than $6 million serviced a line-up of waiting mares.

We were just in time to see and hear the owner of the farm, Kenneth Cox, a commanding figure in his sixties, comment on each stallion. Comeram, a French horse. Star Shower, a never-lose runner as a two-year-old. And Showdown, the farm's leading stallion, an eighteen-year-old of amazing fertility who had "covered" 790 mares successfully at an average of 1.64 services. Showdown's fee was $14,000.

The stipend visitors pay for this once-a-year public tour goes to the Children's Hospital which has received more than $60,000 from the Stockwell show over the years.

We toured the farm in company with Cox's son, Tim, and Jim Bell, a sheep farmer and horse owner.

Stockwell Stud Farm has video cameras which scan the mares in the paddocks constantly. The cameras are equipped with infra-red filters for night viewing. Whenever a mare with foal goes down to give birth, there is a professional handler out of a staff of ten in attendance. The barns and sick bay and hygienic covering shed were immaculate.

We visited the dams that irrigated the pastures and went into green paddocks where the mares and new foals grazed and romped.

If you love horses, there is a special thrill of being in a paddock with a herd of thoroughbreds frisking about, arching necks, stepping high, tossing their heads and manes, showing off.

Out of the car they snuzzle your hand hoping for sugar, nip your coat, shoulder each other out of the way. Handsome, glistening-coated creatures.

Back in the farm manager's house, Kenneth Cox had us sign the guest book just beneath the signature of the Aga Khan who had visited the farm the day before.

"It is over the yardarm. Way past in fact. Tim, pour a drink."

Besides Jim Bell, who we then learned was the owner of our first tip, Red Nose, was Hughie Gage whose horse, Gold and Black, had won the Cup in 1977. He had the cup at the farm and we were given the twelve-inch gold trophy to hold. Actually this trophy was a replica of the original which Mr. Gage had loaned to a leading bank for a window display. It was stolen. They found the thief but not the cup.

"More champagne will be consumed at Flemington tomorrow than in the whole of Australia," said Mr. Cox sipping a beer.

Would Dulcify, the heavy favourite, win?

"The odds are against it. Only three horses have won the Cup when they have been heavy favourites."

Who will win? (The delicate moment.)

"Cubacade," said Cox flatly. "Our manager, here, George Smith says Cubacade. He is never wrong."

We had the horse right here.

The red-coated band shattered the silence of the morning air of the Old Melbourne Inn at eight-thirty. The enthusiastic rock beat set the proper tempo for the Day of Days.

The cobblestoned courtyard of the hotel built to resemble an old country inn was the perfect setting for a champagne breakfast.

Two horses held by riders in hunters' red coats, white breeches and black boots, stood at ease, part of the themed atmosphere.

Formally dressed waiters in black coats and bow ties filtered through the courtyard with champagne and orange juice laden trays.

Guests equipped with binoculars and rain coats, well-tailored men, silk-dressed women nattered enthusiastically. Occasionally a hysteria-edge giggle peaked over the chatter.

Things were beginning to crackle with the excitement of the day.

At the stud farm, Kenneth Cox, known to his friends as "Cackle Cox," had asked, "Have you arranged for a car? No? You'd better do that right away. Expensive, mind you. Cost $170. Get him a car." He paused. "No. That's wrong. You won't get any story material that way. Take the train. Takes you right to the track. Take the train."

So, on the Day of Days, we left the Old Melbourne Inn with our shoulder bags containing notebooks and cameras and Members Reserve tickets and Members Car Park tickets, passed by the hired limousines, the personal Rolls Royces, the Jaguars, the chartered tour buses, crossed the street and took the tram to the railroad station.

The uncrowded, non-stop train got us to the racecourse in ten minutes.

Time: ten-thirty. Just right.

Around eleven the dignitaries arrive with much fanfare and at eleven-forty the first race begins.

The Melbourne Cup was the fifth of eight races and would be run at twenty minutes to three.

"The Melbourne Cup," said the Lady Navigator afterwards, reverting to her Center, Texas parlance, "is a *hoot*."

Our preconceived idea of the Melbourne Cup as a prestigious horserace for the country's best thoroughbreds was correct.

Our other idea that the Melbourne Cup was also the country's most elegant, couturier-fashioned, top-hatted social event was also true. But there were other surprising ingredients.

The course on Melbourne Cup day is a pictorial treat: green lawns trimmed with green hedges, contrasting with white fences. Rosebushes, flagrant in colours, blooming everywhere.

Also, the course suffocates under advertising signs, posters, advertising balloons. Avis won the signpost contest with nine billboards facing the Members' Stand plus one blimp.

"It looks like Picadilly," sniffed one nearby visitor.

The Members' Enclosure was a proper display of good taste in dress, sartorial elegance, a bit of chiffon for the spring weather, a touch of fur for the winter chill.

Outside the Members' Enclosure mocking the fashion event were a number of younger men wearing top hats, white ties, formal coats . . . and no pants. Tennis shoes were big with formal dress. One clan came in costumes from *Star Wars* and *Mickey Mouse*. Another entourage posed as shieks with harems.

The Members' Enclosure was a gentle scene of champagne and sandwiches.

Outside, around the track, families and groups of friends began filling the lawns with picnic tables, card tables, blankets spread on the turf.

Everybody's menu was champagne, chicken, bean salad. With a dash of rum, beer, gin and whisky on the side.

We wandered over to the public car park in the centre of the track. Tents, tables, folding chairs everywhere. Gigantic spreads of food. Buckets of liquids.

"Have a beer, Mate," said a huge thing in a funny cap as we retreated back to the sedate safety of the Enclosure and ducked into the Tea Room for a chicken salad and tea before the crowd swelled — before it was too late.

At eleven, to the sound of band music just outside the tea room, the Governor of Victoria arrived with an entourage. The Aga Khan, the Begum, track dignitaries, Kenneth Cox looking quite smart in his morning coat compared to the open-shirted, slack-trousered farmer of yesterday.

In another twenty minutes the Governor-General of Australia would arrive and we took advantage of the time to inspect the members' car park from the "Big M" public transport wagon pulled by a small tractor. We rode around the periphery of the park.

My! It was one immense party.

Here it was all crystal and damask cloth.

One group was being served out of the boot of their Rolls by black-coated waiters.

Here was a buffet table decorated with potted geraniums.

Over there was an immense canopied tent serving champagne and mounds of food.

Self-contained caravans were strong in numbers and equipped with coloured television sets. It was obvious that many present in the members' car park would never make it inside the track. "Why get involved with all those people in there when the party is out here?"

By this time it became clear that the Melbourne Cup was a festival ... a masquerade ... a carnival ... a *hoot*.

The pageantry ushering in the Governor-General exceeded expectations. A regimental band ump-pah-pahed down the track followed by a huge mob of kilted knees with bagpipes and thumping war-drums. A mounted horseguard of twenty with pennants flying preceded a sleek, black, top-down Rolls Royce. The Governor-General.

The limousine stopped in front of the grandstand. The Governor-General dismounted.

The band played *God Save the Queen*. Everyone at attention.

The Day had officially begun.

James Mason arrived through the Members' Gate carrying a yellow flight bag.

TV cameramen, photographers and reporters staked out a corner of the Members' Stand for capturing celebrities and the ladies whose dress — fantastic, gorgeous, bizarre — caught their attention.

An English cockney designer was dressed in black stetson, jewelled spurs for earrings, black silk shirt, pink hair and chaps slit up the thighbone. If you don't have talent, you have to be outrageous.

As one fashion critic said, "Well, the poor dear is trying."

The number of gentlemen in pearl grey top hats and morning coats were outnumbered by the gentlemen on the other side of the fence carrying styrofoam ice boxes full of grog.

The betting was frenzied, almost desperate. Long lines fronted the totaliser windows for win and place, the daily double, the Trifecta and the Quinella.

Bookies lined the fence along the Members' Enclosure behind the grandstand and people clutching handfuls of bills begged the bookies to take their money.

In the line of duty I researched the Members' Bar — *men only* — which set the Lady Navigator's teeth slightly on edge. "Primeval," I think she muttered.

Very jolly in the Men's Bar. TV sets over the bar solidly lined with tall-type Australians, straight of back, slightly flushed of face.

Excellent draft beer, icy cold, 37c a glass.

A nearby sandwich bar labelled "Nibbles" offered a variety of sandwiches at 95c. Hot dishes were also available at the cafeteria. Nobody seemed to have time for the cafeteria although there was always a line outside the dining room which we never did penetrate — men and women allowed — and an even longer one at the Champagne Bar which was always full.

During the first four races I made repeated trips to the Members' Bar in the line of research with side visits to the win-place window and an early visit to the bookie side of the fence to place a wager each way on Cubacade. (I had the horse.) A token, sentimental wager on Red Nose was added.

The Lady Navigator went her own betting way. She didn't come back with a winner but did gather incidental intelligence: (1) there were windows for lady bettors only. (2) get a seat at the end of the third race and keep it. Solid advice.

A lady in line had visitors from America who thought the Melbourne Cup was a yacht race. Horrors!

Before the Cup race, I made a last reconnaissance outside the Members' Enclosure and was immediately wedged into a non-movable position by the crowds. Almost 100,000 people were in attendance and even elbow room was non-existent. The pick-pockets or "dips" made more money than the bettors according to the next morning's newspaper. I squeezed around and got back in the Members' Enclosure.

The outside venture cost me my seat. By the time I returned to the upper grandstand even the aisles were filled with nervous, chattering, excited people.

I managed to get standing room and was able to see the horses parade in front of the Members' Stand.

Number One was Dulcify, the sweet-looking favourite which had already won over a half a million dollars. Number Six was Cubacade. Number Twelve was Red Nose.

The Melbourne Cup is a two-mile race. The track, a long straightway past the stands to the first turn. The horses race counter-clockwise in Victoria.

Twenty-four horses — too many, it was said — went to the gate without problems.

That momentary hush that occurs before a high-diver jumps . . . before the last putt of a championship golf match . . . before a big horse race.

"And they are away!"

Like a cavalry charge the horses thundered down the straight. Flashing a blur of silken colours, the tiny jockeys hunched low over the horses' shoulders. The yelling of the crowd.

Into the first turn. No idea where Cubacade is. Race announcers are incredible. How can they so accurately call a race with an eye for each horse out of such an immense field?

Down the back stretch. Everyone standing now and screaming. I hear the name Red Nose.

Into the back turn. Bedlam. No mention of Cubacade. No mention of Dulcify.

Here they come into the stretch.

Blood pressures mount all over the place. (Do you think a horse can hear his name being shouted out of a crowd of 100,000 people?)

Good heavens, there in the front pack is Red Nose!

Three horses in the last two hundred metres are nose to nose for the finish line including Red Nose. It must be an omen.

Photo finish. Photo finish between Salamander and Hyperno.

Red Nose has been nosed out.

But wait. The crowd instinctively turns almost as one to look at a point down track. There in the middle of the stretch is a quivering Dulcify. The champion has broken down.

People are in shock. Ladies are holding handkerchiefs to their mouths.

Terrible. For twenty minutes drama is played out behind a screen that protects the crowd from tragedy. "You might hear a shot," a next-seat companion warns the Lady Navigator.

But no. The favourite is bundled into a horse ambulance and removed to the trainer's stable.

The photo finish is now in. Hyperno is the winner. Red Nose third. We win back a dollar.

Cubacade is fifth.

At the end of the sixth race we left. The members' car park parties would go on indefinitely. All Australians can party indefinitely.

We met a lady during our winter tour who had been at the previous year's Melbourne Cup and was involved in a members' car park party until nearly midnight. Went home and found she had forgotten her purse. Her husband volunteered to return and search for the missing article but she said, no, she would go back because she knew exactly where she had left it. When she returned to the scene of the party an hour later, her host looked at her admonishingly and said, "You don't have a drink!"

By the same train and tram we were back in our hotel room in thirty minutes. Easy.

Our entire transportation bill for the day was $6.80. An economic improvement over a $170-a-day car.

A local sales manager who chauffered his visiting managing director to the race course said, "It was hell. It should have taken ten minutes but it took us an hour and a half. Spent twenty minutes at one stop light alone."

As we later told Australian friends, "The only good tip we had all day was to take the train."

Picnic Race at Hanging Rock

In complete contrast to the pomp and ceremony, to the elaborately staged parties, to the show of finery, is the Australian "picnic" race meeting.

The picnic race is without prestige horses and often without grandstands.

As Jim Bell told us driving back to Melbourne from the Stockwell visit, "In my area every farmer used to have a horse that could run and going to a picnic race was one of the few times we could all get together . . . outside of funerals."

Hanging Rock is somewhat unique in all aspects.

Its locale (about an hour north of Melbourne outside the village of Woodend) is in the shadow of Hanging Rock, a pile of stones which starred in a brilliantly written novel, *Picnic at Hanging Rock* by Joan Lindsay. The story of a girls' school picnic and the disappearance of three students and an instructor is a master work. The novel was made into one of Australia's most successful motion pictures. A beautifully directed, photographed and edited film.

The first of Hanging Rock's two annual racing meets is on New Year's Day and is a social event equal to that of the Melbourne Cup. A camp day. More champagne and chicken and all that.

The second meet — the one we attended — is on Australia Day in late January. If the Melbourne Cup is a hoot, Hanging Rock is a romp.

We were to rendezvous with friends in Woodend and after getting lost in the Victorian Railways yards of West Melbourne we finally veered the Green Pony north, arriving shortly after ten, only half an hour late.

The track, about four miles out of Woodend, is quite unlike most with its back to Hanging Rock, a pond in the middle and groves of tall gum trees surrounding it.

The jovial, white-haired gate man (50c a car plus 50c a person) said he couldn't promise any winners but the word was out on Big

Risk in the fifth. (Big Risk turned out to be a bad risk. He ran out of the money.)

We set up an enclosure with the four cars in our party, erected tables, opened the first cans of beer, had tea and biscuits, checked the champagne in the Esky.

Soon the tables were full of cheeses, biscuits, chicken, lobster, salads, strawberries, various jugs of white wine and a perfect quiche.

Around us several hundred families were doing the same.

Cricket batting sessions were going on. A competition among children performing Scottish Highland dances to the shrill music of a bagpiper was in progress on a portable stage.

There were umbrellas and lawn chairs, a few tents, radios playing, children running about, colour, action, food and drink. Picnic!

From the picnic-parking grounds to the Public Enclosure was a short walk, a trip enhanced by the presence of a sleeping koala bear high in the branches of a eucalyptus tree at the entrance. Race course entry tickets cost $2.50.

No grandstand marred the setting. At the finish line was a smaller enclosure where for, an extra $2.50, you were admitted to "Members' Stand" but there was no stand just a smaller number of people in a smaller space. Pointless.

Three units of bookmakers were out for the day. The group lining the fence between the members' enclosure and the public area had the advantage of taking bets from either side. Most of the bookies were located at the edge of the sloping lawn fronting the track. They made book on the Hanging Rock races. Farther up the slope a smaller group took bets on other races around the country.

The principal bookie stands on a box in front of a vertical board which lists the horses in the next race and the odds which he is willing to take. These change constantly. The bookie's assistant, standing on the ground at his feet, scans competitors' boards and reports their odds. A third man sits at a small table faithfully recording the number and amount of each bet placed.

Racing is no picnic for a bookmaker. Eagle-eyed, serious of mien, undertakerish of personality, he carefully scratches his way through seven races.

The races were quite properly run.

A regulation starting gate was used. A sizeable field was present in each race. We didn't witness any foolish rides and there were no spills although one horse, before a race and in front of the enclosure, gave a very serious buck popping his minute jockey about five feet in the air. The jockey came down on his feet and then led the horse to the starting line and remounted in the gate. He finished last.

Between Hanging Rock races the public address system broadcast the running of the races in other places. Lots of action.

For the first time in Australia I picked three winners out of a card, a victory slightly marred by losing the last ticket somewhere between the car and the track and if you find a bookie by the name of Len Griffith tell him that I am still looking for the ticket. (The secret of picking horse race winners is to find a lucky pocket in your clothes in which to store the ticket. Once you find a lucky pocket, you are set for the day. On the other hand, the Lady Navigator uses the close-your-eyes-and-stab-the-race-card-with-your-finger method. Very unprofessional. Laughable.)

In the shadow of their car, four of Mediterranean nationality, played cards the entire afternoon without so much as a glance at the race track.

After the last race we re-assembled around the tables and had the last pieces of chicken, the last slices of quiche, the last bottle of champagne and with the car park almost cleared we turned the Green Pony toward Melbourne with a sense of well being.

Picnic at Hanging Rock. Good Book. Good film. Good race.

It must be reported that on Australia Day there is another picnic race in competition with Hanging Rock and that is the Great Western Race Meeting sponsored by the Great Western Winery at Great Western, Victoria.

The distance from Melbourne is about two hundred kilometres and you can take a bus so you won't have to drive home.

Before the race the winery hosts a small party for a few friends at the winery where between four and five hundred bottles of bubbly are quaffed and during the meet another four to five thousand bottles are purchased and consumed. That's a fair dribble for an attendance of 12,000.

The Great Western has been running for over a hundred years.

A memorial champagne glass was designed for the centenary and 12,000 glasses were sold in an hour and a quarter.

Hobart Cup

Every state has its big race and the annual event in Tasmania is the Hobart Cup, a tradition since 1875 when the race was won by Ella.

At the Elwick Racecourse, spring-bright with floralscapes of dahlias and marigolds in the middle of summer, it was icy cold.

A chilly wind from the southwest brought intermittent sunshine and rain tinged with hail. That evening on the television news we saw it had snowed on nearby Mt. Wellington.

The fortitude-of-the-year award had to go to those in the members' car park who had set up tables and umbrellas and laid out cold chicken and sandwiches and "champers" . . . and stuck with it all afternoon.

In the turn-of-the-century clubhouse built after the 1907 fire that destroyed the 1874 grandstand, there are pictures of the Elwick Homestead and the race course.

Pictures surround the walls of the Members' Bar of races throughout the years.

In a picture display are photographs of the remarkable record set by jockey Geoff Prouse who, on 22 January, 1972, rode every winner in the day's seven races including the Tasmanian Derby.

We had a cool but enjoyable afternoon. Seldom touched a money winner but the beer at 35c a glass and the ham sandwiches for under a dollar were sure bets.

In the first race the Lady Navigator placed a bet on the favourite which headed the field at the last turn but quit in the straight.

The day we left Tasmania three jockeys and a trainer were charged with hanky-panky in connection with the race and the taxi driver taking us to the airport reported that the jockey behind the favourite said, "I thought I saw his brake lights go on!"

Opening Day of the Kalgoorlie Racing Club

The first race meet of the Kalgoorlie Racing Club was in 1896.

Being a gold mining town everything happened with dispatch. Although the first race meet facilities consisted of a tent, by the following year there was a temporary grandstand and the year after that a grandiose, gingerbread two-storey grandstand.

The Kalgoorlie Cup was considered the biggest country race of the year especially during the booming days when gold was pouring out of the mines.

For example in 1903, $65,000 was bet in one afternoon and it was not until 1977 on a Kalgoorlie Cup day that the record was broken.

Of course in those days the admission price was a hefty sixteen shillings and six pence and you could stay at the deluxe Palace Hotel for twelve and six.

We were in Kalgoorlie for the opening day of the season and watched a sizeable crowd spread their bets between the track-operated totalisator and the two groups of bookies operating behind the grandstand. Eight bookies took bets on the race action in Sydney, Melbourne and Perth while a second group of nine handled the Kalgoorlie race betting. A scene rich in colour and in characters.

A public clubroom offered cafeteria hot and cold dishes and two public bars took care of the Australian thirst demand. A Members' Bar was off the public bars.

The requirements of the racing crowds could be measured in the kitchen which had its own bakery capable of turning out 12,000 bread rolls a day.

In the intimate Officials' Bar behind the race committee room we shared a beer with club president Graham Crisp, a bright-eyed bachelor, chemist and entrepreneur and with accommodating Bill Bevan, the racing secretary.

In the town of gold, the traditionally solid gold Kalgoorlie Cup is now sterling silver and plated with gold. The change had been forced three years earlier by the rising price of gold. (They said that the famous Melbourne Cup was going the same route.)

The most renowned horse of Kalgoorlie was Blue Speaker. The horse was walked almost four hundred kilometres to Esperance. Shipped by sea to Melbourne. Won the Melbourne Cup. The year was 1904.

Meetings are held in Kalgoorlie throughout the year. Pleasant track and right in town.

The Great Eastern Steeplechase

The Monday after Easter in the hills of Adelaide is one of the most exciting, glorious picnic races in Australia.

People start assembling three weeks before Easter in the little town of Oakbank. The few hundred resident population swells to 60,000 race goers who camp out in tents and caravans to attend the Onkaparinga Racing Club's annual event.

The two-day meet is held on Saturday and Monday. On Easter Monday the Great Eastern Steeplechase is run . . . a tradition which has occurred since 1876.

One of the favourite stories concerns a non-favourite called Gunn. The horse fell on the first lap and was forgotten until the last lap when who was out in front showing his heels to the rest of the crowd? Gunn!

The punters, it was reported, were furious. Gunn, they claimed, had hidden behind a hedge during the second lap.

The protest was dismissed.

Earlier the race had the reputation of not only being the longest and richest picnic race in South Australia but because of the formidable obstacles, the most difficult.

Many of the obstacles have been removed and the jumps nowadays are mostly brush and hurdle but the famous Fallen Log, fourth on the hill, consisting of horizontal logs piled high on a stone wall, still remains.

Its setting in lush meadows and grassy slopes with the Onkaparinga River flowing peacefully by enhances the charm of the picnic meet.

Another distinctive race is the February Birdsville Picnic Race Meeting. Most of the mob comes in private planes which are parked in the street, a huge refrigerated van arrives filled with beer and the empty beer cans are piled in the middle of the thoroughfare. That's what we heard. Honest.

15. Where Old Locomotives Still Live

The twin rails of the earliest railroad trains were like twin veins circulating life's blood through the widely spread, thinly populated body of pioneering Australia.

Railroads took out sugar and tea and cloth and brought back money-making wool to the wharves.

Railroads carried out iron for nails and pumps for wells and returned to the cities with beef cattle.

Railroads took workers out and brought school children in.

Railroads replaced riverboats and stage coaches . . . replaced cattle drovers' trails . . . replaced camel trains and coastal sailing vessels.

The steam engines of the early railroads had an animal appeal. They were truly "iron horses" breathing like mammoth beasts through their driving pistons — *whoosh — shufff . . . whoosh — shufff.*

The romantic steam engines were replaced by the more powerful, efficient diesel engines which still fulfil a major transportation function in Australia.

The old engines retired but didn't die and today are being brought out of retirement and put back into service by literally thousands of volunteer members of steam locomotive societies who are dedicated to restoring portions of ancient lines.

Now around Australia on weekends, steam locomotives are in motion, pulling carriage loads of screaming, delighted children — and their equally happy parents — over reborn track.

We were frequently aboard along with many other overseas visitors.

Our first experience was in the Dandenong Range, a mountainous area in the resort-commuter town of Belgrave east of Melbourne.

Here is located the Puffing Billy Preservation Society.

In 1900 an experimental narrow gauge railroad opened from Belgrave into the mountain interior to provide service to the small farmers and wood-cutters pioneering the area. It was called the Upper Fern Tree Gully to Gembrook Railway.

From 1900 to 1953 the line was operational but diminishing traffic

ANTIQUE RAILROADS

1. "THE PUFFING BILLY"
2. SUGAR CANE SPECIAL
3. ZIG ZAG
4. THE GHAN
5. PICHI RICHI
6. BELLARINE PENINSULA
   RAILROAD
7. "LESCHENAULT LADY"
8. THIRLMERLE MUSEUM

made it marginal and when the line was struck by a series of landslides, it closed.

Two Melbourne journalists of *The Sun* promoted a final sentimental ride for children before the line's demise. Wildly successful. One final sentimental ride led to another final sentimental ride.

The resultant enthusiasm for keeping the line going led to a call for volunteer membership in the Puffing Bill Preservation Society.

("Puffing Billy" was actually the name given to one of the earlier famous locomotives built by William Hedley in 1813 for an English colliery. The locomotive now resides in the Science Museum in London. On the Fern Tree Gully Line the steam engines were called "Pollys" and "Coffee Pots" and "Hissing Jennys." However, the press latched onto the name of "Puffing Billy" and it became the name of the Society.)

The call for membership was met by an outpouring of railroad buffs from every corner of Victoria's society: doctors, accountants, blue collar workers, retired railroad men, school children all responded to the call.

The volunteers, with the assistance of the army, became slave labourers. They cleaned out weeds, relaid track, built a new terminal at Belgrave, relaid crossings, bypassed a major landslide that had been the final blow in closing the line down.

The first effort took the line to Menzies Creek Station.

The second effort reached Emerald Station where the volunteers had to elevate the entire railroad yard by two feet.

The third and final push took the line to Lakeside in 1975 . . . fifteen kilometres from Belgrave . . . a monumental labour of love.

We arrived at Belgrave on an ideal summer's day eager to ride the Puffing Billy and were greeted by Arthur Winzenreid, the volunteer officer in charge for the day, a teacher of primary school, who took his turn out of several hundred volunteers once a month to go on the work roster.

Besides having a pass to ride on the Puffing Billy I had a permit to ride in the cab subject to the approval of the driver.

I was taken to the change room for the crew and was issued an official blue smock, a pair of thick fireman's gloves and a wiping rag. (I didn't have any idea what I was supposed to wipe.)

My outfitting all the while was being eyed rather enviously by Andrew Harkness, fourteen-year-old junior volunteer for two years.

He was one of a hundred boys and girls between twelve and sixteen who make up "The Student Corps" responsible for the cleaning section. At age sixteen student members became regular members.

The driver, Mike Adams, approved my riding in the cab. Not that there was that much room.

Our locomotive was spankingly clean, brightly polished and small.

Technically, it was a Narrow Gauge Class "A" locomotive, one of six remaining of the original fifteen built in Australia. The first two such locomotives were American-built with high smoke stacks and cow-catchers.

I was positioned standing behind Mike with my back pressed against the wall of the cab, my head level with a speed indicator.

The volunteer fireman, already black with soot, was Brian Sneddon, an electronic engineer when he wasn't playing train on the weekends.

During the fifteen kilometres he shovelled over half a ton of back-breaking black coal keeping the pressure gauge needle at a steady 180-pounds per square inch level. What a hobby. He'd been a volunteer since 1962.

The station master was a volunteer. The guard with a flag at the end of the train was a volunteer. With the first toot of the whistle and the "All aboard" and the flag waving, it came into focus that this was really a step-back-into boyhood ambition come true.

This wasn't a backyard, play with make-believe-boxes train. This was a real, life-sized, live-steam train to play with.

I was tickled to be part of the game.

Mike was a paid professional. He had worked on railroads since he was fifteen, in New Zealand and in Australia. But he shared the same enthusiastic spirit as the volunteers.

"When this job came up, I grabbed it. I'll never leave. To drive a steam locomotive and get paid for it? I'm one of the last lucky blokes in the world!" Mike said.

With a great deal of turning of gauges and shifting of levers, regulating air and steam, we choo-chooed out of the station.

One person was standing at the first road crossing. Never did one person receive so much attention. Every school child waved. Every parent waved. Mike waved. I waved. Only the fireman kept shovelling coal.

Before every crossing "Puffing Billy" would give several toots on the tooter. The fireman would lean out of the cab looking terribly

serious and call out solemnly, "All clear." The driver would acknowl-
edge with one toot. There were many crossings throughout the
journey and it was great tooting fun.

Not long after leaving the station Puffing Billy came to a long,
sweeping, curved wooden trestle.

"This is the most photographed wooden structure in Australia,"
said our driver who I now called "Waving Mike."

Children were leaning out of the front of the train waving to children in back of the train. Cameras were clicking everywhere.

An added bonus of the Puffing Billy experience was the nature
beauty of the ride . . . through lovely trees and towering ferns. Birds
sang to Puffing Billy along the way and by mid-trip we were treated
to sweeping views across mountain valleys to the flatlands below.

Nicely sensitive to the surroundings and familiar with every tree
and bush and view, "Waving Mike" would point out the sights along
the way.

"Here's another one of my girl friends," he said waving to a tot-
carrying mother in a garden above the train. "She is there every trip."
Mike had lots of girl friends.

At the Emerald Station during a ten minute break to take on water,
we were hustled over to a workshed where a carriage acquired from
Tasmania was being stripped as part of a six-month restoration job.
The work was being done by a full-time painter and a full-time car-
penter, two of the few paid staff.

Next to the restoration work was the Puffing Billy VIP carriage
car, a delightful open-ended saloon coach equipped with brass lamps,
etched windows, thickly padded seats and highly polished wood.

The wood for the original carriage had been pre-cut in Tasmanian
forests and shipped to England where the car was assembled.

You can hire the VIP car for parties.

Can you imagine a better time than to have a group of friends
in the VIP carriage, properly provisioned of course, going rickity-
rackiting down the track?

From Emerald Station we steamed down a steep grade, past Nobelius
Siding to Lakeside Station.

Everyone in the neighbourhood knows what is going on with Puffing Billy. Mike said they had had a poor batch of coal the previous
week. "You can tell good coal by the blackness of the smoke coming
out of the stack." When we pulled into the station another one of

his girl friends asked about our slight tardiness, "What happened, Mike? Bad coal again?"

Lakeside Station is where the engine is turned around and the firebox is cleared of ashes.

Passengers go down to Emerald Lake and buy ice cream cones at the kiosk. Families with picnic baskets come in the morning and go back in the afternoon enjoying the atmosphere of the woods and the lake.

The hour's trip back on the Puffing Billy was just as enjoyable.

"See that platform. That is Nobelius Siding. Nobelius came from England and all those trees you see around here are English trees he imported and grew. Shipped trees all around Australia from that loading platform."

Toot, toot, we went through another crossing.

Toot, toot, we crossed the trestle bridge.

Toot, toot, we approached the Belgrave Station.

I took off my smock and surrendered my gloves and my spotless wiping rag.

"You like your engine don't you, Mike?"

He cocked his head and grinned, "You soak the old girl in beer and I'd have her for breakfast."

A Sugar Cane Railroad

The most humpity-dumpity railroad we ever experienced was a restored sugar cane railroad that took us through Sunshine Plantation on Highway 1 south of Noosa Heads on the Sunshine Coast.

The bright red and yellow locomotive pulling open carriages was a photographer's pleasure.

The circuit of the track was less than a mile but we went through a nursery growing examples of the rich basin's fruit trees, pineapple, avocado, sugar cane, macadamia nut trees, etc., etc.

Past a barnyard with animals for children to touch.

Sunshine Plantation is a commercial not a volunteer enterprise but it is worth the stop. Have a fresh fruit sundae with whipped cream. Crushed nuts on top. Skip lunch.

A Cliff-Hanging Railroad

One of the more famous defunct-restored railroads in Australia is the Zig Zag Railroad — official name — because of the sheer audacity of the engineering.

A continuous railroad line from Sydney to the rich goldfields of Bathurst and beyond in the mid-1800's was blocked by cliffs of the west escarpment of the Blue Mountains.

The problem was solved by engineering and constructing a railroad line which switched back and forth across the cliff face. Didn't turn. Just zig-zagged.

The line led from the top of the mountains initially through deep-cut gorges, switched direction and went back across three huge sandstone viaducts, through two tunnels, reversed itself twice working its way down the treacherous mountain face to Lithgow Valley five hundred feet below.

It took three years to build and was proclaimed an engineering masterpiece.

In 1910 the difficult and time-consuming operation was replaced by a direct line that detoured through ten tunnels.

The Zig Zag fell into disuse. The rails were torn out. The cuts and viaducts became overgrown. Derelict. Forgotten.

But then . . . here come the troops again . . . a group of enthusiastic railroad nuts gathered together under the name of the Zig Zag Railway Co-op., Ltd., relaid the line, restored operating steam locomotives and put the line back in the business — the tourist business.

Not only have the volunteers restored half of the line but they have ambitious plans to complete the line to the mountain top and build a new station.

Presently you drive down to the Top Points Station on what was the old railroad bed from the mountain top. This is the next section the society hopes to replace.

At Top Points you buy your ticket from the volunteer ticket seller ($1 for adults, 50¢ for children) and board the carriage behind the panting steam engine.

The Zig Zag descends slowly and steeply for a mile on man-made ledges. After crossing a viaduct the whole amphitheatre of the Lithgow Valley becomes the passenger's panorama. The train goes through a 225-foot tunnel and in ten minutes is on the valley floor.

Riders can take the time to go to the Zig Zag Station and look at the collection of rolling stock including a heavy 400-class Beyer-Garratt steam engine which is considered a super classic among the really fringe nuts. (The Puffing Billy line is also hoping to restore a Beyer-Garratt class locomotive and is trying to collect $250,000 to do the job.)

On the return journey's hard pull the heaving sound of the steam engine's labouring: "I-think-I-will, I-think-I-will" reverberated against the cliff walls. A dramatic sound.

If you'd like to take advantage of the barbecue and picnic areas along the route, speak to the guard before the train leaves and he will see to it that you are left off and picked up again.

Flexibility is an advantage of a volunteers' railroad.

All Aboard The Ghan!

Today a sleek new line goes from Alice Springs south to Tarcoola replacing one of the world's magic railroad legends . . . The Old Ghan. You can take The New Ghan in a trip covering 1,000 kilometres that used to take The Old Ghan two days and two nights . . . or, at times of flood, a week to a month.

The Old Ghan was built on the desert sands without aid of ballast or foundations and the trestles over the dry river beds were made of wood.

Building The Old Ghan to Alice Springs took over fifty years.

The New Ghan was a miracle of construction. It was completed (1) ahead of schedule, (2) under budget and (3) without interference.

All eyes in Australia jerked in the direction of The New Ghan as the construction phenomenon neared completion.

Noel Bushnell reported in Melbourne's excellent newspaper, *The Age*:

"For some inscrutable reason, government, unions, cattlemen, environmentalists, Aborigines, homosexuals, women and whales appeared to have ignored the undertaking.

"Sheer distance probably accounts for the serenity.

"In short, it's not been worth a banner."

The first sod for the original Ghan was turned in 1879 with the ambitious idea of building a railroad through the centre of Australia to Darwin on the far side, annexing the Northern Territory and making South Australia the richest state in the nation.

"Hurrah for the iron horse! Advance Australia!" enthused one correspondent.

The advance took a lifetime and was never completed beyond Alice Springs.

Labour in the new country was in short supply but by July, 1880 there were nine hundred workers on the line. The work camps were not for Boy Scouts. Scenes of illicit profits and violence, illegal grog, rats, gambling, union troubles, women dressed in men's clothes, desertion were part of the daily parade.

Camel trains were the principal means of transporting goods including supplies and rails.

By 1886 the non-European work force had swollen to 3,000 Chinese and Indian labourers.

After the first leg was completed the government had to take over the construction because no private building contractor would offer a bid. World War I caused another serious delay and it was not until 2 August 1929 that the first train arrived in Alice Springs . . . four and a half hours late . . . initiating a tradition.

The entire population (200) turned out to greet the train which above all marvels had a bathroom on board!

By 1930 a trip to Alice Springs on The Ghan, so named after the Afghan camel drivers, was the "in" trip to make and the early law barring women as passengers crumbled as laws so often do when women are involved.

The legends around The Ghan grew in the following fifty years. Weather was the principal factor. First the heat. The train ran through the hottest parts of Australia with the result that the dining room car in the summer was frequently 120°F. and another 10° to 20° in the kitchen.

More importantly was the rain.

The original designers thought it safe to lay the track out on the ground, not remembering that the vast desert acts like a hugh catchment area and it only takes a minimum of rain to create floods.

Flash floods gave The Ghan a reputation of tardiness and disaster. Even in this part of the country known as "the land of lots-of-time and wait-a-bit" the railroad was often referred to in the words: "the poor Old Ghan again . . . "

One writer recalled being stranded for three days by a flood on the south bank of the Finke River until the waters subsided beneath the height of the locomotive's firebox.

The isolated passengers fried under the Simpson Desert sun but, in true Australian tradition, they made do. They showered under the great hoses beside the track used for replenishing the trains.

They organised cricket games, ignoring the dust and prickly

spinifex and when the local pub ran out of beer the passengers confiscated the several hundred gallons of brew consigned to Alice Springs and batted on.

Not all incidents were so droll.

In 1883 during construction a carriage car containing explosives blew up leaving the line in two parts. The explosion could be heard twenty miles away and bits and pieces were found a quarter of a mile away.

A collision in the Pichi Richi pass killed several hundred sheep.

In 1938 the normally dry Alberga River exploded under a rain and washed away a homestead, machinery, livestock, house, out buildings. Nothing was left.

Floods in '48, '49, and '50 created havoc. The 1950 rains saturated the dry beds of Lake Eyre and the trains had to be cancelled.

In 1963 two hundred flood-stranded passengers had to be air-lifted out of the desert.

In 1972 the Todd River rose seventeen feet in places and washed away track, bridges and embankments.

"The poor Old Ghan again . . ."

Still there were moments of charm to enhance the other side of the reputation. The train would stop so passengers could pick wild flowers in season after a rain. And there were other occasions when hot water for the essential tea was supplied by the driver from the scalding water in his engine.

During the last few months of its operation everybody wanted to have a sentimental ride on The Old Ghan. (And hoped for a flood.) We were fortunate enough to get southbound reservations and also permission at some stage in the journey — subject to the approval of the driver — to ride in the locomotive.

Northbound passengers left Adelaide on Monday morning, changed trains in Port Pirie, and in Marree changed to the old narrow gauge railroad of the original Ghan which hopefully arrived in Alice Springs on Wednesday morning.

The ancient, former luxurious German carriages were then gently cleaned, turned around and headed south again by eight o'clock Wednesday evening.

When we arrived in Alice Springs from Ayers Rock to catch the train, the good news we received was that The Ghan, although a few hours late arriving, would leave on time. Passengers would be allowed to board at seven.

No dinner would be served the first evening.

By this time we were professional picnic packers and the hours and the lack of a dining car the first evening didn't faze us a bit.

The first sight of Car Number Five, our carriage, in the weak-yellow-white circles of the station lights was another matter. It sagged. The sides were of wood. They sagged. Built in the thirties in Germany the poor old wagon looked as if it were on its last journey.

Inside, however, Car Number Five were a pleasant surprise. Air-conditioning improved the ambience immediately. Deeply varnished wood gave our private compartment an old-world charm. The pull-out-and-down wash bowl was decorated in Germanic fashion with an embossed lion's head in metal. On the rack above the wash bowl was a thermos jug of ice water.

Toilets and hot and cold water showers were at the ends of the carriage. Men to the north. Women to the south.

We snacked and sipped in air-conditioned comfort and watched the last lights of Alice Springs disappear to be replaced by nothing ... nothing after nothing ... and then went to the luxurious lounge car, also German-built with a picture of Schloss Wilhelmshole at one end, where the formally attired waiter took orders for after-picnic refreshments.

An upright piano was the focus point for late entertainment.

Our conductor was Colin Keith Tuohy, portly, dignified in his immaculate black suit, white shirt and black bow tie; his slightly heavy Irish face set off with spectacles. He could have been the ward leader in Chicago or the village priest in County Cork.

He took fatherly care of us. An extra cup of hot tea. A cold beer on the house. At Marree where some of the first-class passengers had to scramble for non-reserved seats in coach cars he secured a private compartment for us and moved our luggage. A saintly man.

He even turned the sheets down in the upper and lower bunks. With the lights out the riding characteristics of the three-foot, six-inch narrow gauge beds became apparent. The carriages swayed from side to side like lumbering elephants and groaned as they strained on curves, steel against steel, and the wooden sides creaked with the labour of it all.

It was like sleeping in a swaying hammock in a squeaking tree top. Good sleeping.

At dawn I was up and down the hall for a shower . . . a mistake I corrected the second day because water was not heated until later in the morning. Back to the compartment I had an hour to myself before the Lady Navigator stirred, staring out at the flat land, the scrub bush, the occasional trees.

On The Ghan we ate in three shifts . . . the last shift being preferable . . . the table cloth was spottier but there was more time. The white-jacketed waiters were as good as Australian waiters get and the food was also mediocre but the experience of eating in a large-windowed dining car was a pleasure in itself.

The day passed calmly chatting with friends from Melbourne on board, drinking beer, taking naps, eating, reading.

At Oodnadatta, 472 kilometres from Alice Springs, we stopped but were prevented from going across to the pub because the long train blocked the way. "If you miss the train you wait a week before you can get out," was the warning. We didn't go.

Another lucky passenger and I had permits to ride in the locomotive and at Oodnadatta we went to the front of the train and got into the functional cab of the giant diesel.

Stan O'Grady and Malcolm Archer were the driver and co-driver, both sons of railroad men.

On the surface the operation of the diesel is quite simple. The train slowly, slowly got under way as O'Grady pushed the acceleration lever forward. From a lightly cushioned window seat on the right hand side of the caboose, Archer watched the road ahead and behind and every sixty seconds pressed a "vigilant button" which in turn set back a timing hand mounted on the front of the cab to start another one minute count-down.

If the button is not pressed in sixty seconds, a warning buzzer sounds for ten seconds and if the vigilant button is not pressed at that time a loud horn sounds, alerting the entire train.

It is a system devised after an accident caused by the fatal heart attack of a driver whose co-driver was napping.

The cab was a no-nonsense, utilitarian command post for the huge diesel pulling eight hundred and fifty tons of passengers and freight. The only concessions in the glass-walled, grey-steeled cabin were an insulated chest filled with chipped ice, a water container and an electrical pot for making tea.

The hot-and-cold perch was subject to icy desert nights and sweltering desert days.

Driving is an intensive job. The two drivers in the cab change places with two colleagues every seven and a half hours. They bring and prepare their own food.

It was an even more intensive job during these last days of The Old Ghan where track maintenance was minimal and we frequently crept along at twenty kilometres an hour. At this point of The Ghan's service, any major flood or accident would have meant closing the line down permanently.

Despite the mental demands on the drivers the pleasant part of the job was riding along in such splendid isolation and watching the country pass on each side. King of all you survey.

The water courses filled with box gums, mulga, acacia and desert oak, corkwood and eucalyptus.

The birds are yours too, the owls, the hawks, the ducks, the wild turkeys, not to mention the dingos, the rabbits, emus . . . even wild camels and donkeys. We saw them all from the train.

The Ghan was now part of the national railroad system and Michael Archer, like most drivers, was assigned to trains throughout the system. This was his third Ghan run. On his first run he was stranded two days by a rainstorm. On his second run he was in sight of Alice Springs when the train went off the track and he put twelve cars into the bush.

"You might as well do it right," he said.

Boredom is the drivers' main enemy and the relief from boredom can take many forms.

At Mt. Dutton a work train on the siding was preceded by a flagman on foot signalling the track was clear, our cue to proceed through.

Michael leaned out of the train offering a newspaper to the flagman and as he reached for the newspaper Michael dashed a cup of ice water in his face!

Hoots of laughter and knee-pounding followed the caper.

On the last car of the work train another railroad mate in an open carriage door got the same treatment. When the hilarity died down Michael said philosophically, "It may take them twelve months but they'll get even."

When we came to a crossing, the other passenger and I took turns blowing the whistle. Do you think that was fun? Yes, it was.

The whole Ghan experience was a giant party.

The dining car, the lounge car, the circulation of people among compartments sharing experiences was part of the enjoyment. We also had a strong contingent of working and retiring railroad executives on board who were frequently checking their watches against the printed schedule and clucking management clucks.

They knew every stop, every piece of equipment, every person.

"Meet Mr. So-and-So who does such-and-such on The Ghan," the executive would say. "I worked with his father."

At Marree we changed to a standard-gauge railroad and in essence The Old Ghan narrow gauge ride was over.

Also the scenery changed. To the east we picked up the Flinders Range, a grey mass of mountain over a fringe of green.

Houses took the place of emus. Buildings replaced the kangaroos. No matter.

We were late leaving Marree, late leaving Port Augusta and late leaving Port Pirie where we again changed trains, going from compartments into open coaches for the final two-and-a-half hour ride to Adelaide.

Into the hotel at midnight.

Note: The New Ghan offers the chance to enjoy the interior of Australia from air-conditioned, modern railcars. Tours with many combinations of rail/coach are available to Alice Springs and points between/beyond.

Ride the Pichi Richi . . . The Last of The Ghan

Thanks to another group of volunteers in South Australia, a most interesting portion of the old narrow gauge Ghan line through the Pichi Richi Pass has been restored by the Pichi Richi Railway Preservation Society.

With three British-built 1951 "W" Class steam locomotives and carriage stock in operation, railroad buffs and other children can take an historic journey through part of the Flinders Ranges from Quorn. The train operates on holiday weekends and during school holidays. Beautiful scenic ride, too.

One of the engineering details of the Pichi Richi line is the precise dry stone wall embankments built by the precise Chinese labourers.

Bellarine Peninsula Railway

If you have the chance to enjoy Queenscliff and the Ozone Hotel, an hour's drive south of Melbourne, you should visit the operation of the Geelong Steam Preservation Society (250 members).

The Society is responsible for the Bellarine Peninsula Railway which has put down sixteen km of new narrow gauge track to the town of Drysdale. A steam museum in Drysdale is now under construction.

Members sell a "Foot of Track Certificates" for $1 which is matched by $2 government funding.

We enjoyed a ride in a restored Tasmanian carriage behind a TGR M6 engine (4-6-2) built in Darlington, England.

Trains run every Sunday.

The Leschenault Lady

Isn't that a pretty name?

At Bunbury, south of Perth in Western Australia, is "The Leschenault Lady," a regal steam locomotive which hauls just-like-new carriages on advertised occasions, thanks to the volunteer railroad buffs who have made it happen.

Leschenault was the French naturalist who explored the coast of Western Australia in 1803. His name was the winning entry in a name-the-train contest.

NSW Rail Transport Museum

Railroad buffs will not want to miss the N.S.W. Railroad Museum at Thirlmere, eighty kilometres southwest of Sydney.

Caution: it is only open on weekends.

On an eight-acre property there is the country's finest collection of yesteryear's railroading. Over thirty steam locomotives are on display and they run the gamut of tiny, original, century-old steam engines to giant, modern express locomotives.

Antique carriages may also be seen including, as the brochure says: "old dogboxes that everyone remembers ... and a prison van that some may prefer to forget."

Twice a month steam train rides are offered.

For location map and time tables, get a brochure from the tourist office in Sydney. On the right days you can get to Thirlmere by train from Sydney, the last leg behind a steam locomotive.

Take a Ride, Take a Picture, Wave!

One common element of people riding behind a steam locomotive in an old carriage car is that everyone is grinning.

Not smiling. Not simpering. *Grinning*.

Bouncy, contagious enthusiasm is everywhere. You take more pictures than you can ever distribute in the neighbourhood. You wave at strangers standing at the crossroads and driving their cars alongside the train as though they are rich relatives.

And do you know what they are doing? The bystanders are clicking away frantically. They are waving madly. And they are *grinning*.

16. Top of the Mountain

The Big Wrinkle in Australia is the Great Dividing Range.

In a land where the average elevation is three hundred metres — compared to the world average of seven hundred — you don't expect mountain peaks and forests of fern.

But surprisingly the nice little Alpine scenes and resorts you'd like to find *are* found in Australia.

Lamington National Park in Queensland and the Blue Mountains behind Sydney, the Snowy Mountains in the south of New South Wales, the ski resorts of Victoria are all part of the Big Wrinkle.

But there are more mountain pleasures.

The centre of Tasmania is a mass of mountains, unsoiled, unspoiled, isolated, waiting to be experienced.

Victoria has the Grampians, a living laboratory of exotic wild flowers, running streams and waterfalls and Aboriginal paintings.

The Flinders Range in South Australia features Wilpena Pound, a spectacular phenomenon and nature's largest amphitheatre.

The ski resorts of the Big Wrinkle become major alpine resorts in the summer. Cliff climbing, trout fishing in clear streams, mountain trail rides, hiking, water skiing on sylvan lakes.

Every state tourist office is eager to lay hands on you and ship you into the mountains.

It's about time you went back to camp!

Forest-Fair Lamington

Fifty kilometres west of Tweed Heads on the Gold Coast of Queensland and one hundred kilometres south of Brisbane is Lamington National Park where two mountain resorts offer woodlife, birdlife and wildlife. Not too wild.

One resort is O'Reilly's Green Mountains Guest House and the other is Binna Burra Lodge.

To impress you immediately, know that the accommodations at both hospices range from $42 to $65 a day, per person, including all meals and guides.

Binna Burra was on our route south and we made reservations for an overnight stay.

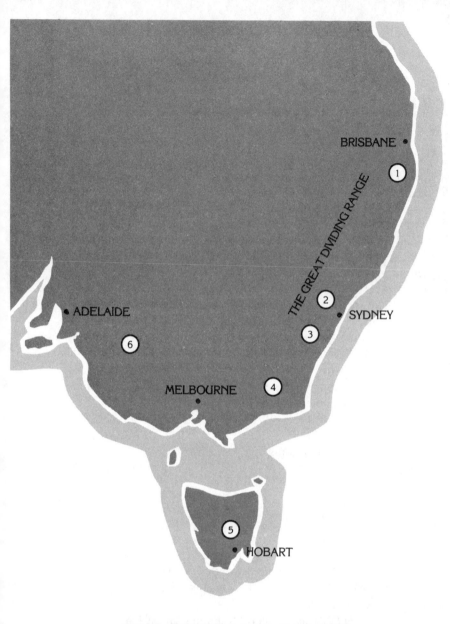

MOUNTAIN TOPS

1. BINNA BURRA
2. BLUE MOUNTAINS
3. SNOWY MOUNTAINS
   (Thredbo)
4. MT. BUFFALO
5. TASMANIA
6. THE GRAMPIANS

Our arrival followed a terrible mountain storm of the night before; rain, thunder, lightning had knocked out the resort's electricity. Binna Burra was still shaking itself clear when we arrived.

We liked our balconied room overlooking a mountain valley. Tea-making facilities, refrigerator, bathroom — no key. No rooms have keys.

A picnic-walking tour was just setting out for a few hours in the bush and we were invited to come along.

Richard Groom, younger son of the founder, was the leader. A likeable, straightforward young man, Richard led us down a mountain trail to Bell Bird Pool. A fire had already been started by an advance hiker-worker to grill chops, steaks, sausages and hamburgers and to boil the billy. Tea flavoured with smoke and ashes is inexplicably delicious.

After lunch the party set off single file into the bush for Picnic Rock, a mile and a half away.

Two young nurses from Brisbane carried their own harnesses for rappelling down cliffs. Richard had slung over his shoulders a coil of rope and additional harnesses provided by the lodge for others.

A rumble of thunder like an off-stage sound effect could be heard in the distance.

Richard peered first over both sides of Picnic Rock, a hundred feet above the forest, elected the easier side, tied his rope around two anchor points and suspended his harness through the rope and walked backwards over the cliff edge.

The two girls followed in turn. Then two men.

Any other volunteers? I get dizzy on the second rung of a stepladder and kept a desperate silence but the Lady Navigator said, "I'd like to try that."

Richard and the nurses strapped her high and low into a harness and then chattering fiercely — she always talks too much . . . constantly . . . questioningly — she walked slowly backwards over the cliff. Heart-stopping.

I have a series of photos of her body gradually disappearing, the last shot being mostly of giant eyes looking pleadingly upwards.

(Some of us have to stay behind and take pictures. That night after a glass of wine, I said, "I could have done it." That's when she hit me.)

After her first success she was all bubbling ready to try it again but I led her to the return path as the distant thunder now sounded closer.

On the trail to the lodge in the moss-slick rainforest the first pitter-patters turned to splats on tree leaves and gradually to a rock rhythm until it was a steady downpour.

At first we were protected by the trees but as the storm picked up in volume and the cold rain turned to hail and the breeze turned into a tree-whipping gale we became drenched and reached the lodge at the height of the storm. After a hot shower, and two sherries, it was a magnificent storm to watch. From the room.

Binna Burra is owned by mountain-loving stockholders who never expect a dividend and also never want to see a tree changed or a bush moved. They are terribly possessive about the resort and form the nucleus of the club attitude of the guests, all of whom are Australian and ninety percent of them are repeat vacationers.

Our presence along with a couple from Boston probably set a new record for overseas visitors.

The guests are nature lovers — walkers all — and the resort activities are mostly "suggested walks for today." Short walks, long walks ... twenty-six mapped hikes including one-night to four-night pack trips.

A six-mile hike including a 900-foot drop, a swim at the bottom of a waterfall followed by a barbecue and a hike out to the natural arch in the area is the most popular walk.

Dangerous? No. "We've been doing it for twenty years," said Richard.

Meals at Binna Burra are constant. 6:30 a.m. Early Morning Tea. 8 a.m. Breakfast. 10:30 a.m. Morning Tea (Scones, Whipped Cream and Jam). 12:30 p.m. Lunch. 3:30 p.m. Afternoon Tea. 6:00 p.m. Dinner. 9:00 p.m. Supper.

Dinner at six? "Most guests like to be in bed early because they will be up early and on the trail in the morning."

The Wine Hatch is open for an hour and a half at lunch and an hour and a half at dinner.

Any part of the year is a good season for Binna Burra and its popularity among so many people who enjoy the relaxation or the mountain life, the majesty of the trees and the beauty of the birds and flowers makes an advance reservation necessary.

Warm, hospitable place. A like-to-go-back-to place.

Mt. Buffalo

The pretty valley resort of Bright in northern Victoria is reached in a day's drive from Melbourne.

Earlier in the morning we had visited Mt. Beauty, a hydro-electric town, headquarters for a completed power generating scheme and now a tree-filled village which serves in the winter as a base camp for skiers at nearby Falls Creek, a ski resort thirty kilometres away in the mountains.

Bright is at the entrance to Buckland Valley, a prominent scene of the 1853 gold-rush days and the place of racial riots against the Chinese miners who were driven out and who resettled in Beechworth.

From Buckland Valley you can see the profile of Mt. Buffalo which does, in fact, resemble a humpbacked bison.

The ranger at the entrance to the Mt. Buffalo National Park charges you a $1 admission fee but gives you a "nature drive" map. Excellent descriptive text concerning the birds, plant life and rock formations which you see as you progress up the mountain.

Mt. Buffalo is an absorbing recreational area. The mountain is singular, not part of a mountain range; it was pushed up out of a sea into a massive sedimentary rock.

Estimated to be 9,000-feet high originally, the granite core was eroded by ice and rain into a plateau 5,500-feet high.

It is a nature-sculptured granite garden. Gigantic rocks are shaped like eggs, torpedoes, whales. Jumbles of huge stones are pushed higgledy-piggledy together.

Vertical facings of sheer granite cliffs make ideal testing walls for experienced grampon and piton climbers.

A rocky wonderland.

The sub-alpine plant life is another wonder.

The rocks and trees plus the birds and wild flowers can be enjoyed in nineteen formal nature walks laid out by the park authorities: short walks, long walks but none too difficult.

From the Tatra Inn we walked across an alpine meadow to the edge of the plateau and Dicksons Falls, following the descriptive brochure and track posts.

A delightful introduction to Mt. Buffalo's nature walks.

One of the most inspiring views is the sunrise from The Horn, the

highest point on Mt. Buffalo, 1720 metres, from which you command
a sweeping panoramic view of the Victorian Alps.

The next morning at five o'clock we awoke to the pinging of our
alarm clock, made coffee in the room and drove the Green Pony
through dense fog up to The Horn, a short distance from Tatra Inn.

At the end of the winding, gravel road we waited in the car, which
was being buffeted by winds, for the fog to lift. Clamped in the swirl-
ing grey mist we decided in the first touch of light that we should
try for the summit.

We climbed the steep trail as the wind continued to blow. The visibility was less than a hundred metres and there was a spooky beauty
in the scene. Our hair was wet by the time we reached the jumbled
pile of granite at the top. The chance of seeing a sunrise was nil in
the creeping grey light.

However we didn't rush going up or coming down, dawdling instead over the many colourful flowers . . . and suddenly the unique,
precious beauty of the mountain flowers came into focus. After reading countless paragraphs praising the mountain flowers, after being
born in the Rockies and after living in the Alps, after playing in the
Sierras, I now saw and appreciated mountain flowers for the very
first time.

Exquisitely small, they had come to life on the barest of soil, a
dirt filled crevice here, a teacup of humus nestled under a rock there.
Having survived snow and sleet, drowning downpours, the flowers
were so triumphant in their bold colours — hey, look at me — and
so graceful in their formations.

It took the confines of a fog to unveil the unique delights of the
mountain flower.

We counted eight different varieties on The Horn, each one a jewel.

On the path we also encountered occasionally a Bogong Moth
which the Aboriginals considered a delicacy.

"It must have been very difficult to make a meal," the Lady Navigator said.

Later in the morning I met Peter Bradle, the park manager.

"Did you see the moths?" he asked.

"Just a few. Little ones. Were they the Bogong moths?"

"Yes, on the path you only see one now and then. Would you like
to see where they live? It's less than thirty minutes from here."

We drove back up The Horn road and parked halfway to the top.
For a quarter of an hour we scrambled through brush, over rocks,

up the hill until we reached a dark cavern formed by granite slabs resting tent-fashion against each other like giant playing cards. An opening to the sky was thirty feet overhead.

"Look in the deep crevices of the rocks, mostly on the underside surface."

He shone his torch.

"See."

Remarkable! The entire surface was layered with brown moths so tightly packed together they resembled a thick, soft carpet. Each crevice. Millions of moths.

Peter said, "The Aboriginal diet of roots and berries was seriously lacking in oil. These moths which come up from the valley below to avoid the summer heat have built solid bodies of oil allowing them to hibernate for the season.

"The Aborigines scooped up moths like you see here, ground them into a paste which was a feast and a needed supplement to their diet.

"For a half an hour at dusk these moths will move out of the cave for exercise; the air will be thick with them. That's why you see so many ravens in the area. The birds are waiting for feeding time."

Later we saw Peter at the Park Information Centre which, in winter, serves as a daytime lodge for skiers.

The rangers put together an excellent, three-dimensional exhibit of plants and encourage the visitor to see, touch and smell: taste the leaf of the pepper plant on the table; look at a specimen under a microscope — that sort of thing. Well done.

At noon we went to The Chalet, a multi-storeyed ginger-bready wooden Victorian structure operated by the Victorian Railways. The hotel accommodates 180 guests in an old-world tradition.

The Chalet is a centre for park activity. Its parking area is an assembly point for non-guests as well. Rock climbers with spikes and picks were taking off for trying some of the most formidable climbs in Australia.

Hikers were leaving on walking tracks.

Hang gliders were unloading their "machines."

Hang gliding! We had never witnessed the nerve-shredding sport of hang gliding at close quarters.

We edged closer.

Mt. Buffalo is considered one of Australia's foremost hang gliding areas because the operators can launch themselves into space from a cliff 1,500 feet above earth and go soaring out over the open plain or up to heaven on the cliff-made thermals.

A week-long hang gliding competition was in progress. How far could a glider travel . . . how high could a glider rise?

On the previous gliding day, ideally hot and clear, a hang glider milking the thermals had reached Benalla Airport seventy-five kilometres away. Another pilot had reached an elevation point more than 3,300 feet above the point of his take-off.

The launch point is called Bent's Lookout and there must have been fifteen kites being assembled by their owners. A previous report had said that there would be no jumps because of the morning fog. Now the fog was lifting. There was going to be action.

We helped one young owner-pilot carry his equipment from the car park over the rocks down to the jump-off point.

Our adopted pilot had curly, sandy hair and a trim, smallish frame. He was calm. His name was Paul and he had come from South Australia for the competition. He wasn't new to Mt. Buffalo. He had been here a dozen times in the past year. "It's a beaut place," he said.

Not dangerous?

He shrugged. "Yesterday there were three bad take-offs. Shakes you up. One fellow went into the tree to the right of the jump. If there hadn't of been people at the spot to grab his machine, he would have gone over the edge, fifteen hundred feet straight down. Shakes you up."

He was bolting the aluminium components together with utmost care.

How long had he had this particular machine?

"Too long. Eighteen months. It's all right in smooth country but around here where the air is rugged you can get metal fatigue." He shook his head.

"No way to check it. The machines are not certified in Australia. The business isn't big enough like it is in America and Europe."

What did his machine cost?

"Seven hundred and fifty dollars. It's a VK-2. Made in Sydney. The initials stand for the V-keel under the wing to give it steadiness."

How did he feel when he stood on the edge of the cliff?

"Breathless. The adrenalin is really flowing."

Paul was meticulous in his preparation.

"This is one place where you don't want to make a mistake."

Surrounding us now were a dozen different models of multi-coloured machines going through the same careful assembly.

"Are you going to go or are you going to wait for the weather to clear?" a mate asked.

"Oh, I'm going," he said. "I'm not going to drive down."

Soon Paul was at the edge of the jump off, donning a helmet, over-alls, knitted gloves.

By this time we felt a parental proprietary about our blond young man and really didn't want him to be the first to go but there he was, crouched, very somber, concentrating straight ahead, waiting for the perfect spot in the light wind, two friends steadying the wing-tips.

"One. Two. Three. *Go!*"

He ran down the slight ten-foot incline and hurled himself into space — safe! He was away and gliding smoothly, held up in his flight by the updraft off the cliff face.

We applauded in relief.

It must take a solid core of steel to make that jump.

Next we watched a sixteen-year-old youth prepare for his maiden jump. Terrifying. He wore a parachute. Once again we experienced that relief of tension when he cleared the cliff and was soaring out into the clear air.

Near Paul during the initial preparation was Steve Moyes, Australia's largest hang glider manufacturer and probably the most experienced pilot. His jump suit was stencilled completely down the back with a chronicle of world-wide competitions in which he had taken part.

He assembled a new machine of his own design and manufacture, a Mega MKII, which cost $940 and among other virtues was extremely easy to assemble.

He launched himself off the cliff with professional ease and when we left the area an hour later we could still spot his hang glider high overhead.

Later we talked with an Australian hang glider pilot who had won the national championship three times, who had broken his leg four times, who said the best hang gliding competition in the world was at Cypress Gardens in Florida.

"They have the best organisation, the best prizes — and they must have four million girls."

Mt Buffalo is also a popular winter sport resort and during the height of the season will have five to six thousand visitors a day.

At Tatra Inn there are four ski lifts. Two additional poma lifts are available at Dingo Dell.

The park has six toboggan runs.

Best of all the plateau nature of the park makes it terrific for the increasingly popular cross-country skiing.

Ski rentals, ski schools and first aid stations are available.

In the snow-less state of South Australia, gangs of skiers crowd aboard ski buses in Adelaide late Friday afternoons, drive all night, arrive at Mt. Buffalo early Saturday morning, ski all day and part of the next day and then drive back to Adelaide, arriving Monday morning in time to go back to work.

The Big Blue Mountains

The popularity of the Blue Mountains is due to its proximity from Sydney — 100 kilometres — and accessibiltiy by train or bus or car.

The mountain area is worth the investment of a thorough exploration because the farther you get off the paved road the more rewarding the rugged country becomes.

Visitors often think that the string of vacation towns along the top of the mountain, Katoomba to Blackheath, comprise the blue Mountains but in reality there are three national parks in the area covering millions of hectares with deep-cleavaged gorges, tipity-toe ridges, rainforests, clear mountain streams.

The Blue Mountain of the resort towns has been popular since the turn of the century.

The moneyed gentry could take railroad trains on sweltering summer days and remove themselves to the cool air, the whispering wind in the trees of the Blue Mountains.

They stayed in ornate hotels and guest houses and took gentle walks and played golf in the afternoon when the temperature had gone down. And sipped tea.

You can do the same.

Modern additions include a scenic skyway cable car and also a breath-taking scenic railway.

We played golf at Leura — nice course — hiked part of the Prince

Henry Cliff Walk which rightly boasts sweeping panoramic views
... and took the terrifying Scenic Railway with its nearly perpendicular thousand-foot drop to the valley floor.

Two restaurants were drawn to our attention by Sydney friends:
The Fork and View at Leura which turned out to be semi-disastrous
... and the Glenella in Blackheath, an excellent restaurant despite
the paper napkins. The Glenella is a BYO establishment and we
brought a bottle of Lakes Folly Cabernet which added considerable
enjoyment to the dinner.

A much more exciting way to enjoy the Blue Mountains is right
at your Sydney hotel-door-fingertips.

Adventure Travel Centre in Sydney offers weekend Blue Mountain Explorer treks with spectacular vistas through the Grand
Canyon, the Blue Gum Forest and the Grose Valley.

The grades are moderate.

Overseas visitors have a chance to see cascading waterfalls, glens
of ferns and rock overhangs, creeks and rivers, forests and walks
along the edge of the Grand Canyon overlooking purple valleys.

The first day starts out at Blackheath and goes to nearby Govett's
Leap Lookout, across Govett's Leap Falls, through a delightful
valley famous for its wildflowers and down to the depths of Neates
Glen, and the Grand Canyon.

From Beauchamp Falls, you descend to the valley floor and follow
the water to Junction Flat and then to the grassy campsite near the
famous Blue Gum Forest.

The next day you explore the most beautiful spot in the Grose
Valley, then along the sparkling Grose River, up to the cliff tops with
many rest stops along the way returning via Pulpit Rock and
Horseshoe Falls and back via the cliff rim walk to Govett's Leap.

Included in the package is all camping equipment including tents,
sleeping mats, sleeping bags and rucksacks and meals from lunch on
Saturday to lunch on Sunday.

Take-offs are every Saturday from March to November.

Also Adventure Travel Centre has other treks for those who like
their adventures on foot. Mountain experiences in New South Wales
involve either the Snowy Mountains south of Sydney or the
Budawang Ranges north of Sydney or the Cradle Mountains in Tasmania. Other treks include a Fraser Island Trek or a Tropical Island
Sea Trek where you spend seven days exploring Hinchinbrook Island
National Park, sleeping on the beach under the stars.

If you'd prefer to enjoy the country but stay off of your feet, check out the Golden West Tour Company at P.O. Box 133, Katoomba.

The company designs four-wheel drive tours to suit the visitor's requirements. Half-day tours, full-day tours or overnight tours include everything needed.

17. Family Beaches Nude Beaches and Number 10 Birds

Australia is a land of beaches.

Being an island-continent there are 20,000 kilometres of coastline. Add to that the off-shore islands and the reefs.

Beaches for swimming ... for sunbathing with and without suits ... for surfing ... for underwater diving ... for fishing. Beaches are everywhere.

Also as a beach occupation there is the attraction of looking at beautiful people.

The pot bellies go to bars and the beautiful bodies go to beaches.

If you think Australian beaches are filled with Bo Derek Number 10 types, you're correct. Simply marvellous.

The Lady Navigator reports that the men, particularly those participating in beach carnivals, are magnificent specimens ... if young.

An overseas visitor should make every effort to take in an Australian beach carnival which pits various Surf Life Saving Clubs against each other in gruelling ocean events, not only to enjoy the sight of all those magnificent specimens but also to see surf skills at their best.

The surf clubs were born of necessity. So much surfing around the cities, particularly where rip tides and giant waves caused havoc with swimmers, created a need for life guards — volunteer life guards — to protect those who so frequently get in trouble.

A world-famous organisation resulted.

"You have to know," Ernie Davis, executive secretary of the New South Wales Surf Life Saving Association told us one afternoon in Sydney, "that sixty percent of the people on beaches can't swim fifty yards. Yet, within twenty miles of Sydney where there are thirty-six swimming beaches, we haven't had a death from drowning on a guarded beach since 1936."

The message to visitors is simple. Swim on a guarded beach which is recognised by its coloured flags.

How big in the volunteer life saving movement?

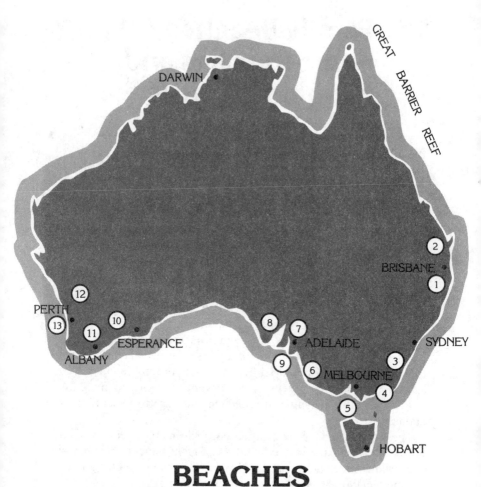

BEACHES

1. GOLD COAST
2. NOOSA HEADS
3. BATEMANS BAY
4. LAKES ENTRANCE
5. PHILLIP ISLAND
6. GREAT OCEAN ROAD
7. FLEURIEU PENINSULA
8. PORT LINCOLN/
   EYRE PENINSULA
9. KANGAROO ISLAND
10. ESPERANCE
11. ALBANY
12. PERTH
13. ROTTNEST ISLAND

"The total? Throughout Australia? Counting actives, active reserves and associates, there are *thirty-three thousand members*. Our state, being the most populated, has one hundred and eighteen affiliated clubs with a membership over twenty thousand. Last year our clubs were involved in some five thousand rescues and two thousand of those were made without the use of any life saving gear."

We later read an annual report where the case histories for merit awards read like fiction stories.

Speaking of gear, we asked Ernie about the famous Australian surf boat. We had heard it was no longer used in surf life saving but was still part of the beach carnival competitions.

"That's true. Our training and our equipment are both increasingly sophisticated. We have rubber boats with engines and torpedo tubes and a radio network tied in with helicopters.

"One of the factors that keeps the clubs together and the membership strong is the beach carnival. Among the fifty-two carnival events the surf boat is one of the most popular. A third of the membership wants to row because that is what the Australian male likes . . . the challenge, the danger, the excitement. So we keep the surf boat."

Before leaving Sydney, which we must do because this book is about The Country, the overseas visitor should pay a visit to the two most popular city beaches: Manly to the north of the harbour and Bondi to the south.

Also our intelligence sources report that the official nude beaches in Sydney are Lady Jane, Obelisk and Reef.

On the outer edges of most major family beaches it is considered acceptable to go topless. Discreetly.

A friend recounted an experience which is hard to erase from our minds. He had gone swimming at Lady Jane, the nude beach which is serviced by an ice cream vendor who arrives by boat. The sight of the nude bodies lining up for their ice cream cones with their change jingling in their hands has to be a classic cartoon.

North of Sydney . . . The Gold Coast

A very long day's drive north of Sydney (1,000 kilometres) is one of the most famous beach resort areas in Australia, Surfers Paradise on the Gold Coast.

We were prepared for a junky, over-built resort. A place full of oiled bodies, fast food operations and tacky shops appealing to tacky vacationers.

Erase.

Surfers Paradise is a resort of many modern high-rise buildings properly spaced out; a resort with gorgeous beaches. Long. Broad. Soft, golden sands.

Behind the beach area is a vast development of high priced homes where owner occupants demand shops and restaurants to meet their tastes and pocketbooks.

Surfers Paradise is impressive.

We stayed in a modern high-rise development, the thirty-three storeyed Golden Gate, and we didn't mind the air-conditioned comfort, the two bedrooms, the two baths, the fully equipped kitchen at all. At $65 a night on a weekly rate, we loved every minute of it. One of the world's great travel bargains.

Two-thirds of the year the Gold Coast days are sunny, the temperature is moderate. Little wonder that the coastline is studded with apartment buildings although surprisingly no new hotels have been built in twelve years.

The place is filled with to-do action.

Tourist authorities know that the number of people at beach resorts who actually go into the ocean is small regardless of the quality of the beaches and the warmth and cleanliness of the sea. So there are swimming pools everywhere and visitor attractions to occupy vacation days.

One of our first activities was hiring a U-drive putt-putt boat to gawk at the luxurious homes and gardens bordering the 150 kilometres of canals back of the coast. Eye-opening.

(A nice touch is the friendliness evidenced by signs directed towards sight-seers: "Hello!" "Have a good day." A third eliminated all unnecessary letters: "Aveagooday.")

The six-horsepower boat we picked was reasonable to rent by the hour — cheaper by the half or full day. Our only regret was that we didn't take a champagne picnic.

The canal also borders Cascade Park where you can beach your boat, picnic, use a restroom or get a free pot of boiling water for your tea.

In the Gold Coast vicinity for the punter are three tracks for flat racing, harness racing and greyhound racing.

Three golf courses.

Probably the largest family attractions are Sea World located at the end of the sandspit a couple of kilometres north of Surfers Paradise and its nearby sister attraction, Bird Life Park/Koala Bear Village.

Both attractions are first rate.

We have seen so many shabby marine and bird displays that we approached both parks with a "must we?" feet-dragging attitude.

Although they are operated independently, the parks are owned by the same company whose attention to Disneyland principles is obvious. Everything is pin-neat. Uniforms are bright and fresh. The personnel young and cheerful.

Our guide at Sea World was Lyn Moore, a former Miss Queensland. I wanted to take her home as a souvenir. A Number 10.

Sea World encourages families to come for the entire day by scheduling multiple free shows: shark feeding, seal acts, aquacade on water skis and, best of all, a dolphin show.

At Bird Life there are cockatoo and reptile shows, an immense aviary, a fixed-rail tram ride in a horse pulled wagon. The heartwarming, heart-throbbing thrill at Bird Life is to cuddle a koala bear. So soft, furry, loving. They cling to you like babies and smell slightly sweet like freshly crushed eucalyptus leaves, which is all they eat.

I wanted to take one home as a souvenir but the Lady Navigator said no. She said I couldn't have Lyn Moore either.

Behind the Beach

The Hinterland is a nearby mountain area with a major dam, deep wooded valleys, spectacular waterfalls. A pleasant rural contrast to the coast. In The Hinterland you can also visit a War Museum and a Boomerang factory.

The antique car museum, Gilltrap's Yesteryear World, a few kilometres south is a winner.

The museum not only has a superb collection of cars which they demonstrate in operation in a participatory show but they also have a 1936 Supercharged Auburn. (In my childhood, if you died and went to heaven, we believed that you went in a supercharged Auburn convertible.)

The star of the museum is a 1904 Darraco, built in France, which starred in the 1953 film *Genevieve*. It is a charming car and can do seventy kilometres per hour today without a struggle.

There is a classic 1914 Detroit electric car with cut-glass vases at the windows, a 1907 Cadillac designed by Henry Ford before he started his own car company (the Lady Navigator got to drive it and went into laughing hysterics trying to shift forward and backward) and a 1909 Model "T" the revolutionary car that changed the face of America.

If you appreciate automobiles, take it in. Good show.

Noosa Heads

The second Queensland destination was Noosa Heads at the north end of what is called the Sunshine Coast, 200 kilometres north of Surface Paradise.

Much of the southern part of the Coast is given to real estate developments but as yet Noosa Heads is low rise, low key and highly desirable.

Lovely beach. Lovely girls.

We stayed at the Pine Tree Motel, a growing-like-topsy complex with three seasonal rates too complicated to explain except that you should avoid the Christmas and Easter holidays. The motel runs at over ninety percent occupancy per year.

The manager is Tom Morrison, a handsome young man who hires only smashing looking ladies.

Next door is Belmondo's where we dined on fresh oysters, Greek salad, white snapper in champagne sauce. Delicious.

Luc Turschwell, the Alsatian manager of the restaurant, told us to return for lunch the next day. We did and had grilled fresh reef fish dressed in lemon butter with fresh fennel on the side. Mango sorbet. Pistachio nuts served with hot bread.

He buys the fish fresh every morning. Ages his own beef. But he overcooks the vegetables. Incongruous. Why? He apologised by saying when he does crisp vegetables, they are sent back. Terrible.

Noosa Heads abuts Noosa National Park. Good walking.

You can walk along the cliff face past the Boiling Pot Lookout, Tea Tree Bay and Dolphin Point to Granite Bay which is the "nudie" beach.

In Queensland it is forbidden by government attitude to sin and we were somewhat shocked to find a legitimate run-around-in-the-buff beach.

Taking off your clothes in public is not a habit of my generation, the mind having formed nicely defined do's and don't fences which must not be jumped.

When the Lady Navigator said, "You wouldn't dare," I looked at the challenge with little enthusiasm.

Skinny dipping with the right person at the right time has a dashingly romantic appeal but public nudity too often is a spectacle of wholesale flapping parts which are best covered if only from an esthetic point of view.

But no prudery here. Onward.

I unfrocked in three seconds and was in the water up to my neck in two with a strong inclination to cover my privates with one hand and dog paddle with the other.

It can't be done. To die of shame is one thing. Death by drowning is another.

The humility of the former is quickly over-ruled by the finality of the latter.

It was the fastest dip in my life.

"If anyone on the beach blinked, they missed you," said the Lady Navigator that night in recalling the event.

"Not so. Did you see that blond Lorelei on the rocks?"

"Vaguely."

"I think she waved at me."

She howled. Sometimes I don't understand her. She howled.

An excellent place to research what-to-do at Noosa Heads is in the Seven Flags Tourist Centre on the Tewantian Highway.

(Incidentally, the Seven Flags operation gets a round of applause for being open seven days a week. We are constantly astounded by tourist centres around the world that are open only five and five-and-a-half days a week. Information assistance during the weekend, the most popular travel time, simply is not available.)

The Centre offers an audio-visual presentation of the area — beautifully done — a three-dimensional electronic location directory, a plethora of printed material and a booking service for motels, apartments, caravan parks, houseboats and tours.

We booked a lake-river Everglade cruise for the next morning at eight.

The Intruder was a powerboat that skimmed over waters only fourteen inches deep into Lake Cooroibah and then, carefully following a marked channel, into Lake Cootharaba, a low-tide lake swarming with pelicans, sea eagles, hundreds of black swans and cormorants.

We turned through a narrow channel at the end of the lake past a new national park centre built on stilts, and into the Noosa River bordered with ferns, vines of morning glories climbing to sunlight on cotton trees, their own blossoms a bright yellow.

The best picture, however, was the water itself, a coal black reflecting surface. Discoloured by decomposed vegetation, particuarly the bark of the gum trees, it was a perfect mirror for the imposing gum trees and mangroves and melaleuca and the paperbark tea trees.

The reflected trees made everyone in the party reach for cameras. Clickety, clickety, clickety.

At a place called Kin-Kin Creek we disembarked on a river bank under guard by a three-foot sand lizard which slid off into the bush. We took a ten minute walk in a rain forest distinguished for the number of different kinds of palm trees.

No snakes. Bern, the guide, said he was afraid of snakes and the only thing in the vicinity were carpet snakes, a type of python. (They don't bite. They hug you to death.) The largest specimen he had seen was fifteen feet long. How quickly we returned to the boat.

Back at the ranger station one of the putt-putt tour boats was just pulling in when we finished our morning tea and biscuits and took off for home in the twin-80-horse-engined cruiser. (It is much faster to go in a cruiser.)

That evening we took cocktails to the top of the Noosa Heads Lookout where we could see the Everglades and up the coast to the beach of the coloured sands.

Noosa Heads is a calm, tucked out of the way peaceful place.

You can buy all the property you want for a million dollars an acre.

South of Sydney

The Princess Highway takes you south of Sydney along the coast and if you are driving to Canberra, you can inspect myriad lovely, lonely, luxurious beaches as far as Batemans Bay and then turn west to the nation's capital.

The popularity of beaches for family vacations varies with the weather. In the winter those from the cool south go north to the Gold Coast, Sunshine Coast and to Cairns.

In the summer Sydney families go south to their favourite beaches: Bulli, Wollongong, Kiama, among many.

We drove out Jervis Peninsula to see the Naval College and picnicked at St. George's Bay . . . a detour we don't recommend.

But a detour worth taking for the ideal setting is to Mollymook where there is an inviting crescent of white sand, a nine-hole golf course (an eighteen-hole course is at Hilltop), tennis, bowls and fishing.

The best fishing reputedly is at Ulladulla.

Our destination was Batemans Bay where we had a reservation at the hilltop Country Comfort Motel overlooking the broad waters of the Clyde River.

The river and the ocean beaches flanking it are the focal points of Batemans Bay as a resort area for visitors from Sydney (a half day's drive to the north) and Canberra (a two hour drive to the west).

The river offers excellent fishing, water skiing, cruising.

The beaches offer surf-boarding and swimming. The manager of the motel told us that there are many isolated beaches along the way where you can go with your favourite friend, take a picnic, take off whatever you want and enjoy nature all alone.

We drove to Batehaven and Malua Bay and peeked at McKenzies Beach and Burrin Point along the way.

Our best morning was at the Catalina Golf Club. Fun golf in the early hours.

Our best evening was at the Lobster Pot.

On the way to dinner, crossing the bridge, was a sign: "No Fishing From Bridge." Each side of the bridge was *solid* with fishermen. Local knowledge is bigger than the law.

At the Lobster Pot we had superb Clyde River oysters. Then a main course fish, the lightest, tastiest, best-grilled John Dory in Australia.

East of Melbourne

East of Melbourne along the coast is Lakes Entrance, an ocean resort for the metropolitanites. Avoid it in the summer. It is a hamburger-haven-fried-chips-little-Athens-Adriatic mess.

De-peopled, Lakes Entrance is a place of spectacular works by Mother Nature.

Waters flowing out of the mountains of east Victoria formed a series of sizeable lakes, rich with fish and fat with vegetation. Lake Wellington, Lake Victoria, Lake King, Lake Bunga, Lake Tyers.

Along the oceanfront, storms from the Bass Strait have piled high sand dunes farther than the eye can see, forming Ninety Mile Beach.

The Forest Park at Lake Tyers is a haven for fishermen with its bream, whiting and flathead . . . the largest flathead on record being twenty-one pounds.

The huge landlocked lake area was settled by the Dutch in 1838.

The first attempt to cut an entrance to the sea began in 1869 and then stopped. In 1881 work started again and in 1889, nearing completion, the entrance was opened by an angry storm which swept away the last barrier of sand-bar.

Within the peaceful harbour today, safe from the Bass Strait storms, is Australia's largest fishing fleet which nets ten million pounds of fish annually. But not during the summer-Christmas season when the resort is full of visitors hungry for fresh-from-the-sea fish.

The fishing fleet goes on vacation.

At Lakes Entrance you have many cruise options on several excursion boats: all day, half day, cocktail-sunset, charter.

Or you can hire your own little powerboat to explore and fish on your own at a reasonable cost which we were going to do but a summer rain spoiled the day for boating so we went instead to the Gippsland Aboriginal Art Museum, one of the most absorbing Aboriginal museums we were to find in Australia.

A map at the entrance to the museum shows the location of five hundred Aboriginal tribes. The folk art inside is primarily from the north and central tribes.

Fascinating stuff. How the Aboriginals painted and carved. Displayed were the symbolic references to their "dreamtime," the other world of legend and religion from which so many of their customs flowed.

Spears were thrown from a *woombra*, a wooden sling-shot which gave the spears more length and accuracy. Aboriginal "bread" was made from fungus found underground. Shoes of emu feathers. Painted bones to induce death. The making of the *didjeridoo*, the hollowed wooden musical horn. The *corroboree* (dance) headdress.

A taped guide and several strategically placed video sets in the one-room museum brought the exhibits to life.

For the overseas visitor, it is an edifying stop. (The group in front of us spoke Polish and the people behind us spoke Dutch.)

One plus factor we found at Lakes Entrance was the Tres Amigos Restaurant which has a fantastic enchilada made with fresh scallops.

At the time of our visit there was no outstanding seafood restaurant. Inconceivable at such a seaport.

Our most satisfying visual was the gently rocking colourful fishing boats at sunset.

South of Melbourne

From Lakes Entrance we drove west along the coast to Phillip Island and the resort town of Cowes.

Phillip Island was crowded with vacationers from Melbourne enjoying the beaches. We had an ocean-front room with a bed that sagged like a hammock in the Continental Hotel.

Two attractions brought us to Phillip Island. Seals and penguins.

The Australian fur seals were almost wiped out by the avaricious seal hunters in the nineteenth century but a successful attempt to re-establish them has brought their population back to 20,000.

Near Cowes is Seal Rock where a colony of 5,000 seals reside, mostly immobile . . . just sunning.

At the kiosk you can look through powerful binoculars to see the rock island humped and bumped with seals.

The bull seal comes to the island in early November to set up camp and stake out his territorial area. The female follows and in the November-December period gives birth to pups. Within six days she mates again and for the next eleven months raises one pup while carrying the embryo of another.

Walking on the rocks below the Lookout is a tempting sport but signs warn the visitor to be careful. Several unwary walkers have been washed away.

Great views up and down the coast.

Port Phillip is probably best known for its fairytale of the sea: the Penguin Parade.

At dusk every day of the year, winter and summer, the march of the fairy penguins, smallest of the seventeen penguin varieties, begins. They come out of the ocean reluctantly and after flitting in and out of the small surf, finally waddle up into the tussock-covered reserve and burrow in for the night. Two hours before dawn they waddle back into the ocean for a full day's fishing.

A fairy penguin can swim underwater at a 45-kilometre clip and has been seen 64 kilometres out at sea.

The penguin reserve at Summerland Beach is operated by the Port Phillip Shire Authority. They also operate an immense car park and a large kiosk selling films, books, light snacks and souvenirs.

Admission is $1.50.

The penalty for using a flash camera is $200 and confiscation of the camera.

The penalty for littering is $500.

We never saw a flashbulb go off and we never saw a piece of paper on the ground. The supervision of the entire Australian countryside should be turned over to the Port Phillip Shire.

At the beach there is a concrete grandstand but people who want to get closer to the action go down to the beach, which is roped off to allow a free passage for the birds of the sea to reach the reserve.

Visitors are advised, even in summer, to carry blankets, ski jackets, seat cushions, warm hats.

We arrived early when the car park was nearly empty. It was 8:15 by the time we were bundled into the concrete grandstand. A chalk board announcement at the entrance said the probable time of the penguin parade was 8:50.

The sun was just setting behind the hills. The summer crowd filled the stand and overflowed to the beach.

Announcements were made in Japanese, Spanish and English.

It was after nine o'clock and the beach was floodlighted before the first finger pointed to the surf. "There!" a voice exclaimed.

Out in the shallow of the tide a dark blob bobbed and eventually stood on its feet ... the fairy penguin was soon joined by its brothers and sisters in a flock of about twenty-five.

On either side of the grandstand more penguins emerged from the sea, playing tag with the surf, straggling toward the lights between the caged-in people and wandering freely into the reserve.

And so the parade went — more than a thousand penguins were estimated to be returning home from the sea hunt.

We left as late-comers were still arriving . . . and the car park was absolutely filled.

One to two thousand people come every night, waddle down to the beach to be herded into pens to watch a thousand penguins waddle out of the water in freedom to their evening homes.

People parade. Penguin parade. A delightful show for a dollar.

At Ocean Grove on the southwest coast from Melbourne 15,000 people camp tent-peg to tent-peg during the summer.

Farther down the coast is the prime surfing area of Torquay and, just beyond, the most desirable surfing beach in Australia, Bells Beach, an uninhabited stretch of sand at the foot of a tall cliff, where big, steady rollers come in off the Bass Strait.

It was a cold, windy, rain-blown day. Were there surfers down there in the ocean? Of course.

We were on our way to Anglesea to attend the Anglesea Beach Carnival, traditionally seen by 10,000 spectators in warm sunshine.

That December day was a disaster. A shivering handful of relatives and friends of competitors came to watch the surf races, the iron men contests, the boat races as the contest among the clubs went on in spite of grim weather.

As guests of the Anglesea Surf Club we enjoyed a pleasant buffet lunch in guilty comfort before going down to the beach and getting in the middle of the action.

The ocean was rough. Surf boats capsized. Surf canoes capsized. The waves were high. The winds were cold. The competitors seem to thrive on it.

We were grateful to new-found friends who took us to their impressive beach cottage and fed us hot tea and gave us sound advice for the next day's drive, one of the most impressive coastal drives in Australia.

The Great Ocean Road

From Anglesea we drove along a rugged coast to the resort town of Lorne with large guest houses and hotels and a pleasant Victorian ambience. Immaculately starched white bowling members made their way to their green-lawned club at the ocean's edge.

Farther down the coast at Apollo Bay the Lady Navigator checked in with the local automobile club representative who advised her to take the route across the peninsula through the Otway Mountains to the coast.

Although it was a gravel road the scenery was delightful. Tall, lush ferns bordered the route. Towering trees. We always were astounded to find "rain forests" comparable to those in Hawaii.

On the west side of the peninsula we detoured a couple of kilometres to Melba Gully. You should do the same and find a verdant grove of sloping lawns and trees filled with wild birds. We arrived to hear the voices of a vacationing bible-student group doing a finger-snapping, pre-picnic prayer song "God is Great — God is Good" before settling into sausages and things.

We returned to the coast in an area sparsely covered with heath. It was lunch time and we followed the traffic into a treeless, unimpressive Port Campbell Park.

Wham-O!

Below the lofty cliffs where we parked was one of the most staggering, stunning sights in Australia — a series of incredible sea sculptures pillared in the surf. The high noon light cast just the right shadows down the length of the cliff-high statues called "The Twelve Apostles."

The action of the sea has washed away the softer parts of the sandstone cliffs leaving these gargantuan carvings standing in frothy waves, their multi-coloured layers of sandstone backgrounded with sparkling blue sea and sky.

(A bright lad went by our parked car and turned back to his mother and said, "The biggest one must be called Peter.")

We stayed riveted to one spot for more than an hour watching the changing shadows on the Apostles.

Farther down the park other spectacular formations are cut into the sandstone cliffs: Thunder Cove, Blow Hole, London Bridge, Island Archway, Mutton Bird Island.

If I had only one place, one visual, one scene to take my overseas friends to, it would be here. Port Campbell Park.

Tasmania

Tasmania doesn't promote its beachside resorts although it is surrounded by ocean with many fine beaches.

The cooler weather removes Tasmania from being a year-around aquatic playground but we watched a television beach carnival in

Hobart. There is excellent surfing and skin diving in Tasmania but the tourist literature, like most Australian visitor information, simply takes beaches and surfing for granted. If you are interested, you will find ocean action everywhere.

South and West of Adelaide

Immediately south of Adelaide thirty minutes from the city a string of white sand beaches stretch from Brighton clear down to Rapid Bay.

This jutting of land into the Great Australian Bight is known as the Fleurieu Peninsula and besides the wining and dining, the Southern Vales region offers an array of museums and galleries, historic buildings, parks and reserves, golf courses, deep sea fishing, surf fishing.

Most of the beaches are well protected.

The best known beach is Maslin Beach which is South Australia's first nude bathing beach.

We drove there after lunching at "The Barn." A sizeable parking lot sign reads:

WARNING
The reserve for clad and
unclad bathing
is 500 metres
south of this car park.
Unclad person outside
the reserve
shall be prosecuted

It was a beautiful day and we were tempted but our destination was Victor Harbor and not knowing how long our driving time would be we hitched up our clothes tight around our Barn-filled bellies and drove on. (It turned out that we had plenty of time.)

Another famous peninsula in South Australia is the Eyre Peninsula and is an alternate route prior to driving across the Nullarbor Plain. (I always pronounced Nullarbor incorrectly putting the accent on the second syllable while the local usage places the accent on the first syllable. *Nool*-ah-bur.)

After leaving Port Augusta a highway goes south to Port Lincoln where foreign flag ships load grain from huge silos and live sheep and frozen meat. Yachting, fishing, swimming, surfing abound.

Also at Port Lincoln is Rodney Fox who is an authority, writer and photographer of the great white sharks. He mounts expeditions — you'll want to take one of these — for photographers who are lowered in baited cages among the enormous man-eaters. Baited with fresh, bloody meat! You'd love it.

Following the main highway northwest along the Eyre Peninsula there are many side roads to hidden coves and beaches. At Point Labatt, a narrow strip of coastal cliffs, you can sometimes see the only mainland colony of Australian sea lions.

Streaky Bay is a popular seaside resort with fishing and sandy beaches. *Blue Fin*, a film, was produced here.

Shortly after Smoky Bay you rejoin Highway 1 at Ceduna.

The Eyre Peninsula alternate route, if you stay one night at Port Lincoln and another at Streaky Bay or Ceduna, adds only 260 kilometres to your Nullarbor crossing and one or two days, depending on how much time you give to sightseeing.

Kangaroo Island

Adelaide's most popular seaside resort is a king-sized island 80 kilometres south of the capital called Kangaroo Island which is too large and too varied in attractions to take in on a day-trip although it is possible to fly over in the morning and back in the afternoon.

Kangaroo Island is a place where you want to hole up for a week, take off your shoes, your mental girdle and enjoy the many leisurely activities the island offers. Lots of wonderful beaches — many of which you can have to yourself — fishing, seafood, walking, strolling, sleeping, drinking.

Kangaroos and emus and sea lions.

The Kangaroo Island brochure includes in the attractions: "At night one of the unforgettable sounds is that of penguins mating in small caves in the coastal cliffs."

A car ferry services the island in addition to aircraft, according to the popularity of the season.

Western Australia

At Esperance, having driven south from Kalgoorlie 390 kilometres that morning, we picnicked at the hilltop Rotary Lookout. The many off-shore islands in a blue-on-blue sea was balm for our eyes.

It is easy to understand why this is a favourite week-end and holiday destination for the miners and the farmers inland. What a gorgeous ocean scene after the parchedness of the goldfields.

Esperance, a properous port town for the goldfields in the early days, now is a major shipping depot for grain which is grown in abundance in the surrounding country since the introduction of modern irrigation and fertilising techniques.

David Rockefeller and Art Linkletter are among others who put large amounts of investment capital into the farming enterprises.

The prosperity of modern Esperance is apparent in the modern shops and the new, expensive houses.

We drove west along the coastline looking down on fantastically beautiful rice-white beaches, some with posted warnings of rip tides — "don't endanger the rescuers" — others warning about fishing off the rocks.

But also there were tucked-away cove beaches. Perfectly safe.

Twilight Beach, one such cove, protected on one side by a sand dune made for sliding young children, is probably the most perfect swimming beach we saw in Australia. Silken sand softly sloped into emerald green water. Ideal.

Farther along the coastline is Observation Point where the first French exploration boat anchored on December 9, 1792. Later its commanding sister-shop came into a calm bay to the east of Observation Point and Entrechateau, the commander, named the anchorage after his ship, *Esperance.*

Near the centre of the beach resort is a new local museum. A major exhibition dates from the time when the name of the town was heard all around the world. Instant international fame came to Esperance on the 12th of July, 1979 when Skylab, the giant U.S.A. space machine fell to an earthly demise and scattered its parts over southwest Australia. Major chunks were found near Esperance.

"It sounded like a sonic-breaking airoplane," said the lady at the ticket window. "A giant wind. Oh, yes, we heard it!"

Among the museum's Skylab mementos are a frozen food locker, a tank made of titanium to hold nitrogen, bulkhead material, a gear part and a melted regulator of an electrical power circulator.

Nearby is Pink Lake. It is pink. Sometimes it turns purple.

This what's-going-on-here phenomenon is caused by eosion, a natural dye created by the action of bromine on fluorescein.

In the Pier Hotel, notable for a giant police dog which roams the corridors, I ordered a bottle of beer for dinner.

"You can't have a bottle," said the barmaid.

"No?"

"You can have a stubby."

The laws and nuances of beverage sizes vary throughout Australia. My fail-safe habit was to go to a bar and point to a neighbouring glass or bottle (or stubby) and say, "I'll have one of those."

South of Perth

When it is summer-sizzling in Perth, a large segment of the population runs south to the cooling breezes blowing off of the Southern Ocean at Albany. Which explains the line of motels leading into the city of 18,000.

By April 1 we had missed the summer crowds but without a reservation we turned to the tourist office for help. We needed a kitchen where we could enjoy a simple meal of our hand and design. We were directed to the Albany Holiday Flats, two blocks from Middleton Beach and two blocks from the Albany Golf Course.

Our self-contained unit had a double bed, colour TV, generous sized bath and a modest but glorious kitchen. It was our 107th abode, our least expensive accommodation and one of the most enjoyable. We immediately extended for two additional nights.

Middleton Beach faces King George Sound and extends from Princess Royal Harbour to Emu Point at Oyster Harbour. Emu Point is also the location of several holiday motels.

The beach gets an "A". Broad, clean, long and safe.

The golf course gets another "A" if only for the "birdie" bonus. It is a beachside course, simply laid out, first nine holes out and back between the sand dunes, second nine holes out and back between sand dunes. The birds in the bushes and the trees on top of the dunes include multi-coloured, yellow-winged honey-eaters, green parrots, black cockatoos, ravens, swallows. During the first light of the morning, it is a stimulating, God-is-wonderful golf course.

When we were there, Albany was having a local artists exhibit in the old town hall from which the city had purchased a very avant-garde painting for $1,000. You could hear the clucking in Perth.

Highly recommended is The Residency, formerly the home of Albany's Government Residents, located on the point where Major Edmund Lockyer landed Christmas Day, 1826 with a handful of militia and convicts — two-and-a-half years before Perth was born — to establish the first British foothold in the state.

A replica of Lockyer's brig *Amity* is set in concrete nearby.

The Residency is a fine museum now, a branch of the West Australian Museum, with excellent presentation of life in a remote colony including an educational exhibit on the evolution of discovery of "New Holland" as Australia was called.

The local history is an example of the everlasting fear of the English that another country might claim the new continent first.

My accompanying historical reference book was *A Short History of Australia* by Ernest Scott, 1920, Oxford Press.

He wrote:

> "As long as foreigners could be kept off other portions of the coastline by waving the Union Jack, dumping down a few convicts at points like Westernport, Albany and Melville Island, and saying firmly in diplomatic language, 'This is all ours' — that was sufficient. The lion lay couchant after a heavy meal with his paws on what he intended for his supper."

Across the street from The Residency is the Old Gaol, another historical museum, and in the centre of the city is a handsome farm residence, The Old Strawberry Hill Farm, built in 1831 by Captain Sir Richard Spencer. The original slate roof came out from England. Not much on the inside but a classic exterior.

(The local newspaper as an April Fools' joke, reported the official decision to demolish the old farm. The resultant hue and cry sent the editor into a tailspin of apologies.)

Perth

Perth with the graceful Swan River wandering through its middle is a visual piece of cake.

The frosting is made up of beaches.

Unlike the city beaches of the East, the open, sunny beaches of Perth are almost lonesome they are so uncrowded.

When they are filled, it is with tanned, slim, sexy birds for which Perth is famous.

I summered in Perth many years ago during those days of youth when one never thought of the size of one's waistline. Afternoon after afternoon was spent at Cottesloe Beach at an outdoor pub table that expanded to accommodate more and more drinkers . . . more and more empty beer glasses.

Occasionally a member would get up and go diving in the surf. But not often.

A glorious summer when the uncluttered sands of Perth's northern beaches stretched into the countryside.

Most ocean beaches today — Leighton Beach, North Beach, Watermans and Sorrento, Scarborough, Rockingham and dozens more — support healthy-sized communities.

The official nude beach is Swanbourne between Cottesloe on the south and City Beach on the north.

At City Beach where we ran at dawn on our last trip, a group of hardy individuals swim every morning all year round. They are looking for new members.

A little more than twenty kilometres off the coast is Perth's favourite playground, five by eleven kilometres Rottnest Island, contracted Aussie-style to "Rotto."

During the summer months you can be sure all of the accommodations are taken: brick-built flats and villas, wooden bungalows, and a 160-guestroom lodge.

The bulk of visitors are day-trippers who go over on a two-hour ferry or in the faster, more luxurious comfort of an hour hydroflite. Convenient air services get you from Perth Airport to the island even quicker.

The attraction of "Rotto" is in its simplicity.

You can't take a car. You can't rent a car. Not a traffic light or a parking metre.

Lots of bicycles.

Many appealing deserted beaches for romantic swimming.

Fishing from rocks or hire boats, a nine-hole golf course (sand greens), bowls and tennis courts.

A little bit of imbibing, of course, at the Quokka Arms, with no worries about driving home.

Wild life includes peacocks and quokkas, a bitty-sized marsupial, and sandgropers. Sandgropers are humans who occupy "Rotto" ... very wet but not dangerous.

18. Hey, Sport!

Scratch an Australian and you'll find the original sports lover.

The Australian Tourist Commission's *Special Interest Manual* has sections on inland fishing, game fishing, saltwater fishing, golf, horse racing, horse riding, lawnbowls, motor sport, skiing, tennis, underwater sports and yachting.

Cricket is not mentioned but if you are in Australia during the summer season and you don't understand the rules of cricket go to a bookstore and buy a simple book on the rules to preserve your sanity because newspapers are filled with cricket stories and the television stations show hour after hour of cricket and the radio stations broadcast the lengthy cricket matches.

And cricket, after a summer's immersion, is intriguing. The skills of bowling and batting and fielding are subtle and finely honed. (The bowling ball travels at ninety-mile-an-hour speeds and is dangerous. Two school lads were killed playing cricket during our stay.)

To report on all Australian sports would take books and books.

Like the cross-section of safaris we can only share with the visitor a few samples ... three participatory sports: golf, skiing and lake fishing ... and one unusual spectator sport: Australian Rules Football.

Come along.

Hey, Sport!
Take Golf as an Example

In Australia there are over 1,300 golf courses ... ranking third in the number of golf courses behind the U.S. and U.K.

For overseas visitors the welcome mat is large and the reception enthusiastic. The green fees are most reasonable. The exception would be the "Royal" courses which tend to be a bit crusty and where you need to be introduced by a member and usually play with a member.

Our original intention to play only country courses was changed by the chance to play the Royal Melbourne through an introduction by Peter Thomson, the five-time winner of the British Open. Royal Melbourne is considered one of the finest golf courses in the world and it was an opportunity we couldn't pass up.

Playing the West Course of the club's 36 holes with singer Johnny Mathis who was on an Australian concert tour added to the experience. My notebook contains the memo that Johnny Mathis can make a par and a triple bogey with equal ease.

Although the Royal Melbourne fairways were reduced to the thinnest turf, or no turf at all, by an extremely severe summer drought, still the variation of holes was more than pleasurable. The layout commanded admiration and respect.

The Royal Canberra — introduced by a member — we found to be one of the prettiest golf courses in Australia. Here the fairways in the nation's capital city were lush and green and, in the afternoon, shadowed by the many trees, it was a joy.

With two "Royals" in the bag, we began to collect them.

The Royal Hobart in Tasmania was a pleasant, flat course which we played with a public relations friend out of London and a member.

In South Australia we played the Royal Adelaide, near the sea, which is also a flat course unique in that a railroad crosses two holes and a local rule states: "The railways system is an integral part of the course and a ball lying on it must be played where it lies or declared unplayable with the appropriate penalty." That'll hurry up your back swing.

The Royal Perth in Western Australia was the most expensive: $7 each. Members of golf course greens committees note: signs at four of the greens advised players, "Every Player Is Invited To Repair AT LEAST One Plug Mark On Every Green." The greens were immaculate.

With all of these Royal Courses behind us, we felt it mandatory to play the Royal Sydney and we extended a day in Sydney to see if we could get it tucked in. Very difficult. The Royal Sydney would prefer that you didn't know that it was there . . . and certainly doesn't want the knowledge leaked to strangers.

Phil Tresidder, editor of Australian Golf Magazine, was our introducer and we taxied out to the course to meet him.

Old wood, old brass clubhouse. *Polished* old wood. *Polished* old brass. Members to match. Breathing tradition, money and status.

After being introduced by Phil to the secretary and assistant secretary we teed off on the manicured course which swarmed with greens keepers. Everywhere. Beautiful golf on what must be the most expensive real estate in Australia.

No charge for anything. Except the telephone call for a taxi to come and get us. Twelve cents.

Our first golf experience in Australia had to be the most memorable.

At the south end of the Gold Coast are the Siamese twin cities of Coolangatta and Tweed Heads.

Coolangatta is in Queensland and Tweed Heads is in New South Wales but they are separated only by a boundary marker in the middle of a city thoroughfare.

A major difference to visitors is that Tweed Heads, being in New South Wales, has slot machines ("pokies") and Coolangatta being in sinless Queensland has not.

The Coolangatta-Tweed Heads Golf Club is in New South Wales and it is simply eye-popping.

Modern, three storeys, glass and concrete with a gaudy giant golf ball on top, the super clubhouse offers three bars, a first-class dining room, a bistro restaurant, a snack bar, entertainment seven nights a week, music in the lounge every afternoon and, incidentally, outside there are thirty-six holes of golf.

Four thousand members pay $50 initiation fee and $50 a year in dues.

What makes this bargain possible is a game room where there are — if I counted correctly — one hundred and forty-eight slot machines.

According to the club's annual report, the ten and twenty cent coin machines gross over two and a half million dollars in a year! The net take after half a million in taxes and maintenance costs, and re-placement costs is over one and three quarter million dollars.

If you belong to the usual golf club which is forever struggling financially to make it all come out even, you simply shake your head in amazement at the Coolangatta-Tweed Heads Golf Club.

No wonder they call it the Gold Coast.

Another financial note about a golf club which qualifies for the "Best Bargains in Australia" list: the Dubbo Golf Club charges $1.50 green fee for nine holes. But that includes a free drink at the bar.

Two of the prettiest golf courses we found were on opposite sides of the country: at Orange in N.S.W., the Duntryleague Golf Club with its incredible Victoria-Edwardian guest house and in the south-west tip of Western Australia at Albany, a delightful seaside course populated with rare birds, the Albany Golf Course.

Avoid the faux pas I made early in my Australian golf. It is considered improper dress to wear golf shorts with short socks; shorts are proper but *long* socks, please.

Another tip. In Sydney I called the secretary of the New South Wales Golf Association and told him our itinerary in his state and asked his advice about the most interesting golf courses. It proved a short-cut to good golf.

Every state in Australia has a state golf association.

A true horror story we clipped from a sports section: a Queensland golfer, a former state holder of a PGA title, was playing the par-four, 395-metre third hole in the Australian Open at Melbourne's Metropolitan Course.

After parring the first two holes, he was on the edge of the green on the third hole and looking at a long putt for another par.

His first putt was off line and after two more putts he was still not down. When he saw that his fourth putt was going to miss, he hit the ball in frustration while it was still moving and thereby incurred a two-shot penalty.

Now boiling, he putted again . . . and again hit the ball on the run. Another two shot penalty.

He finally finished with a twelve, after nine putts!

When asked to comment on the hole later he said in a classic understatement: "I lost my head."

Hey, Sport!
Take Fishing as an Example

"New" Lake Pedder is a mammoth man-made lake in southwestern Tasmania.

In addition to its physical size, twice that of the Sydney Harbour — everything is compared to Sydney Harbour — the lake is famous for the size of its brown trout.

The fish stories about the lake invoke a combination of "ah-come-on" disbelief to spine-tickling "let's go" reactions.

Examples: Six weeks before our trip a twenty-five pounder had been caught.

Four weeks before our trip one of Australia's most noted fishing writers, John Sautelle, with fifty-nine years of angling around the world, caught his first double-digit trout — a fraction shy of fourteen pounds — fishing on the east bank of Mt. Solitary with a dry fly using a Felmingham Dry Fly Special.

The Inland Fisheries Commission has netted and thrown back thirty-three pound trout in the lake.

"A dedicated Lake Pedder fisherman returns anything less than five pounds," we were told.

AH-COME-ON!

The success of the brown trout in the seven-year-old lake is due to the enormous food supply including the innocuous dragonfly.

The female dragonfly in her twenty-four hour existence as a winged insect mates with her partner and then they both die.

Her eggs drop to the bottom of the lake and a cycle starts with the birth of the "mud-eye" which works its way up from the bottom on lake reeds until it reaches the surface, blossoms into a dragonfly for one day, mates and dies.

During its cycle, the mud-eye provides food for the monstrous brown trout.

One look at the frame of Allan Felmingham, fishing guide, made us think that everything to do with Lake Pedder came in giant proportions.

Six feet-four inches, he has the look of a man who is still growing despite his forty-odd years. A former public servant, he saw in his hobby of trout fishing Lake Pedder the need of a guide service, quit his job, invested $40,000 in equipment and, in addition to being a trout fishing adviser to the Tasmanian Government Tourist Bureau, established a company, Island Water Safaris.

In his first year of operation ninety percent of his available time was booked!

He squeezed through the door of our holiday apartment in Hobart one evening to see how he could help us experience Lake Pedder even though he had no free time left before departing that week for a Tasmanian promotional tour in California and Washington. He, however, arranged for us to be taken to the lake for two days under the guidance of his week-end back-up, Tim de Haan. Allan would join us there with other fishermen.

Promptly at nine Saturday morning, Amsterdam-born de Haan, manager of the popular Westside Hotel, appeared in a four wheel-drive Toyota Land Cruiser, metal dinghy on top, towing a small caravan-camper which was to serve as our sleeping quarters at the lake. Little did we know how little we were to enjoy the caravan.

Because fishing at Lake Pedder during the latter part of the summer dry season is done principally at dusk and after dark, we took our own car to give us touring flexibility during the day.

From Hobart the drive to Lake Pedder is through beautiful hop-growing fields, bordered by tall poplars. At the gate of the national park Tim paid our entry fee and we went along a sealed road until we turned south on a forty kilometre cut-off over a gravel road to the south end of the lake. Through alpine country. We reached our destination at Scotts Peak Dam and at nearby Huon Camping Ground set up camp among tall gum and myrtle trees.

After a light lunch we drove to the top of Red Knoll to look across the spread of the "new" Lake Pedder. When the Serpentine and Gordon Rivers were dammed, the minor Lake Pedder along with adjacent Lake Gordon became the holding waters for a major hydro-electric generating operation at Strathgordon at the north end of the lake.

Around five o'clock Tim put on "tea." The Dutch guide with a career in the tourist-food industry starting with cruise ships and resorts and big and small hotels proved an excellent chef.

The steak was rare, zucchini crisp and onions properly browned. The steak was topped with fresh mushrooms and for dessert we were served fresh strawberries and cream. The kind of rugged camp life we enjoy.

By six we were in the Land Cruiser to Huon Inlet reached by a jeep trail around or through a lot of mud holes. When we finally stopped we put on rubber chest waders, assembled the spinning rods, grabbed a flashlight and hiked the last mile down the trail to the lake bank.

It was now almost seven and the last of the summer sunset. For an hour and a half we fished a healthy portion of the lake front without a nibble.

No matter. All was not lost because the scenery of the surrounding mountains at dusk was gold and peaceful.

A cloud started to form around the top of a mountain behind us and Tim reported, "The local people say that this is the country where clouds are born."

After dark, Tim switched our spinners for a lure called a "fish-cake" an unholy lure which is designed to simulate a small animal on the surface of the water.

An inch and a half wooden plug, painted polka-dotted yellow or black or red or white, has a metal propellor fixed to its nose which creates bubbles and a whirring noise when it is reeled slowly across the surface of the water.

Attached to the plug are four huge multi-pronged hooks. A monster!

The night before, our guide told us, the fish had gone berserk along this stretch of beach.

We fished without seeing, hearing or smelling a fish. But again there is something so satisfying about a skyful of stars ... a faint glow of a never-seen moon behind the mountain.

At midnight we packed it in. Quit. Weary. Cold. Trudged back to the Toyota and took off for camp.

At one of the mud holes Tim had skirted on the way in he went straight through. Halfway. Stuck.

The first attempt to gun the Toyota forward and backward only settled the vehicle further in.

"No problem," said Tim. "We'll winch it out."

There was a problem. In the flat scrub-covered land there was nothing to anchor the Toyota front-end winch to.

An attempt to put the winch cable around a thick roadbank covered with vegetation proved fruitless. The cable cut through the heavy turf like a piece of cheesecake.

When the cable finally did tighten, the load of the mud-trapped Toyota proved too heavy and the safety sheer pin on the winch gave way. A make-shift pin was inserted. It gave way. The jeep was now up to its bumpers, the axles resting on mud. Two o'clock in the morning.

"I'll go get help," said Tim.

"At two in the morning?"

"Fishermen around here are on the road at all hours of the night."

He ended up walking twenty kilometres back to Huon Camp. In mudboots.

For four hours we huddled frozen in the front bucket seats. Scrunched together, one bucket seat was too small. Separated, we iced over. We twisted, turned, contorted, cramped trying to get snatches of sleep.

At quarter to six a flashlight beamed through the front window. Tim had found Allan's son and two mates sleeping in a station wagon and brought them back to get us. The station wagon couldn't pull us out but it did get us back to Huon Camp where we crawled into our sleeping bags in the camper and, still chilled, went into exhausted sleep.

Three hours later the little toddlers in the camp (it was the last weekend before school started), banged on the caravan and rattled the door. When I opened the door, bloody-eyed, a little angel asked innocently, "What are you doing?" She is still living only because I was so weak I couldn't catch her.

Allan came to the camp in the late morning with two fishing clients from California and after sausage and eggs for lunch we put our gear into the five-metre *Safari Queen*.

We launched the boat at Scotts Peak Dam and took off for spots on Allan's air-photo map which was coded with accumulated intelligence: location, lures, dates, times and size of fish and successes in fishing for the giant browns.

In the late afternoon we fished portions of the Edgar Basin, banks of Mt. Solitary and Huon Inlet without success. I tried the spinner and the dry fly. Nothing.

Near sunset we re-grouped for tea on the boat. Chicken in butter, fish curry, sausage, bacon, bread and beer. Substantial but you never know how long the fishing night might be.

At dusk the California fishermen were set adrift at Little Bays in the dinghy for a try at dry-fly fishing, hoping to catch the last of the evening rise.

We were taken to another part of Huon Inlet where for an hour we cast without success.

At another part of the lake, now dark, we splashed ashore. The Lady Navigator said she'd rather read a good book and stayed on board while Tim and I went off into the night.

The greatest challenge while casting in the lightless night with a vicious "fish cake" is not to catch yourself.

Once on the slippery lake bank my foot went from underneath me and I found myself on my rear-end sliding backwards into the lake. I remember saying to myself as the water came into my rubber waders, "This is not the approved position."

I had no sooner emptied my rubber jacket pockets of water than Tim gave a yell twenty feet away.

"I've got one! Come and play it."

Now playing and, hopefully, landing a trout hooked by your guide is like having Mother cut your steak. It's for children.

So like a happy child I went over and played the fish. Tip up! Don't give it any slack! Careful! Let it run!

Tim was a very nervous mother but then he had never caught a double-digit fish after trying for eight years in Tasmanian waters.

He focused the light of his torch on the water as the splashing neared the bank and, *migawd*, there was a monster! Tim eased into the water, got behind the fish and then caught it by the tail and heaved it onto the bank.

It *was* a double-digit fish. They *were* there!

We went back to our posts and ten minutes later he yelled again. Another one. Again I obeyed his summons and again had hold of a fish. This one had more fight and gave a good struggle. When it was near the bank the torch revealed the line had become wrapped around the brown's gills. Bad. Denotes that the fisherman had given the trout too much slack.

"You'll be lucky to get it on shore," said Tim. But through great skill, cunning combined with experience . . . aided a bit by Tim getting behind the fish and booting it onto the bank . . . the fish was landed. A real beauty. Deep in the belly, broad at the back, the fish was in excellent condition.

When the *Safari Queen* returned near midnight we each toted a fish to the appreciative gasping of the Lady Navigator.

One fish weighed nine and a half pounds. The second fish, twelve pounds!

One of the Californians had also landed a fish — with the "fish cake" — and now everyone wanted to fish the entire night. Almost everyone.

The sleepless night of the evening before had caught up with me. I had fallen down again. Fouled my line a dozen times. Hooked my thumb. Bruised my ego.

Let Tim land his own fish!

While the rest went trudging off into the cold night, the Lady Navigator and I nestled into sleeping bags in bunks in the bow of the *Safari Queen* and slept soundly until six o'clock when we awoke to the tramping of heavy boots on deck. Our frozen companions had caught one more fish.

The fishing season in Tasmania is generally from the first of August to the end of May.

Lake Pedder is only one of several excellent fishing grounds. Western Lakes on the central plateau is a wilderness of a thousand lakes and is stocked with rainbows and browns. Another area south of Launceston consists of the Lagoon of Islands, Lake Sorell and Lake Crescent.

"They pulled a thirty-three pound brown trout out of Lake Crescent," a fisherman told us, "but that was the odd one.

For full information on Tasmanian fishing, get a Tasmanian Trout and Game Fishing booklet from Tasmanian or Australian tourist offices. Also there is a Tasmanian Professional Trout Fishing Guides Association, care of Mrs. Lois E. Jetson, secretary, 78 Main Street, Cressy, Tasmania 7302.

Her husband, Noel Jetson, is one of the leading river fishing guides in the state.

It is our last understanding that Allan Felmingham has merged his services into Tassy Highland Trout Tours (Bill Beck), 2/45 Landsdowne Crescent, West Hobart, 7000. Current costs are $100 per day per person for a party of two or more.

Two other members are Hay's Tassie Trout Tours, P.O. Box 75, Roseberg and Tasmanian Trout Expeditions, Bothwell, 7411.

A private lake offering fly fishing only is London Lakes, August through April. Day angling only, $70 a day. Everything including all meals and accommodations: $140 per day per person. Write London Lakes, Post C/O Post Office, Bronte Park 7464, Tasmania.

Hey, Sport!
Take Skiing as an Example

Between Sydney and Melbourne are mountains of snow.

Naturally, in sports-nutty Australia downhill skiing is another excuse to break an arm or fracture an ankle. Cross-country skiing is gaining in popularity.

The Snowy Mountains ski centres in New South Wales are Thredbo, Perisher Valley and Smiggin Hole and Victoria's ski fields include Mt. Buffalo, Falls Creek, Mt. Hotham and Mt. Buller.

Popular? The Australian ski fanatic will ski on a shaven ice cube if that is all there is and when the snow falls in the June to September winter, the resorts are full. Chock-a-block.

The Snowy Mountain resorts are reached from Sydney or Melbourne in an easy day of driving.

We had a pleasant drive from Sydney, with a brief tour of Canberra, to Thredbo Village.

Thredbo was started as a ski resort in 1957 with one ski rope tow and a small lodge.

It is now a major resort representing an eight million dollar investment with another four million dollars being added. There are a host of commercial and club ski lodges, restaurants, shops, a nine-hole golf course and four tennis courts.

Fifteen lifts carry 11,000 skiers an hour . . . three times the capacity of the hotel and lodges.

"What do you want to do first?" asked Derek Browes, the hotel manager at that time.

"Get up the mountain," we said.

Derek called Ludwig Rabina, the mountain manager who outfitted us with ski gear and lift passes. He then introduced us to our Information Guide.

When we go to unfamiliar ski resorts, the first thing we do is to hire an instructor, not to teach us how to ski — we are too terrible to be corrected — but to show us the mountain.

With fifty kilometres of trails the Thredbo management knows that it is not an easy terrain to understand and that the faster a new skier to Thredbo knows the mountain the more enjoyment he and she will have and the faster they will come back.

So Thredbo provides a Ski Information Guide, free, who shows newcomers the trails. Not an instructor. Just a guide.

We had a great companion-guide, Geoff Goodwin, who took three hours to show us the chairlifts, take us down the beginners and intermediate trails, locate the restaurants. The fifty kilometres of trails range from wide novice slopes to challenging championship runs.

(On the first run the Lady Navigator went out of control and ended up in a huge pile of rocks with her skis above her head. One doesn't laugh at these times. Later I skied onto a ski-lift platform which was only partially covered with snow. I was going too fast and when the snow became wood the skis stopped and I continued doing a swan dive onto the platform. She fell down laughing.)

Thredbo has an army of ski instructors who come from all over the world when winter skiers in the northern hemisphere are out of snow. French, Swiss, German, American, they are all here . . . also a major contingent of Australian instructors.

Also there are ski hostesses on the mountain and at the base of lifts to answer questions.

That night we had dinner with Ludwig Rabina and his wife, Sharonne.

"In the official mountain guide and map, there is a paragraph about 'sno-cat touring.' What is that?" we asked.

"Just what it sounds like. When the weather conditions are right ... not too much wind ... we take a group of skiers to the top of the chairlift, put them on tow ropes behind a sno-cat and take off above the chairlifts to the mountain tops. On top of unbroken slopes, the skiers let go and ski down virgin snow to the bottom where the sno-cat picks them up and back to the top of the next slope.

"You want to go?"

Together; "YES!"

"It will be arranged."

Ludwig was born in Slovakia. He is fifty years old and looks thirty-five. Sharonne is thirty-five and looks twenty-five.

The couple has hiked into the Himalayas twice using Sherpa guides and Nepalese porters. On their second trip an awesome animal noise came out of the night terrorising the porters who crowded into the Rabina tent. They were certain it was a *Yeti*, the unseen Himalaya animal-man. The noise only subsided with the lighting of a fire with valuable, hand-hauled wood. "I don't know what it was," said Ludwig.

They trained for their trek from Katmandu to the top of 15,000-foot Himalayan peaks by running up the Thredbo mountain roads five miles every day for five months.

The next morning we were on top of the mountain.

The sno-cat was broken.

Two sno-mobiles were brought out, called "skidoos," and tow lines were passed back. The Lady Navigator had a skidoo to herself. The second machine towed the Information Guide and me. Off we went like little Eskimos behind a team of running dogs.

It was stupendous.

For two hours they pulled us across open snow fields on the top of the mountain range.

We went to the edge of the mountain overlooking Tom Groggin cattle station, a speck down in the valley. We looked up at Mt. Kosciusko in the distance which cannot be seen from the valley of Thredbo Village.

"Actually," said Gary Connors who was in charge of the expedition, "they have surveyed a mountain next to Kosciusko which is several feet higher but it is an embarrassment because Kosciusko has always been publicised as the highest mountain in Australia."

Winds on top of the range where we were standing often reach a velocity of sixty kilometres an hour. They create fabulous, award winning snow sculptures on rock outcroppings. The intricate designs and frozen snow swirls deserve a museum showing.

From the various elevations we released our tow ropes and skied down gentle slopes through fresh, virgin, unbroken powder snow, a skier's greatest fantasy.

That morning was an absolute lark, ranking with our experiences of shooting the shark-infested Tiputa Pass in Rangiroa (French Polynesia) and hiking the Milford Track in New Zealand.

After it was over the guide asked us if we wanted to ski the regular trails around the top lifts. We declined. We didn't want anything to detract from the flavour of the two glorious hours skiing the top of the Snowy Mountains.

The day before we had turned down the chance to run a time trial over what is known internationally as a NASTAR course. What we didn't know is that each runner is videotaped and that evenings, tapes are shown on the hotel television screens. Who could resist such opportunity? Neat promotional idea which is a Thredbo trademark.

We played two sets of tennis in our track suits and would have gone golfing but the report came back that the course was still too frozen.

The outdoor swimming pool had been closed in an effort to save energy but two outdoor hot tubs were in operation and when we left to play tennis a gorgeous redhead was holding court in one tub with a cadre of laughing young men and several bottles of champagne.

We thought when we came back that we would order a bottle of wine and take the other tub but that tub was also full with soakers and imbibers when we returned. It was a party that went on and on with men and women in various sizes and loosely draped towels leaving and joining the tubbers. The champagne bottles were heaped high. My!

We settled for a sauna.

Derek and Rei, his wife, had us to dinner.

He recalled a tub party that went on until three o'clock in the morning.

"An irate guest overlooking the pool shouted and screamed at the revellers to knock it off.

"I went down and tried to close the party. I ended up in one of the tubs.

"Coming across the lobby floor, drenched, the irate complaining guest appeared, took one look at me and said, 'You are drunk! Who do you report to?'

" 'The managing director.'

" 'Where is he?'

" 'He is in one of the tubs.' "

The next morning after counting the hundreds of dollars in champagne receipts signed by the tub party, Derek reported the incident to the managing director.

"Tonight, send the guest a bottle of your best French champagne compliments of the house and when he checks out of the hotel, there will be no bill."

The guest accepted the champagne with grace. When he checked out and was told there was no bill, he paused. (Now this I found to be quite consistent with the Australian character.)

"Thank the management for the champagne. People come here to have a good time and I shouldn't have lost my temper the other night. I was wrong. I'll pay my bill."

In the summer Thredbo promotes its fair weather activities: hiking, horseback riding, pack trips, tennis, trout fishing, water skiing, sailing, canoeing, golf.

Two other ski resorts, side by side, in the same Snowy Mountain area are Perisher Valley and Smiggin Hole.

Both areas have completed major improvements in ski lifts and facilities.

Perisher and Smiggin are higher in elevation and catch more snow. Thredbo claims that being lower in the valley the driver doesn't have the problem of reaching the lodges and hotel in snow conditions. Take your choice.

We left Thredbo impressed. Excellent professional facilities and an attitude that the first objective is to give the guest the greatest satisfaction. Everything good flows out of such an approach.

Hey Sport!
Take A Spectator Sport as an Example

One shouldn't be surprised by Australian Rules Football.

In a country which has a beer can regatta, a dry-river regatta, an annual cow-chip throwing contest; in a country where you can attend a cockroach racing derby, you could expect Australian Rules Football.

Many years before on my first visit to Australia I passed through Melbourne during the summer and heard about this winter game which is played in all states except N.S.W. and arouses such passions that little old ladies beat each other over the head with bumpershoots and players and referees have to be separated from the frothing spectators by snake pits and armed guards.

The latter proved somewhat of an exaggeration.

Following the skiing exercise at Thredbo, through the offices of the Australian Tourist Commission we obtained Members' Section tickets to a Saturday afternoon contest at the Melbourne Cricket Ground which is *never* called the Melbourne Cricket Ground but is *always* referred to as "Emseegee."

After a Friday night Chinese dinner — excellent Chinese food in Melbourne — we separated the next morning so the Lady Navigator could take a city sightseeing tour — "such exquisite parks and gardens" — and I could have the morning for antique book collecting which is a terminal disease.

We who are giving to snuffling out antique books in by-way shops are prone to wide bottoms, soft stuttering and to petting Persian cats. We immediately recognise each other and exchange information. Shop owners are eager to recommend the next book shop and the next. I found and bought a Golden Cockerel edition of *Matthew Flinder's Journals* for $275. The lady in the book store said it was a steal and I must have it for my South Pacific library. I believed her. A disease.

But back to the game at the Emseegee.

The first rule is that you, the spectator, "must have a pye with soss at the footy and a shout of beer."

We did what we were told. You hold a hand-sized round pastry filled with meat chunks and brown gravy in a paper container and pour soss — tomato ketchup — on the top of it. It is a mess.

The other food item is a "footy frank" — a long sausage wrapped in a soggy bun and plastered with soss.

To get a beer I went into the Men's Bar by showing my member's badge. The Lady Navigator couldn't go. Her eyes narrowed, her claws showed, but she didn't say a word.

Back to the game.

Australian Rules Football is played on a huge oval, not rectangular, field.

At each end are four posts. A ball which is kicked but not run through the taller centre posts is a goal and worth six points.

A ball which is similarly placed through the side posts is a "behind" and worth one point.

Eighteen players on each side kick or pass by punching the ball, tackle, run and generally beat the hell out of each other.

You need field glasses to follow the action on the far part of the field but it is one of the most exciting spectator sports we have ever witnessed.

The players are in superb condition. On the immense field they go, go, go with never a sign of flagging.

We were told to cheer for North Melbourne. We found ourselves sitting in a cheering area of the opponents. We kept very still.

There was much flag waving. Little boys wore club hats and club scarves and club coats and ate footy franks. Their fathers drank beer.

At half time we went to a lounge in the Members' Section where ladies were allowed if accompanied by a male member.

The contest was excellent. North Melbourne, trailing during most of the contest, brought it together in the last ten minutes to win the game.

We walked back to the city centre along with a few thousand others.

In the hotel room I said, "That was great. I particularly like the camaraderie in the Men's Bar. Jolly good."

Bristle.

"And having a lounge where women are not permitted alone is proper. The way things should be. Don't you agree?"

Double bristle.

"Degrading!" she exploded. "Primitive! Yesteryear! If you think we are not strong enough to get a cup of tea without a man's arm . . . or not good enough to have a drink in a man's company. . .!"

The Lady Navigator then made noises like a hissing, clawing tiger.

I don't think she liked it.

19. Found and Treasured By the Lady Navigator

"New game," I suggested on one of our final days of research.

"Let's name the 'Ten Best Buys' we've experienced. We will alternate and I'll start with 'opals.' (God knows I had bought enough of them and needed to justify the action.)

My friend concurred. (Thank heavens.)

"Woollies," was his first nomination.

"You mean hand-spun, hand-woven wool sweaters?"

"Yes."

We had outfitted kith and kin in winter climes for sure and bought a tunic jumper for skiing for ourselves.

Chocolate at the Cadbury factory in Hobart was second on my list. You eat your way through the factory on the $3.50 escorted tour — they lost money on me — then, how glorious, they permit you to buy at employee discounted rates. Whopping savings.

The game was enlightening. To probe our own minds for the best-of-the-best was an exhilarating way to put Australia into perspective.

It did not surprise us that opals topped the list. The opal is as synonymous with Australia as the topaz is with Brazil. It is the number one take-home souvenir. The rich buy opal as a hedge against inflation, convinced that its past annual twenty-five percent escalation rate will continue.

About ninety-six percent of the world's opals and practically all of the "precious" opals are mined in Australia. Precious opals are distinguished by a combination of translucence and fiery colours that flash changing patterns as the stone is turned in different directions.

In ancient times precious opal was among the most noble gems, ranked second only to emerald by the Romans. It is said that Mark Anthony banished the Senator Nonius in order to acquire his magnificent opal "as large as a walnut."

Throughout the middle ages the opal was thought to bring luck.

Just what is a precious opal?

We could tell you that it is a mineral of amorphous silica and variable amounts of water. That it comes from Australian desert lands that once were covered by a huge inland sea, creating an environment suitable for the formation of opals.

We could tell you that there are nine basic types of Australian opal. We could simplify the nine to three: solids, doublets and triplets. We could explain that the solid is a stone that is entirely natural. A doublet is a sliver of opal glued to some darker rock or glass, perhaps even more opal of the potch variety. The triplet is a doublet with a dome of clear crystal quartz.

We could confuse you with fiction. The black opal isn't black; it is dark grey or grey-blue. If it *is* black, and it *is* solid, be impressed. It is extremely expensive because it is extremely rare. Coveted!

We could further confuse you with fact: the inexpensive doublets and triplets look like black opals!

You can buy an opal for any amount of money you want to spend, from less than $10 a carat to more than $6,000 a carat. I bought triplets the size of pencil erasers at $3 each and they have a strength and colour vitality you cannot believe. I also bought a solid, not much bigger, that cost $150.

Our strongest advice is to do a bit of comparative, competitive shopping before buying. It's not only educational, it's fun.

Talk to the opal dealers, the cutters, the sales people. They are enthusiastic to share their knowledge and generous with their time.

I confided in a sales lady at The Opal Bar, a shop in Adelaide, that we were going to Coober Pedy, largest opal depository in the world, and asked if prices were cheaper there than in the city.

"Depends upon whether or not you meet a miner in the right frame of mind. Go to a pub; let it be known that you are interested in buying and someone might volunteer to show, and sell, from his private collection. From him, you could get a real bargain.

"Tourists who have shopped the stores in Coober Pedy tell me that city prices are cheaper, especially since the Hong Kong merchants have moved in and will buy everything in sight. Also, more tourists flow through Adelaide which makes competition keener. Come back in when you return and share your reaction with me," she said as I left the store.

That was about forty-five minutes later, after she had staged a private show-and-tell programme for me. I learned, by comparing stones of similar sizes, that the brilliance of colour and the depth of colour and the uniformity of the colour patterns make the difference between a $30 per carat and a $500 per carat stone.

"I'm sorry I haven't a really good stone — an 'investment' stone — to show you. Stones appraised at over $500 we ship off to Sydney or the U.S.A."

She paraded stones with the various traditional patterns before me: the "pin-light" opal with myriad tiny, fine dots of ever-changing colours spaced uniformly throughout the stone; the "broad-flash" whose colours are bold and sweeping as the stone is turned; the rare "harlequin" that is a collector's item with its precise computer-chequered mosiac.

You will find as many names for colour formations as there are miners, dealers and merchandisers . . . the theory being that exciting labels build exciting sales.

"Whatever the pattern, the more colours visible when rotating the stone in light, the better the quality of the stone."

I also got some opal care tips. Take off your opal ring when you wash and don't expose opals to sudden extremes of temperatures — like unpressurised baggage compartments in aircraft. The stone is slightly porous and contains a small percentage of moisture which contributes to its brilliance but which water-logging or ice solidification may damage.

Opals are comparatively soft and will scratch if exposed to abrasive substances. This characteristic makes a good case for buying triplets, especially for hard-use items like men's cuff links. The quartz dome protects the opal.

Solid opals that Di Crossing, our farm holiday hostess at Quirindi, had purchased for $30 and $60 per carat in Coober Pedy from a service station attendant first seeded a greed to go straight to the source. And when she told us about "noodling" for opals I went berserk.

We arrived in Coober Pedy about noon Saturday. Spent the day touring. Some noodling, mostly disappointing. Too late to hit the opal shops upon return. Everything closed. Pubs too crowded with rowdy Saturday nighters to "mine" for direct sales.

Sundays during the summer months, when most miners have turned from earth-digging to sand castle building down south, few stores even bother to open. Thin inventory. Few tourists. I found a single shop open, The Purple Shop. Eugene Peck, a Polish immigrant, had been an opal cutter in Melbourne before he staked his own claim in Coober Pedy and opened his own business.

My bonus from Mr. Peck was a new appreciation for the triplet which, I confess, I had denigrated.

"I was a solid opal snob too once. I felt that only the solids had intrinsic value until I discovered the 'images' in some stones which cannot be seen unless they are backed with a darker substance. Let me show you," and he disappeared through the door to the family residence.

The triplet pendant he rotated in his hand flashed blues and greens in a brilliant array of neon intensity. Then as he turned it ever so slowly, a crimson olde English script "7" blazed across the face. It was like watching Walt Disney's *Fantasia*.

"I've been offered thousands for it but my wife would divorce me before giving it up."

Interestingly, seventy percent of all the opals purchased by tourists passing through Coober Pedy are triplets, Mr. Peck estimated.

"North Americans buy the solids, Germans and Dutch go for triplets in a big way."

"How competitive are Coober Pedy prices?" I asked.

"You'll get a bargain here. Most dealers work their own stake. Some of us cut our own finds. There are no middle men and there is sufficient competition to make us price our gems fairly."

Back in Adelaide I took the Coober Pedy prizes I'd bought to four different opal dealers for appraisal. The triplets seemed to be duck soup for them; each appraiser priced them within a couple of dollars of actual cost. The solids, however, pose a perplexing situation. One beaut — not of "investment" quality but crystal clear with bursts of chartreuse and lilac, coral and pink — was alternately valued at $150, $160, $250, and $450. Quite a spread for professionals in the same city!

Most states have a luxury tax on opals. The amount of the tax varies by state. International visitors, upon presentation of their passports and on-going transportation tickets, are exempt from this tax or any portion of it that the dealer elects to discount. Some do not discount at all. The largest mark-down I received was twenty-nine and a half percent from The Opal Bar in Adelaide where my lady-counsellor also accurately appraised to the penny every opal I had purchased in Coober Pedy.

Of the four opal mining centres in Australia, only Coober Pedy is geared up with several accommodations, restaurants, attractions for tourism. Lightning Ridge, the home of the black opal, has a hotel, the Diggers Rest Hotel. Singular. Fly in during a winter month. Don't drive. Long and dusty. Don't go in the summer. You will melt. A feature of the hotel saloon bar is a set of dentures made of black and white opals and mounted on the wall.

The opal fields of Queensland, where most of the "boulder" opal originates, are in semi-desert regions; South Australia's second mining town, Andamooka, peaked its production several years ago and the town has shrunk.

The Hand Mades

We bought the woollen ski tunic, number two in our "best buys" list, in a restaurant, the Kilikanoon Cottage, in S.A.'s Clare Valley vineyards. Ian Bennetts, serving her delicious cucumber soup, said of wife Molly, "best weaver in Australia" whose rebuttal was "just compulsive."

The tunic was $110 from which $10 was arbitrarily deducted. (It seemed to be an Australian habit to "round off" prices, especially in small owner-operated stores.)

Finding superb craftshops in quaint restaurants is typical in The Country. Matter of fact, you will find craftstores in any number of interesting buildings from abandoned factories and warehouses to abandoned churches and schools, movie houses, even service stations.

Historic places — oasthouses, corn mills, pubs, prisons and convict cottages, noble estates and modest bluestone townhouses — are the craft hounds' bonuses. They supplement the more predictable shops in town centres and malls, in museums and in funky street markets, of which there are many.

Quality?

It is as wide ranging as there are people involved.

A diverse collection of ethnic influences has been grafted to the basic British rootstock through a surge of migrant artists in recent years.

Some of the most professional work we found — and the best quality — was in Tasmania where the notion that prices are half those of mainland Australia is aggressively promoted. It just might be true.

The "Tassie" crafts community, in cooperation with the Government Tourism Bureau, publishes a directory of shops and galleries with interesting related data: the historical significance of buildings occupied by some of the galleries and biographical profiles of the artisans, their specialities and nationalities. They are a cosmopolitan clan.

Tasmanian Craft led me to, among others, Saddler's Court Gallery in Richmond just across the bay from Hobart. The owner Mrs. Krongaard, has earned the respect of artists and customers for her constant vigilance for product excellence.

She won my respect through price as well.

I spotted an enchanting piece of jewellery, a poignant three-dimensional face of silver by Hobart-artist Jon De Jong. Its price — $86 — was just high enough for me to waver, just high enough for Mrs. Krongaard to apologise for "the inflated, escalated cost of silver."

Later I saw the pendant featured in *Vogue* and, still later, visited the artist's workshop at Salamanca Place where the same piece was priced at $145.

Jewellery and metal work in general are the beneficiaries of both the various migrant cultures and the abundance of semi-precious gemstones. There is just so much to work with: agate, topaz, sapphire, chrysoprase, jasper, garnet, zircon, ruby, tourmaline, amethyst, turquoise, petrified wood, fossilized shells, gold, silver.

A speciality of Western Australia, believe it or not, is iron ore jewellery. Shines to a lustrous black pearl finish.

The Classic Brown Jug

Australian craftstores, like those throughout the free world, are full of brown pottery. (Why can't potters pot in livelier colours?)

Bendigo pottery, the granddaddy of Australian crockery, is brown but recommendable. During last century's gold-rush days a young Scottish potter supplied the country's pioneer kitchens for over half a century. Today his nine huge bottle kilns are outfitting Australia's — and the world's — cupboards with both traditional Bendigo pottery and new microwave ovenware.

In the Stables Gallery savings up to fifty percent are available through "imperfects" (tagged orange and green) or "seconds" (tagged yellow). Even at the source, a coffee mug costs from $7.

The Bendigo Pottery complex won the first Victoria Government Award as the best tourist attraction in the state.

An aspiring crafts-tourist operation is The Mohair Farm just outside Bendigo. Built around a reclaimed ancient fibre mill and a few angora goats, the Farm's salesroom features more woollen than mohair items and their guides need to learn a lot more about their subject.

Sovereign Hill, in addition to being one of the most professional, historically authentic tourist attractions, is a shoppers' delight. In re-created 1850's stores, craftsmen forge steel, iron and brass into Chinese woks, candlesticks, andirons and fireplace accessories; they fashion in leather and fabrics, lathe woods into furniture and sell licorice sticks from apothecary jars, homemade jams, jellies and cookies. A great way to taste the best of yesterday.

The Specialities

Each of the states has crafts that are special if not exclusive. For example, Tasmanian Huon pine is an aromatic, smooth-as-glass-when-polished, champagne-toned wood that is made into all things small, like souvenir and home furnishings items. Its sawdust or chips are sold in small packets, alongside those of lavender which is grown commercially only in Tasmania. Both are suggested sachets: heavenly lavender to scent your dainties; the pine to discourage crawlies. The pine won't kill silverfish and spiders and their friends but it irritates them so much they nest elsewhere.

Bark pictures — or, more precisely, bark mosaics — is another Tasmanian specialty due to the profusion of multi-coloured bark-shedding trees on the island.

Bark "pictures" are not to be confused with bark "painting" as crafted by the Aborigines using vegetable dyes on large strips of rough bark to depict totemic symbols or ceremonial abstracts.

We spent our Aboriginal art budget at the Centre for Aboriginal Artists and Craftsmen in Alice Springs. The Centre is a cooperative that benefits the artists. There are powerful and dramatic hardwood sculptures of burial poles, carved birds and spirit figures from the Tiwi tribe on Bathurst and Melville Islands, images painted on paper bark with ochres and decorated with feathers and seeds from the

Northern Territory's famous Arnhem Land tribes; the carved animals of the Pitjantjatjara tribe of Western Australia — lizards, snakes and life-size perenti. There are bark-fibre string bags, twined or coiled pandanus baskets and mats, war spears and boomerangs.

You can pay a little or a lot for boomerangs. Most are frankly fake — just for souvenirs. The authentic version — the one used as a weapon — will fly and return to its origin. It is distinguished by grooves at both ends. Also, there are left-handed and right-handed boomerangs. The way to tell the difference is by the painted decoration. Symbolic animals or stick-figure people face *in* to the holder when the instrument is held for throwing.

Albany, W.A. is a rich larder of specialty crafts items. Firstly, there is the "blackboy" woodwork. This blackboy looks like a giraffe with whiskers but is, in fact, a member of the Lily family. The *X. Arborea* alone has a hardwood centre suitable for turning. Blackboy grows around Albany at an eighth of an inch per year and when it dies naturally the centuries-old beauty lives on in black-ringed bowls, plates, lamps and small specialty tables: chess, checkers and backgammon boards.

Crestafurn, a crafts workshop opposite the Old Gaol, was our best source (prices from thirty to fifty percent cheaper than in Perth!). In addition, they sell small, resin-surfaced tables and other pretties made of native tree roots and shavings.

We had a field day at Amity Crafts across the street which stocked a wide selection of well-styled woolen goods, leather and pottery.

Two other W.A. notes: Broome cultured pearls, heretofore exported, are now being made into jewellery and sold in the Broome Pearls workshop and through a few jewellery stores in and around Western Australia.

Gold "nuggets" were advertised in *This Week in Perth*. Wouldn't you love to have an authentic gold nugget? I investigated. "Sold out. Come back next week when we'll have another batch made up."

Not exactly what I had in mind.

Every state, city, country town has skins and skin products for sale. There are the predictable souvenir items: miniature kangaroos and koala bears made of kangaroo skins, sheepskin rugs, car seat covers, and all kinds of wearing apparel. There are the skins themselves. A tip from a sheep station owner: examine the hide side for tanning rough spots, thin spots, nicks and cuts made by the shearers. These will harden and break, tear easily and wear out too fast.

A Customs tip: souvenir skin items entering the U.S. *as accompanying baggage* will encounter no problem. The Customs corps is only after the commercial importers.

Another U.S.A. Customs note: don't believe it when someone tells you there is no duty levied on unset Australian gemstones.

I confess that we found prices generally high with one exception: international telephone calls from post offices cost less than $8 for three minutes. Now that's a bargain.

20. Country Inns and Country Pubs

"Hotel" in Australia is a public building where you can get a drink. Out in the country some of them carry a sign saying "accommodation." A few add the word "private" which means you can't get a drink.

All hotels, big and small, are known as "pubs."

Across the country many hotels are collectors' items either for the ornateness of their Edwardian-Victorian architecture or for the colour and character of their owners.

Take, for example, a turn-of-the-century resort hotel which was built for the new moneyed who derived their fortunes from the goldfields.

An hour's drive south of Melbourne is the seaside city of Queenscliff, an historic holiday resort and fishing town still dominated by antique hotels and guest houses — guest houses were very popular in the old days — and terrace houses.

Across from the cliff-top park overlooking The Rip are three old-world beauties: the Lathamstowe Building constructed in 1884 as a gift from the founders of the Carlton Brewery to the Church of England. Farther down the street is the Queenscliff Hotel (1887), two storeys of gingerbread plus a tower. The lobby is potted palmed and golden-glass skylighted.

Sandwiched between the two is the third building, the Ozone Hotel, which was the pioneer hotel (1882) of the resort town. I think it was because of the pristine condition of its lacy ironwork that we stumbled into the Ozone out of the rain to have a refreshment. We found a snug restaurant in a back room, the Boat Bar, and stayed to lunch ending up with the best whiting, a long, delicate, white fish, we were to find in Australia.

The Ozone Hotel had surprise after surprise. Obviously it had been refurbished with much care and much money.

Across from the Boat Bar Bistro, done in dark woods with old shipping and passenger vessel pictures on the wall — the Ozone was named after a paddle-steamer — was a cafeteria able to serve mobs of weekend holidayers.

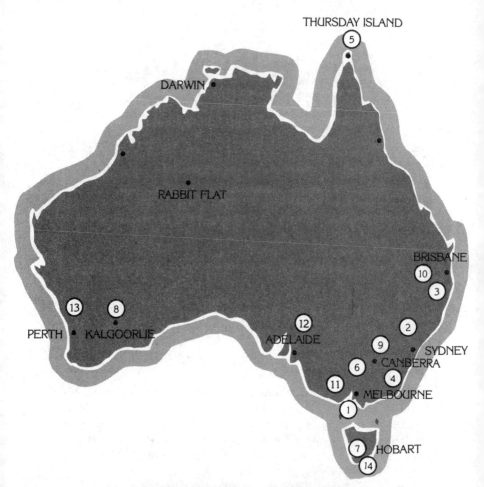

COUNTRY INNS &
COUNTRY PUBS

1. OZONE HOTEL
2. HYDRO MAJESTIC
3. WALLABY BOB'S
4. DORA DORA PUB
5. GRAND HOTEL
6. STAR HOTEL
7. BALL & CHAIN
8. BOULDER BLOCK
9. GUNDAROO PUB
10. FARMERS ARMS
11. SPORTSMANS ARMS
12. OLD LIONS BREWERY
13. PALACE HOTEL
14. BUSH INN

The original building was erected by James George Baillieu who jumped ship in Victoria, found his fortune, sired sixteen children and for ten thousand pounds sterling—a fortune—he built the Baillieu House which later became the Ozone Hotel.

Another resort hotel which dates back to the turn-of-the-century which we enjoyed was in the Blue Mountains an hour out of Sydney.

At the train-stop station of Medlow Bath is the unbelievable, two-storey, white Hydro Majestic Hotel which stretches a quarter of a mile along the top of the cliff.

Built originally as the Commercial Hotel in 1895 it was changed into a hydropathic hospital in 1904 modelling itself on the famous European spas at Baden-Baden and Aix La Chapelle.

The natural mineral water springs at the site were the first inducement for locating the hostelry at Medlow Bath. Electrotherapy was considered an advanced medical technique and a hydroelectric plant was set up to run the X-ray and electrotherapy machines imported from Germany along with two German doctors.

Among the famous visitors were Bertha Krupp from Germany who expressed her satisfaction by presenting the hotel with a Steinway grand piano.

May Hope came wearing the Hope diamond. Tommy Burns came and trained for his world heavyweight championship fight with Jack Johnson. (He lost.)

In 1923 a disastrous fire swept through half the building . . . and the hydro cures were dropped. The Hydro Majestic never fully recovered its lustre, but it became a tremendously popular family hotel.

"At that time," reads a newspaper story, "all the waiters in the Dining Room were Chinese and coffee was served by two small Turks dressed in National Costume."

Too much.

The flavour remains today.

We stayed at one end of the complex and went to the dining room at the other end of the hotel through the Belgravia Wing passageway, through the large lobby, past the cocktail bar with the marble nymph on a marble pedestal, through the ornate ballroom, past what must have been a chapel, past more guest rooms, past a recreation room (pinball machines!!) and into the dining room.

The golf course laid out by Scottish experts from Gleneagles is gone now but the two tennis courts are still in use.

There is no longer an orchestra for evening dancing in the ballroom but there is a coin-operated record player and one night after dinner, under the dome ceiling with its noble frieze — and with the constant vigilance of Red Indians Shooting Buffalo and Ibex Hunting in the Alps, and Moors and the Leopard in North Africa we had the room to ourselves and we danced and danced and danced.

A number of pubs have become famous because of their proprietors.

If you are in the Gold Coast area, you have to make a pilgrimage to Wallaby Bob's a dozen miles inland, which used to be out in the bush but now a Gold Coast bypass highway to Brisbane almost runs by the front door.

The Wallaby Hotel is a typical country pub: a one-storey, white-painted wood structure with a corrugated iron roof and a broad veranda for summer imbibing.

The walls of the public bar are covered with photographs of Wallaby Bob in his days as a professional wrestler, pictures of the Wallabies versus the All Blacks in bygone rugby matches, pictures of U.S. naval ships whose crews have visited and marathoned at the bar with Wallaby Bob, and signed pictures of celebrities: Judy Garland, Red Skelton, Mickey Rooney, Abbott and Costello.

Wallaby Bob was out playing golf the afternoon we dropped by.

Another famous character pub is the Dora Dora in northern Victoria where the proprietor, Alfie Wright, a round, bespectacled man has covered every square inch of space in his tiny two-room pub with oddities. Mr. Wright is considered the chief—oddity is the wrong word—object of talk.

It would be useless to tell you how far Dora Dora is away from civilisation because you'll never get there. Nevertheless it is eighty kilometres from Albury up a dusty, dusty track in the foothills of Talmalmo alongside the Murray River where it is so quiet, according to Alfie, and so healthy that they had to shoot somebody to start a cemetery.

Anyway if you did the unexplainable and looked up the pub at the expense of an entire day, you might find it wall to wall with people who would also never go to Dora Dora — and one of them would be a photographer or a reporter doing another spread on Alfie Wright and his nut house.

Our visit coincided with a stop by half a dozen "bikies," Hells Angel types, scruffy, torn, obscene, at whom the remainder of guests stared, transfixed, as if rattlesnakes were next to their boots.

When we arrived the old barrel of beer had just run out and the pipes to the new barrel were frozen over.

The bikies, impatient with the non-flow of draft beer, bought six-packs of tinnies, helmeted themselves and, with the disdain of mounted warriors, barrummed off. The tightness in the air disappeared like the snap of fingers.

Alfie's collection of "things" accounts for his notoriety. The bar walls are plastered with pennants, war guns, bayonets, Aboriginal spears, skins, branding irons, foreign notes, gold mining tools, handcuffs, pickled snakes, samurai swords. You get the picture.

The door stop is a mastodon tooth.

The lounge, twelve-foot square, has a table in the middle, an assortment of odd beat-up chairs and an upright piano against the wall. More photographs, an assortment of military insignia, framed foreign monetary notes, and even the ceiling is papered with calendar covers of yesteryear.

At the door the sign says "Free Beer Tomorrow." It is a safe promise. Tomorrow came to Dora Dora long ago.

Many hotels are attractive as symbols of history.

The Grand Hotel on Thursday Island was a grand old lady of a hotel in the colourful days of pearling which brought prosperity to the little island. Its wide verandas must have catered to a gentry of a different sort then.

It was a place for Somerset Maugham, for infamous intrigue and tropic-inflamed romance.

Now it is crumbling at the edges but the air of old maid elegance still clings to it.

History too is the attraction at another port-town pub, only this one is on the Murray River in Victoria and dates back to the time when the city of Echuca was the centre of a tremendous river trade.

The pub was built in Echuca by an ex-convict, a Lancashire lad who had lifted a silk handkerchief and instead of being hanged he was sent to Tasmania.

As a free man he went to Echuca and first constructed a bridge and charged a penny a sheep for crossing. Millions of sheep crossed his bridge. He was an arrogant, parsimonious man who built the Bridge Hotel, now open for inspection. There's a restaurant downstairs. Beautiful bar.

When the hotel was new, the owner advertised the hotel with: "As this is already known as the best hotel outside of Melbourne no other comment is necessary."

Farther along the river front the Star Hotel was built in 1867. Its advertising is also worth quoting:

"To meet the exigencies of the case, and cope fully with the peculiarities of the Echuca climate, more particularly during the summer months, a large underground bar, twelve feet below the surface has been excavated so those who may wish to indulge in the luxury of a cool drink, can be supplied with the same at the above hotel and the very best liquor."

Later the hotel was de-licensed but a tunnel was created in the underground bar for the escape of the illegal drinkers.

The Star Hotel is now a museum.

In Tasmania we recall with pleasure a pub in Hobart along the old waterfront, Salamanca Place, where its thick stone ex-warehouses have been restored and used for arts and crafts and antique shops. The Ball and Chain is a popular restaurant which keeps the flavour of the early times of this southernmost outpost.

The Boulder Block Tavern outside of Kalgoorlie is the last remaining pub out of six hotels in the middle of the Golden Mile known as "The Dirty Acre."

The hotels never closed. The grimy, hardworking miners spent their money there where beer was almost as cheap as water.

The Boulder Block, formerly Powell's Hotel, had a history like the others of gambling and drinking and chorus girls joining in . . . and a mine shaft in the basement.

Another good country pub experience occurred one evening in Canberra when we joined a Murray Coach Tour to the Gundaroo Pub Restaurant, twenty kilometers outside of town.

The bus is a relief of the drive back after consuming too much wine or beer. The dinners are held on Thursday, Friday and Saturday. Sundays are family days with a theatre in a nearby barn for the kids. Tickets must be purchased in advance.

There is a nice hot-diggity-dog Australian flavour to the whole evening enhanced by the casualness of the host directors, waiters, musicians.

Ron Murray, the handsome, tall, thin manager gave us the background of the operation.

"It was the tradition in the bush if you went by a house and stayed for two minutes you were served a cup of tea. If you stayed a half an hour, you were served a meal.

"We try to recreate that spirit here. No money changes hands. Eat as many steaks as you want. Drink as much wine or beer as you want. No one hawks pictures. No flower girls.

"I bought this old pub to live in and then friends started to borrow it for parties and the 'pub night' just grew out of that.

"Everybody loves it. The band, for example, has been with me for eight years." (They were good.)

Most of the crowd was made up of Canberra groups with a sprinkling of tourists. There is much tub-thumping dance music. Table hopping musicians doing Australian mining songs and bush songs. A sing-a-long.

Good steaks.

And a sleep on the bus on the way home.

In the rich farm centre of Toowoomba, the largest inland city in Australia with 75,000 people, there are antique shops, schools, flowered homes and clipped hedges . . . and lean farmers in pork-pie hats, neat cotton shirts and ties, twill trousers, shined shoes accompanied by rounded matrons in flowered dresses.

In the centre of the city is the White Horse Hotel, an appealing pub on the exterior with many straight white columns and white spirals and rounded window tops, curve on curve on curve of white, contrasted against the walls of red brick. Don't go inside. It is a shambles. Enjoy the outside. True at many picturesque pubs.

A famous pub, the Royal Bulls Head in suburban Drayton, a former stage coach inn, is now closed.

North of the city about twelve kilometres is the Farmers Arms, a local favourite.

Last year the dart throwers in the pub had a long-distance, play-by-wire dart match with an English pub, the White Swan in Great Yarmouth.

"The Poms won," sniffed the bartenderess, "but they cheated."

On the bulletin board was a notice: "The Old Bastards Christmas Party will be held in the Lounge on December 9th starting at 4:30 p.m."

The Sportsmans Arms at Boggy Creek looks like a low-lying Irish cottage tucked into the river valley. The pub which lies inland down a country road between Port Campbell and Warrnambool in Victoria is known for the Boggy Festival held at the nearby Curdies River bridge crossing in January. It has axemen and greased pole climbing and fishing and costumes. A country ball.

Although Sportsmans Arms derives a certain revenue from big city fishermen and curious tourists, the main source of revenue is from the local farmers.

When we were there, a major inter-club dart match was in progress and the pub owner (and team captain) was leading his valiant and thirsty team to another victory.

At one time in the early history thirsts were assuaged with illegal whisky and the hills abounded with homemade pot stills and distillers and an equal number of revenue officers and customs detectives.

The most notable bootlegger was Boggy Creek's Tom Delaney, a member of a family of farmers whose talents were not given to farming but to distilling a high grade of whisky and eluding the law. The volume, it was said, ran as high as a hundred gallons a week.

Troopers never found the source of this production but they scoured the bushes in constant search and the story is told of a time when troopers hitched their horses to trees and went on foot, again in vain, to find the illegal booze.

When they unrolled their waterproof capes that night at camp, every cape was found to hold a jar of whisky! Funny.

We spent the night in a remodelled double room with its own bath, fresh flowers everywhere, whitewashed farm walls and had a steak dinner with lots of red wine shared with a honeymooning couple from Melbourne and a country-style breakfast the next morning.

Our total bill was $38.

You'll find in Australian bookstores a coffee-table photograph book called *Australian Pub Crawl*. It's good. Catches much of the flavour . . . but not all.

The Seacombe Hotel in Port Fairy, the Rose Hotel in Bunbury, Tanswell's Commercial Hotel in Beechworth, the Kangaroo Hotel in Maldon, the Imperial Hotel in Castlemaine, the George Hotel in Ballarat, Fitzpatrick's outside of Launceston, Barossa Brahaus Hotel in Angaston and Bentley's Hotel in Clare were among our favorites.

We have long lists of country pubs that date back to the pioneering days of the country and stacks of photographs of these architectural gems . . . the Kurri Kurri Hotel in Kurri Kurri . . . the handsome Shannon Hotel in Bendigo. And you'll do the same.

"Country pubs" can also be found in cities because the cities started as country towns . . . the iron-laced Britannia Hotel in Adelaide . . . or in the same city, the Old Lions Hotel, once a brewery which has been converted into a fine restaurant, a disco, a subterranean restaurant, etc.—a complex which on Saturday night will host two thousand people!

In Perth we must refer you to the Palace Hotel, a nostalgic memory pub where I spent more than a month after the war in a small top-storey room for $6 a night. The rooms were called "dog dens," but the price was right.

Even then before Perth's postwar population-prosperity explosion it was a regal hotel of the Victorian motif. New management has completely refurnished the hotel, closed the guest rooms but redone the restuarants and the same dining room of my youth has black-dressed waitresses with white bonnets serving tables. On Wednesday, Thursday and Fridays they have genteel luncheon music and the evening dinners are booked out a month in advance.

One should be aware in Australia that the best food buys are not at fast food establishments but "Counter Lunches" at country pubs.

It is possible to combine history with a solid repast at a remarkably low price.

For example we stopped in a little town of New Norfolk on the way back from fishing at Lake Pedder.

The Bush Inn overlooking the Derwent River dated back to 1815 — the first licensed hotel in Australia — where in 1838 William Vincent Wallace wrote the opera *Maritana* and where in 1924 Dame Nellie Melba sang an aria from the opera from the balcony.

All very good but the best part was having lamb chops with bacon and salad and chips for $2. But that is real history.

21. The Last Night

It was our last night of the Australian adventure and we were wallowing in luxury in Perth.

It was our one hundred and tenth bed!

The past was a blur of dark motel rooms with humming air-conditioners, hotel rooms with breakfast orders hanging from the door knobs. We remembered the woodshed bedroom on the Bogong High Plains and the river beach mattresses on the Nymboida and the Toyota Land Cruiser bedroom and the night on the houseboat when the thunder crashed and the crackling lightning lit the Hawkesbury waters.

Now we were in fantasy land.

Peter Thompson, then manager of the Sheraton Perth Hotel, put us in the Presidential Suite to celebrate the Last Stop.

(Peter has since been elevated to the manager of the Sheraton Wentworth in Sydney and vice president in charge of a growing string of Sheraton Hotels in Australia. A most capable young man.)

Stretching the entire width of the top floor with ceiling spotlights, mirrored walls, a furnished bar, fresh fruit, stereophonic music, two colour television sets, personal terry cloth robes in the two bathrooms . . . it was good enough for us.

We poured a libation and toasted all the warm, unassuming, helpful Australians who had made it happen.

Dramatic changes had occurred in Australia since we first visited the country many years ago.

The "White-Anglo-Saxon-Only" barrier had been dropped and Italian war prisoners who knew good farm land when they saw it initiated a rush from Italy which now is strongly represented in farms and wholesale markets.

The Italians were joined by Vietnamese and Koreans.

All taxi cab drivers in Melbourne are Greek, part of an ethnic community larger than most Greek cities.

Dalmations are wine producers in the Swan Valley.

Chinese restaurants flourish in most towns and cities.

New bloodlines are being introduced which will change and expand the characteristics of Australians.

The results are already to be seen in ethnic newspapers, ethnic broadcasts, ethnic foods.

Physically, the cities have exploded outwards and upwards.

Perth, the former country town where I had lingered as a young man while wandering around the world, is a high-rise city of concrete and glass yet it retains, and has restored, much of the glory of yesterday's architecture.

The former lonesome beaches are now bustling suburbs crowded with expensive homes and modern condominiums.

Still there is much room in The Country in every sense.

Opportunities abound on all sides.

How many visitors to Australia, during our stay, confessed to us, "If I had to do it all over again, I'd come to Australia."

Almost self-sufficient in oil, rich in coal, the prosperity of Australia is both now and in the future. It is the America of tomorrow.

A key characteristic remains.

The come-in kindness of the Burnetts is an example. Easy hospitality is part of the take-for-granted graciousness born of open country where strangers meant someone to talk to besides your horse. It's still there.

So is pride.

Woe is in store for the new arrivee who displays any signs of superiority. "Cutting down the tall poppies" is a national pastime.

I still sting from a remark thirty years ago at a party in Sydney where I met a newspaper sub-editor.

"Where are you from?" he asked suspiciously over his beer at the first sound of my accent.

"The United States," I said innnocently.

"Oh," he said turning away, "you are the people who invented the bathroom."

Yesterday there was a greater sensitiveness of being "backward," a common trait found throughout the Pacific. Today there is a sense of "having arrived" in accomplishments. No feeling of a "second rate" country. It is first rate.

Winning the America Cup in 1983 was the cherry on the top. It was a huge psychological boost for the entire country.

I went sailing on Sydney Harbour on my last updating research trip and every other yacht was flying a green pennant of the fighting kangaroo with boxing gloves on, the pennant of the winning Perth yacht.

Fortunately other early virtues remain also: the ruggedness, the self-reliance, the courage in overcoming obstacles.

As we said in the beginning, if you go to war, go with an Australian. If you go to a party, they aren't bad either.

I picked up one of the six phones in the Presidential Suite and called a few friends. What's a furnished bar for?

People Who Made It Happen

There are so many people to whom we owe our thanks. Kindness was shown to us at every turn.

Thanks to Gordon Stepto, to Gary Court and all of the girls in the office at Air New Zealand, Sydney, who thought I lived there. And to John Oxley in Melbourne and John Mason in Adelaide.

To Stan Marks and Alan Jones of the Australian Tourist Commission in Melbourne. To state travel officers Miriam McMillan, our godmother, Graeme Atkinson, Geoff Reynolds, Colin Byfield, Brian Price, Sue McFarland, Barry Haines, Colin Haley, Ian Anderson, Les Robertson.

To Phillip Burford, Peter Castle and Nigel Kingsmill, Clarrie Bennetts, Richard Power, Marilyn Zweck, Marilyn Ascot, John Mulcair.

Also thanks to Duffi and Kelli for silent understanding during their annual visit which was limited to watching father staring and snarling and pounding at the typewriter.

I apologise to all the vignerons who shared their time and vintages with us only to be so severely edited down — just like this list — because of limited space.

Lastly, we thank Rosalie Char Tam again for putting order into a mangled manuscript and to Bill Ewing for a most sensitive pre-publication reading.

INDEX

THE
How To
Get Lost
And Found
TRAVEL EXPERIENCE
SERIES

The first book in the Lost and Found series was about New Zealand and was published in 1977. It has since gone through four editions. The other books added to the series in their order of publication include Fiji, Tahiti, the Cook Islands, Australia, California, and Japan.

The San Diego Tribune reviewer wrote: "The books are chatty, insightful, humorous, and make splendid reading. If you are planning a visit to any of the destinations, these books are *must* reading."

The books are available at many local book stores, or may be ordered directly from the publisher at $9.95 each plus $1.00 for bookrate postage when ordered in the United States. Allow five weeks for delivery. If airmail in the USA is preferred, add $3.00 for the first book and $1.00 for each additional book mailed to the same address.

Overseas distributors are listed in the front of this book.

ORAFA Publishing Co., Inc.
1314 S. King Street, Suite 1064
Honolulu, Hawaii 96814, U.S.A.

How to Get Lost and Found in New Zealand
  294 pages, 23 maps, 4th edition, 125,000 copies in print. ISBN: 0-912273-00-3
How to Get Lost and Found in Fiji
  208 pages, 12 maps, index, 4th edition. ISBN: 0-912273-08-9
How to Get Lost and Found in Tahiti
  262 pages, 13 maps, index. ISBN: 0-912273-02-X
How to Get Lost and Found in The Cook Islands
  212 pages, maps, illustrations, index. ISBN: 0-912273-03-8
How to Get Lost and Found in Australia
  320 pages, 13 maps, index. ISBN: 0-912273-07-0
How to Get Lost and Found in California and Other Lovely Places
  308 pages, 14 maps, index. ISBN: 0-912273-05-4
How to Get Lost and Found in New Japan
  288 pages, 16 maps, index. ISBN: 0-912273-06-2

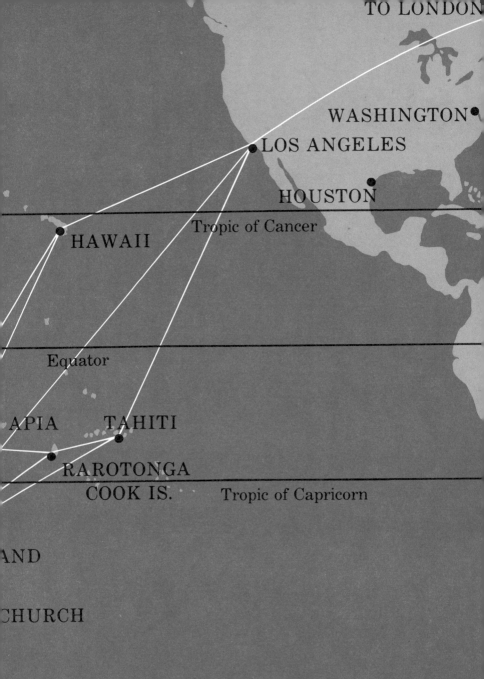

TO LONDON

WASHINGTON •

LOS ANGELES

HOUSTON

Tropic of Cancer

HAWAII

Equator

APIA   TAHITI

RAROTONGA
COOK IS.   Tropic of Capricorn

AND

CHURCH

Air New Zealand International Route Network